RUN WITH THE WOLF

Rainbow

ON RECORD

MARTIN POPOFF

RUN WITH THE WOLF

Rainbow

ON RECORD

MARTIN POPOFF

WP
WYMER
PUBLISHING
Bedford, England

First published in 2024 by Wymer Publishing, Bedford, England
www.wymerpublishing.co.uk Tel: 01234 326691.
Wymer Publishing is a trading name of Wymer (UK) Ltd.

Print edition (fully illustrated): **ISBN: 978-1-915246-64-6**

Edited by Agustin Garcia de Paredes.

A catalogue record for this book is available from the British Library.

Typeset/Design by Andy Bishop / Tusseheia Creative.
Cover design by Tusseheia Creative.
Cover photos © Alan Perry Photography / Rich Galbraith

TABLE OF CONTENTS

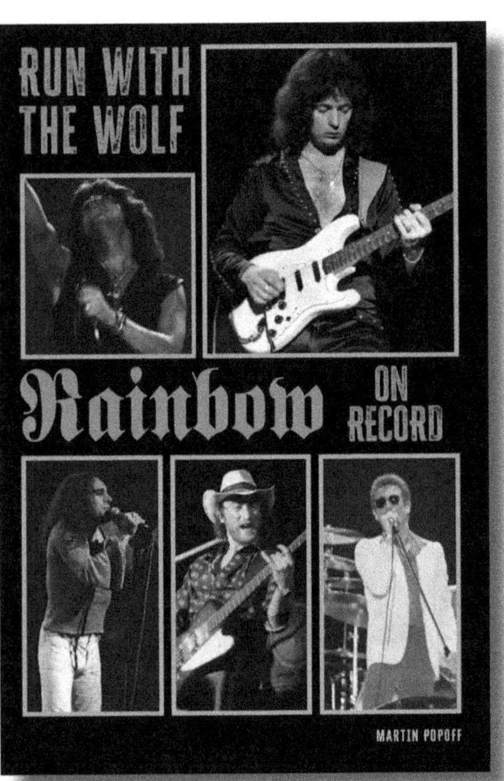

RUN WITH
THE WOLF
Rainbow ON RECORD
MARTIN POPOFF

INTRODUCTION

Hey medieval minions, welcome back to another instalment of these personally very rewarding panel books I've been doing. It was with trepidation that I decided to tackle the legend that is Rainbow, first, given the brief catalogue but second, given that I'd already done a book on the band. But *Sensitive to Light: The Rainbow Story* is your traditional rock biography (available to this very day from Wymer Publishing, as is the boss' *Rainbow: A Visual Biography*) and *Run with the Wolf: Rainbow on Record* represents my time-honoured gathering of wise music swamis, with the expressed purpose of squeezing from them their thoughts on this enigmatic band of four eras.

And I gotta say, man, these panel books continue to inspire me, pointedly through the new concepts proposed and then bantered back and forth until myriad new ways to experience and enjoy the band's catalogue emerge. Along the way, I found myself continually impressed with the level of scholarship spoken back to me as I conducted the interviews that form the lifeblood of the book.

Like many of these classic rock cats, my journey to the pot of gold at the end of the rainbow began with the debut album, *Ritchie Blackmore's Rainbow*. I recall being somewhat impressed but not "over the rainbow" (last one, I promise) with the album, other than the two obvious monolithic metal-munchers on it (I was 12, granted). But then *Rising* arrived and for me an' my buddies, *Sad Wings of Destiny* was still light years more sophisticated, but this was the first album ever that was hard rock from start to finish, no mellow or "lousy" songs, which was an official term in our airtight rating system. No "so-so" songs either (a category between lousy and "good"). In fact, there weren't even any "lousy goods," with only "Run with the Wolf" and "Do You Close Your Eyes" coming closest at "average good." This made it a "perfect" record, like I say, the first, until it was joined by *Let There Be Rock, Never Mind the Bollocks, Here's the Sex Pistols, Overkill* and *Bomber* to close out the seventies.

It was back to a regular record for the next one and the next one, and then we got the Joe Lynn Turner years, after which the band hung it up so that Ritchie and Roger could participate in a successful Deep Purple reunion. Messing up the catalogue, the Man in Black would deliver one later "stranded" album, credited to Ritchie Blackmore's Rainbow, and that is discussed here too, arguably with less enthusiasm. And by the way, breaking with tradition, given the modest catalogue, I've also included the band's two "proper" live albums as part of this discussion, namely *On Stage* and *Finyl Vinyl*. After that, legitimacy degrades, although one can argue that's already happening with *Finyl Vinyl*, given its posthumous placement and descent into the concept of compilation.

But I was pleasantly surprised at the depth of analysis of these last two rag-tag releases showered upon by my friends collared for this journey. In fact, listening to them articulate their way through these records might have been the most productive part of this exercise for me as a Rainbow fan, given how little I had invested in these two albums over the years.

And then along the way, all manner of cool insights arose, flung at my temples like Chinese throwing darts, at which time, after the imbedding, my adrenalin kicked in and I responded with a sharpening of many of the isolated concepts proposed. As I've learned to do with these panel projects, I've deliberately stuck myself into the conversation beyond the role of mere moderator, making sure that in my question zone, if I had something smart to say, it got said. And I can't stress this enough: at the end of the book, I was pleasantly surprised at how productive this was, and how much I had learned about the band, with trends spotted, solos analysed, the messaging of the album covers decoded, the philosophical milieu of JLT revealed.

As a final note, distinguishing this book from the four in the series previous (on Blue Öyster Cult, The Cure, Robert Plant and Thin Lizzy), I love that these chapters are comparatively much longer and more involved, constituting a significantly deep dive into the band's eight studio albums and two live albums. It is my hope that at the end of this journey, you'll find yourself as newly enriched about these records as I was. And with that, without further musing, let's step back in time and revisit the golden age of what my buddies and I used to call… moat metal!

Martin Popoff
martinp@inforamp.net; martinpopoff.com

RITCHIE BLACKMORE'S
RAINBOW

September 5, 1975
Oyster/Polydor PD-6049
Produced by Ritchie Blackmore, Martin Birch and Ronnie James Dio
Recorded at Musicland Studios, Munich, Germany
Personnel: Ronnie James Dio – vocals, Ritchie Blackmore – guitars, Craig Gruber – bass, Mickey Lee Soule – keyboards, Gary Driscoll – drums, Shoshana – backing vocals.

Side 1
1. Man on the Silver Mountain (Blackmore, Dio) 4:38
2. Self Portrait (Blackmore, Dio) 3:18
3. Black Sheep of the Family (Hammond, Dio; arr. by Blackmore) 3:20
4. Catch the Rainbow (Blackmore, Dio) 6:40

From Deep Purple to a totally new spectrum.
RITCHIE BLACKMORE'S
RAINBOW

RITCHIE BLACKMORE'S
RAINBOW

Ritchie Blackmore. One of the founders and driving forces of Deep Purple. He went in search of new colors. He found the voice of Ronnie James Dio.
Together, they entered into a new spectrum of sound. Exploding with a rainbow we can hear. All hues. All tones. Every color in music.
Ritchie Blackmore's Rainbow. The first album from 1975's rock super group.

polydor
On Polydor Records and Tapes

Side 2
1. Snake Charmer (Blackmore, Dio) 4:30
2. The Temple of the King (Blackmore, Dio) 4:46
3. If You Don't Like Rock 'n' Roll (Blackmore, Dio) 2:36
4. Sixteenth Century Greensleeves (Blackmore, Dio) 3:35
5. Still I'm Sad (Samwell-Smith, McCarty) 3:53

RITCHIE BLACKMORE'S
R-A-I-N-B-O-W
DP 1996
MAN ON THE SILVER MOUNTAIN
STEREO
銀嶺の覇者
へび使い
SNAKE CHARMER
レインボー
Polydor

Polydor
STEREO
PD 14290
(75 NP 1287)
2066 623
Time: 3:54
Owl Music
Ltd./
Armchair
Music
(BMI)
℗ 1975
Deep Purple
(Overseas)
Limited
Arranged by
Ritchie
Blackmore
Produced by
Blackmore/
Birch/Dio
From Polydor
Album PD 6049
"RITCHIE
BLACKMORE'S/
RAINBOW"
MAN ON THE SILVER MOUNTAIN
(R. Blackmore - R. Dio)
BLACKMORE'S RAINBOW
MANUFACTURED BY POLYDOR INCORPORATED, NEW YORK, N.Y.

A *Ritchie Blackmore's Rainbow* Timeline

1967. Ronnie and the Prophets change their name to The Electric Elves. By the end of the year they are The Elves and later, Elf.

May 1970. Quatermass issue their self-titled debut. It contains a track called "Black Sheep of the Family," the covering of which will cause Rainbow.

August 1972. Elf issue their self-titled debut. Producing is Ian Paice and Roger Glover. The band consists of David Feinstein on guitar, Mickey Lee Soule on piano and organ, Gary Driscoll on drums and Ronald Padavona on vocals and bass.

August 31, 1972. Ritchie meets Judith "Shoshana" Feinstein, who will feature on the debut Rainbow album. The occasion is a Deep Purple concert in The Bronx, New York.

December 16, 1972. ATI acquires the booking rights for Elf. The company's Bruce Payne (also Deep Purple's manager) is also framed by Elf's Dave Feinstein as the band's "unofficial manager."

April 1974. Elf issue their second album, entitled *Carolina County Ball*, produced by Roger Glover. Ronnie has ceded the bass position to Craig Gruber. Replacing David Feinstein on guitar is Steve Edwards. There's a song on the album called "Rainbow."

December 1974. Roger Glover issues *The Butterfly Ball*, an elaborate concept project. Included on the album are Ronnie James Dio and Mickey Lee Soule.

December 12, 1974. In Tampa Bay, Florida, Ritchie Blackmore records tracks for a solo single, amidst time off during Deep Purple's US tour dates, working with Ronnie James Dio and other Elf members, plus Hugh McDowell of ELO. This follows upon sessions a few days earlier in Minneapolis, Minnesota, where "Sixteen Century Greensleeves" is purportedly fleshed out. Both Elf and ELO had been part of the Deep Purple tour package making the rounds at that time. It's the Quatermass song, plus newly minted original "Sixteenth Century Greensleeves."

February 20 – March 14, 1975. Ritchie Blackmore and most of Elf work on what will become the *Ritchie Blackmore's Rainbow* album four months later. The line-up that creates the record never plays live.

March 16 – April 7, 1975. Deep Purple Mk. III perform their final dates, closing out in Paris. Supporting is Elf.

April 12, 1975. Deep Purple issue a press release explaining that the band is taking a three-month break to work on solo projects.

April 24, 1975. Oyster Records, a subsidiary of Purple Records, is legally incorporated. The first two Rainbow studio albums as well as the *On Stage* live album will bear the imprint.

May – June 1975. Deep Purple fulminates over the hiring of a replacement for Ritchie Blackmore, discussing the likes of Jeff Beck and Clem Clempson before settling on Tommy Bolin.

June 1975. Elf issue their third and final album, *Trying to Burn the Sun*. It is produced by Roger Glover and the album cover depicts only one member of the band, Ronnie James Dio.

June 19, 1975. It's announced to the UK press that Ritchie has quit Deep Purple, with Tommy Bolin named as his replacement.

July 1975. Rainbow issue their first album, *Ritchie Blackmore's Rainbow*. It reaches No.11 in the UK and No.30 on the Billboard 200. The album goes gold in France and silver in the UK.

November 10, 1975. Rainbow perform their first live show, in Montreal, Quebec, supported by Argent, after the first four slated dates, in the US, are rescheduled for later in the month and December. The band's personnel is now Ritchie Blackmore, Ronnie James Dio, Tony Carey, Jimmy Bain and Cozy Powell, the line-up that would record the *Rising* album.

Early December 1975. Rainbow wrap up their short first tour, a completely American jaunt of about 20 dates, excepting the inaugural show in Canada.

Martin talks to Marco D'Auria, Peter Jones, Pontus Norshammar and Matt Thompson about *Ritchie Blackmore's Rainbow.*

Martin Popoff: All right, Marco, open the discussion for us. How do we wind up with the first of two Ritchie Blackmore's Rainbow albums, and a bunch of Rainbow albums in between?

Marco D'Auria: Right (laughs). So yeah, with Ritchie Blackmore's Rainbow, Ritchie had become disillusioned with Deep Purple. It's like it had become a job to him and I think he missed being part of a band. Plus there was a lot of politics in Deep Purple at that time, in terms of songwriting credits and things, division of duties. Simultaneously, he'd heard Ronnie's voice and something about his voice attracted Ritchie. And the result. I think it would be erroneous to consider *Ritchie Blackmore's Rainbow* a solo album. I don't think it was; it really does feel like a true collaboration between Ritchie and Ronnie, at least, with the Elf guys backing it up. But definitely, he was very generous on that album. Every song was credited to Ronnie and Ritchie, other than the two covers on it. I think he appreciated going back to being part of a band and starting a new band and I think that was reinvigorating his career.

But it's interesting that he talks about how he didn't like the direction of Deep Purple's current music, because it hasn't changed appreciably here. I think maybe he used that as something of an excuse to not have to say that it was personalities, and put people down. Because some of the material on *Ritchie Blackmore's Rainbow* is reminiscent of *Stormbringer*, which is the album that he says he wasn't happy with. But yeah, it's now known that the songwriting credit issue had bothered him and that they weren't getting along and he just wanted to start something new and fresh. As for the name of the band, Ritchie Blackmore's Rainbow, I'd say his name is in there to give the band that extra bit of push, through that recognition that this famous guitarist is running things. But at the end of the day, it really was a band effort.

Peter Jones: Exactly. As the timeline goes, here we are, early 1975 and Ritchie's left Deep Purple—rather acrimoniously. He doesn't like the material, he's not happy with the direction, stories are that he's got tracks that are already written but he's not going to let Purple have them. He's holding onto them for maybe a solo project. And so he grabs basically the band from Elf, minus their guitarist Steve Edwards, and puts together a single that he likes so much he decides, well, let's make a whole album here. And what we get is *Ritchie Blackmore's Rainbow*.

What kind of album is this? It's a mystery. It's a strange record. Where it fits on a timeline makes sense, but I'm not sure the material make sense in the timeline. And I'll get into that as we go track by track. It's both an exciting album from the prospect of what is potential and what may come, but I think at the actual time—and retrospectively—it may not be as shiny a diamond as maybe we think it should have or could have been. That's the way I look at it. You have Ronnie and his strong vocals, but now they're coupled with the more fantasy realm kind of lyrical content that we start to associate with him, and that balance is very pleasing. He is a tremendous singer, of course, but on the material that he was working with in Elf, that big, full, aggressive voice doing more honky-tonk or boogie things, that doesn't mesh. It's like looking at Judas Priest's pre-leather era—your ears say one thing, your eyes say something else and they don't mix. But we now have this bigger voice with some subject matter that seems to work better.

Pontus Norshammar: Yeah, it's an interesting one, because the usual story is that he got tired of the Mk. III line-up while recording *Stormbringer*; he felt the record was too funky. And he also wanted to do the cover song, "Black Sheep of the Family," and the band said no. And here's the interesting thing. I've been thinking about this a few days now. Dio comes into the orbit of Purple around late '72, early '73, I think it is. And he's there and Glover is producing the Elf albums, and actually Ian Paice and Roger on the first one. He's touring with them; the band is actually an opening act on several tours. And I just can't find out why he didn't grab Ronnie for Purple. Why doesn't he grab him when they search high and low for Coverdale and find Coverdale and they end up with a compromise that is two singers, one that can sing the high notes and one that can sing the bluesy stuff Ritchie wants to have? So Purple have two singers and that becomes the dynamic of the band.

At the same time, they know this enormously good singer from New York who could do both parts, easily. And you wonder, why didn't they just hire Ronnie? Was it just that at the time Ritchie wasn't the one in charge? It becomes a wonderful "what if" story.

If you had the Deep Purple *Live in London* two-CD reissue, there's a story that during those shows in England in '74, Ritchie goes off stage. I think Paice is having a solo and Blackmore goes off stage and a fan runs up to him and says, "Oh, I just heard that you're going to do a solo album. And I hope it's not going to split up the band." And he goes, "Solo album? What do you think I've been doing for the last seven years?"

So it's really his band. He could have easily kicked out Coverdale and Hughes if he didn't like it. Well, something happens during those sessions. I don't know if he wanted to do a single and then it turns into an album, or if then and there he had it in mind to do a full band. Let us put it this way: what would Elf have become if Ritchie wouldn't have come along? Elf was the ultimate sort of opening act. If you listen to the albums, they're okay, but they're not really a standard. They are a group among other groups and there's a lot of those. There's another band on the Purple label called Silverhead, right? No one's remembers them, with Michael DesBarres.

But suddenly he wants Dio in. And I think Dio has two things that he can contribute to this; one is that he has the band, he has the musicians, he knows they are together and they can easily play this sort of "Black Sheep of the Family" stuff. Secondly—and this is an interesting one—Dio knows Bruce Payne and he becomes the manager later of both of Rainbow and Purple, right? So, there is some inklings about, we could do this if it was possible.

In the process he loses Paice and Lord, who he's played with for seven years. And they are playing at the highest level—Paice is playing like a god at the time and Jon is at his best as a keyboard player. And why does he want to lose them just to go with this ramshackle group, just to record a solo album? So yes, the question is, what would have happened if Dio had joined Purple? Would we have had *Rising* with Purple?

Matt Thomspon: Pretty interesting, yeah. But just to fill in the gaps, I guess the breakup song for this is "Black Sheep of the Family." Ritchie wants to record that song with Deep Purple. The rest of the band is not keen at this stage of their career doing cover songs and that becomes a point of discontent. They're touring with Elf and they become friendly with Ronnie, so he reaches out to him to record what would be a solo single, and that then they collaborate further.

They're still, of course, doing *Stormbringer*, which continues in the Coverdale/Hughes preferred styles, which includes more R&B

and funk, which is not what Ritchie wants to do at that time. So the continued discontentment with Deep Purple coinciding with exploring making music with Ronnie results in him deciding to record an album. Which, again, it's not breaking up Deep Purple yet, right? It's supposed to be just a solo project. But then they start to do the *Stormbringer* tour and things are still not well and Ritchie leaves the band. The Rainbow record's done, but he's still technically in Deep Purple at that point, and it's pretty shortly thereafter that he bails.

As for the record in a general sense, I would say it's halfway there to becoming Rainbow. Some of the things that Ritchie says he wants to do, he does. And the other half of the record, he's still sitting in a world that really isn't that different from Elf and really isn't that different from *Stormbringer* either. So it's a little surprising. It's not fully realized in terms of where he ultimately goes and, really, where Ronnie wants to go. That probably doesn't happen until *Rising*.

But it's interesting because *Ritchie Blackmore's Rainbow* become important, really, to the whole history of hard rock music right? This collaboration. Dio's on the Mount Rushmore of heavy metal singers and this is his first thing where he's really getting known. And then you've got Ritchie Blackmore, who's on the Mount Rushmore of heavy metal guitarists. And of course he's coming from Deep Purple, who are on the Mount Rushmore of the start of heavy metal. That's the coming-together of some important elements. Together, Ritchie and Ronnie create some music that is extremely influential to future bands and genres and the fans that adore them.

Martin: What do you think of the production?

Peter: It doesn't seem to have the ambience or the level of cut or aggression that Ritchie certainly had on *Burn* and to a lesser extent on *Stormbringer*. It's a reduction in the intensity of his tonal qualities here. There's keyboards; they're nice, but they're really buried in the mix; they're just for ancillary support. You get the sense that Ritchie wants to be the one that's featured here. So this is not Deep Purple from an equitable standpoint, with respect to the balance between keys and guitar; it's much more guitar-driven.

But the bass is very upfront, and it's got a thick, good, natural seventies sound to it and that's actually pleasing. The drums are very dry and they can tend to sound a little bit dated to the seventies. Not much resonance to them, kind of thuddy. But of course we get

Ronnie, and his vocals are exceptionally strong.

Martin: What do you think of this idea that it sounds this way because this is Ritchie on an even tighter budget than he's used to? What I mean by that is I've done piles of interviews with Deep Purple members, and there's always this undercurrent of how they were worked like slaves for low pay. And now Ritchie is knocked down a peg and his new organisation is decidedly B-league. If you think you had it bad in Purple, wait until you see how we're gonna treat you as a solo artist!

Peter: I like that (laughs). It's almost like demo Deep Purple. You would not expect an album like this from someone with that pedigree, which goes back even pre-Purple. This is something where you go, did he do it at his house? (laughs). You sit there and go, well, there's Martin Birch. He certainly isn't a novice; he knows what he's doing.

Martin: Although he's just beginning to be credited as a producer. The lion's share of his crediting has been as an engineer.

Peter: Yeah, maybe he's just going, "Okay, let's try that again, please." Maybe he's not having the kind impetus or influence or control he'd have later on. But clearly, through his early stuff with Purple, he's established a certain kind of sound with them, albeit, like you say, likely on the larger budgets. Plus I want to say that those records aren't as sonically opulent as other albums by other bands during the same period of time. You and I have talked about how the Uriah Heep records sounded much more full and vibrant than their Purple counterparts.

Pontus: The production has a warmness to it. I know that it's going to be heavier with *Rising,* but I do think that's down to Cozy's drumming. This is warm and it has breathing room in it; you hear things very clearly. There's a lot of layers of guitars, there's layers of keyboards, it's very solid. The production is quite inviting. I always liked the sound of it. One thing is very clear. Ritchie, having worked with two singers prior to this for two albums, that actually rubs off here, because we get a lot of backing vocals. Dio does backing vocals with himself a few times and he does a very good job of it. So Ritchie's recent experience might have inspired him into thinking he could do with some backing vocals here.

Martin: What are your thoughts on the album cover? Personally I always liked it, but over the years, it's been edging into a sort of children's book realm for me.

Marco: Funny, yeah, I didn't know that the cover was supposed to be a guitar! In all the years of enjoying this album, I didn't notice that until I read the first edition of your Rainbow book. I just saw it as a sort of fantasy-themed castle. I just thought it was this fantasy cover. I see what you mean though. It's very colourful, whereas *Rising* looks more heavy metal, with the mountains and the clouds and stuff.

Martin: Okay, let's get past the cover and into the music, beginning, sensibly, with the opening track.

Marco: Yeah, "Man on the Silver Mountain" is a classic Rainbow song, riff-wise, as they say, their "Smoke on the Water." It's one of the first songs I ever heard from Rainbow and it instantly attracted me to the band. The medieval and sword and sorcery and fantasy themes hadn't been done to this level up to that point in rock music, and that definitely gave the band a distinction. And since then, a lot of people have disparaged the lyrics in Rainbow, including David Coverdale—he was never a big fan—and Graham Bonnet and Tony Carey as well. Tony just thought it was nonsense. But I thought it was awesome, and very visual. Yeah, they get the ball rolling with "Man on the Silver Mountain."

Basically, it's a story about a powerful man who lives high up on a hill who can see the unseen and he comes down with vengeance. It also foreshadows future songs about powerful beings who are worshipped and are cast out. And there are religious undertones to the song as well, with that "I can show you the way" idea and "Come down with fire/And lift my spirit higher/Someone's screaming my name/Come and make me holy again."

Peter: Right off the bat, this song opens with a riff that's familiar for anybody who's ever listened to anything Ritchie's ever written. If Ritchie is guilty of one thing, it's serious plagiarism. But he robs from himself. He has a very strong habit of recycling riffs that are usually in the same key and in the same position on the neck. He just rotates which order he plays things and this is one of them. It's a very similar riff to how he opens "Spotlight Kid," it's similar to "Smoke on the Water," it's similar to "Burn." It's familiar and it's Ritchie and from that standpoint, it's comfortable. At least he's not ripping off anybody else at this point. He's got a little flanging on his guitar. It's a medium to slower tempo for an opener, which is against the norm of what he had established with Purple. They were usually more aggressive, up-tempo songs that would open albums. That was pretty consistent their entire career before this record. It's a straight eighth-note feel in pattern. Ritchie's tone on this is a little muted.

As for Ronnie, he's a little more aggressive here. There were moments of it in Elf and it didn't fit. That raspy, throaty thing doesn't work on "Black Swampy Water" (laughs). The verses are straightforward, with simple drumming. I like the pre-chorus, that "Come down with fire" part. Ritchie adds a nice, pizzicato classical guitar riff to that, which is nice, which live, he had to be doubled by keys, of course, because he couldn't do both parts. So we get classical elements there. But the song doesn't really have a proper bridge, nor are there keyboard solos. So it just rides straight through for its 4:42 duration. Ritchie's solo is strong; it's melodic and very tasteful and it's got moments of his flash and his technique. In particular, he sounds really great. But the backing material is pretty average and really doesn't push you into any new territory. It's a good opening track, but as I mentioned, it certainly doesn't compare to "Burn" or "Stormbringer" from his previous two records. The material's there, but somehow it's lost in the translation.

Pontus: Still, what a great way to start. It's one of his best riffs, maybe his best since "Burn." It presents Dio as a very solid singer—he kills on this one. The arrangement with the backing vocals, when they come in, is very good, the solo is good, lots of guitar textures and the band is solid. There's a clavinet in there, courtesy of the band's keyboardist, Mickey Lee Soule. Also introduced is the way that Dio ad-libs at the end; he almost rewrites the lyrics in the end. That's a forte for him. That's a thing he will always do until he dies. He comes up with these lines that just fill out the song. He doesn't have to wail, he doesn't have to put in oooh-oohs or anything. He just comes up with some new words, which is an attractive thing.

But you wonder, where were those riffs during *Stormbringer*? Did Ritchie just write it then or did he have a pile of those? So it's a smash, a great opening track. He has now worked with Martin Birch for five years, since *In Rock* and they both know they need a solid track to open with and they choose the best one.

Matt: What's interesting is that "Man on the Silver Mountain" gets released as a single, although the initial purpose of the band was to create a single for "Black Sheep of the Family." So the management and band and powers that be must have thought that this was the best opportunity for a song that people will like. It's got a great riff to it that's in that plucked style of "Smoke on the Water." So you immediately start the album with a good riff and then he gets those muted arpeggios going. Essentially, Blackmore's giving us some cool extensions of things he'd done in Deep Purple.

Martin: Could you explain that plucked technique a little more?

Matt: With a traditional power chord, where you eliminate the third, you've played the first and the fifth of the chord. So that's like a bar chord, which is sort of the heavy metal thing to do. But he's not really playing the bass part of the note at all. He's playing the middle parts of the chords, and he's playing them at the same time. So when you play a normal chord and are strumming downward, even though it's quick, you're technically playing one note at a time. In this case, he's plucking the strings so that they're simultaneously being played. It gives it a different attack to those riffs. So instead of striking down, he's simultaneously playing two notes at the same time and so it gives it a different voicing for the chord but also a different type of attack. That's one of the things that makes his rhythm playing unique, because he does that a lot. Even when he's playing the voicing of a bar chord, he doesn't bar his finger across, right? He's holding it in more of an open position, which, again, changes the attack, offering a little less on the bass end.

Martin: When he plucks, do you think he's got a pick on one of those ring picks? Or is he using his two bare fingers?

Matt: It looks like he just uses his fingers to do it, right? I think it's like the magic trick where you palm the pick and then do it. He also has this slide technique where he holds the slide and you can't even see the slide. It's really different too. He's a very unique player, not just for what he's written but just his technique. And for "Man on the Silver Mountain," the song itself becomes very important in that it's a big stage number for the band. It becomes associated with Ronnie James Dio as well, right? It becomes a live staple for him in his various solo bands. So it becomes part of the canon of both Rainbow and the Dio band.

And then lyrically, Ronnie's explained it as being a semi-religious song that you've got this godlike figure who's going to come down and save us. And I think there's some built-in scepticism and cynicism in there, an anti-authoritarianism. It's a clever thing that goes away in the live versions. I guess his philosophy is to not be dependent on the man on the silver mountain to just tell you what to do, right? Think for yourself would be in alignment with his overall philosophy. In concert, it becomes a bit more of a "come together" thing. "We're all men on the silver mountain!" (laughs). I'm not sure what that means, in that case, but maybe just that we're all our own gods. And we all have our own opinions and freedoms.

Martin: Nice. Next is "Self Portrait," a bit of a proggy one, or at least a fairly ornate rock waltz, given its swinging, 3/4 time structure.

Marco: Yeah, and "Self Portrait" is a hidden gem, I think, not only in the Rainbow discography, but just in rock in general. Is Rainbow a hidden gem band? Fans of classic rock and hard rock, I don't want to say they ignore or aren't aware of Rainbow, but if you take a guy who loves the radio hits of AC/DC and Led Zeppelin, they probably don't even know who Rainbow is. And you can forget about "Self Portrait" and in fact a few on this album. Anyway, this one's rich of melody and it's hooky and catchy. "Nothing is real but the way that I feel." I don't know, I take it to be a song about seeing ourselves for who we really are. "There's only the devil to pay," meaning we see ourselves with all our faults or we choose to see nothing. "Paint me a picture with eyes that never see the truth, or see the lies" thing. It's left vague but that's what I get out of it.

Peter: At the music end, "Self Portrait" opens with three cowbell hits and a drum fill. And to me that is much more reminiscent of the Elf albums than it is a Purple record. It's a slower tempo that languishes at times, but they're doing a waltz-like 6/8. There's two tambourine hits (laughs) that he plays throughout this entire song. They're signalling that it's a 6/8 rather than a 3/4 by accenting with the tambourine only on the alternating notes, so on the six and the eight. And he carries that through the entire song without any break and it's like Chinese water torture after a while. It's like, okay, back off on the tambourine thing. Give me something that changes (laughs).

Ritchie's love of classical music is on display here. It's loosely based on Bach's "Jesu (Joy of Man's Desiring)" from his Bach

"Cantata;" there's some elements of that in there. The tempo, Ritchie has said that it's a combination of Bach and Hendrix's "Manic Depression." I'm not really sure I can stretch into that one, only because it's got 6/8, so maybe that's where the similarities end. Dio's vocals are strong. I like the double-tracked harmonies. The keys are way buried in the mix, and usually they're just there to reinforce or double Ritchie's lines that already exist. Gary Driscoll's toms are just dead. They all sound similar. And there's no contrapuntal or counterpart or point to anything like you get in Purple; a contrasting line, a unison line, something.

I love the bass playing here and I want to mention that I think Craig Gruber's bass playing on this album is really strong. He might be my favourite musician on the record (laughs). And going forward, he actually may be my favourite Rainbow bassist, which sounds odd, considering who Blackmore's had. But his playing is so tasty and it's very musical.

The lyrics are dark, about depression and falling into despair. And Ritchie's solo is very fluid. It's legato, it's got great phrasing, it's classical and I love his tone on the solo. I love his vibrato. I think it's my favourite vibrato of any guitarist I've heard. It's very classical in its oscillation and its speed. It's just perfect like a violinist or a concert cellist or something; it's just really, really nice. "Self Portrait" was not a concert staple by any means. It was only played ten times live. It's a safe track. But safe doesn't make good rock 'n' roll.

Pontus: I love "Self Portrait." It's a great riff and melody and I love the sort of jazz waltz rhythm in it. Again, plenty of guitars, which build texture. There's also a bit of percussion, which is very, very soft. I think it's a very good song, well written. For me it's the deep cuts that redeem this record.

Martin: And with the first two songs in a row, lyrically, we're seeing the creation of this world, and even a certain poetic use of language, that Ronnie would continue to flesh out for the rest of his career.

Pontus: Yeah, and it's a very interesting world because going from the Coverdale world, which is very basic, very sort of chasing girls and all that, you enter this world of storytelling but with fantasy lyrics, right? But it's well crafted and you're right, he's set the tone across two songs. It's almost like a novella. It also mirrors Ritchie's guitar playing and even his tone a bit, and together they create a different world.

Matt: It's got a very strong vocal—what a good introduction to Ronnie. Of course there was Elf, but this is putting Ronnie on a platform. The Rainbow album and the breakup of Deep Purple were covered in the rock magazines very heavily. There were big pieces in all the rock journals around both the new Rainbow album and wondering what was going to happen with Purple. And so what a great introduction, right? He comes out with the first two songs and both with very strong vocals. It's a well-crafted song, and it's got a really unique guitar riff and a melodic solo. So the first two songs are successful in establishing this as a new band that has merit on its own. It's not earth-shattering in terms of change for Ritchie, but certainly it's a progression. You can see with the first two songs that they're doing something different beyond the legacy bands they come from.

Martin: Next is "Black Sheep of the Family," like Matt says, the song that got the whole thing rolling.

Marco: Yes, "Black Sheep of the Family" was the cover that basically started Rainbow because Ritchie apparently brought it to Deep Purple and they rejected it. They were already touchy about song credits and here was Ritchie introducing a cover into the situation and you wonder how that would have gone down politically. Anyway, this was on the one album Quatermass ever did, from 1970, and they didn't even write the song (laughs).

This one and "If You Don't Like Rock 'n' Roll," even though you might consider them generic, throwaway tunes or filler songs, the performances by Ritchie and Ronnie make them interesting enough that they're not skippable. I appreciate those songs and they're hooky in their own way. I suppose it's valid in terms of being here because it's the song that started Rainbow but also because Ritchie had been the black sheep in Deep Purple, pretty much, at the end there. And lyrically, it's about being an outcast to society, a drifter, even homeless. It's about all the things that this guy has or doesn't have. He talks about sleeping on floors, having nothing, not wanting to go on. I really like the lyric, "I've got a pocket full of dust/And eating is a must" (laughs). But yeah, I picture this vagabond sleeping on floors and hopping trains and stuff. It's pretty bleak.

Matt: As Marco said, it's a song most recognized as a Quatermass song, but they didn't write it—it was originally done by Fat Mattress.

Fat Mattress did a more folky version, and Fat Mattress was founded by Noel Redding. So it's interesting. It's written by Steve Hammond, and also gets recorded by Chris Farlowe. For this obscure song, it actually has quite a bit of history to it already. And Chris Farlowe does this over-the-top version.

What's interesting to me is that Quatermass influences Judas Priest. The year before, K.K. Downing is really influenced by them. And they're a proto-heavy band, and Judas Priest, even as early as *Rocka Rolla*, the year before, what they take from that album is to be a little heavier, and to be sparser, right? In the sonic mix, everything's got a place. Those Judas Priest records, even though there's two guitarists, each one has a very sort of precise place in the audio sphere. They don't conflict with each other. It's not messy. Everything's tightly recorded.

For the first Rainbow record, they're not doing that at all. It's quite messy, right? You've got keyboards and the guitar and a busy bass and busy drums that are all really competing for your attention. And that tends to bury the guitar in the mix and it buries Ronnie at times in the mix. The result of which is that the album is not that heavy-sounding. It's not fully a heavy metal record. It evokes this old, loose, jammy side of Purple and of Elf at times. The busy-ness reduces the power of the songs.

So in the end, Rainbow's "Black Sheep of the family" is not as heavy as the Quatermass version. And it's a song that in and of itself, it seems so strange that this is the song that breaks up Deep Purple, because there's not really anything that makes the song stand out, from a lyrical standpoint or from a songwriting standpoint at all, where you could say, well, this is the one to go to bat for because it's so different than what Deep Purple's doing. It sounds like they could have recorded it for *Stormbringer*. And, in fact, it's more funky than heavy, their version, that ends up on the Rainbow record. So it's just strange and interesting to me that at this point they haven't learned the same lessons that Judas Priest has learned when they're coming from some of the same sources.

Martin: So Priest was influenced by Quatermass?!

Matt: Yeah, in K.K.'s book he talks quite a bit about how they played with them a lot in the early days. So they're seeing them play live and it's definitely an influence.

Martin: Interesting. Peter, your thoughts on this one?

Peter: As Matt says, there's a long lineage here. And it's one of two covers on the album. That seems to be a thing—you get a lot of debut albums that have cover tracks on them. We can go on forever about albums that have that, *Van Halen* and so forth. But yes, it's from Quatermass and an extra connection is that band's drummer, Mick Underwood. Mick played with Ritchie in The Outlaws and later played with Episode Six, so he knew Gillan and Glover. And the story, as Marco explained, is that Ritchie presented it to Purple and they said no. So he did the demo with Elf and that was the impetus to say, well, hey, this turned out pretty good; let's go do a full record.

Again, it opens with cowbell, which previously you got only sparingly. "You Fool No One" is the cowbell track for Deep Purple. This is more of a straightforward rock track, but it's got a bit of boogie to it. It's not really hard rock in any of its flavours. Ritchie plays a rhythm part that is reminiscent of other tracks that he's played with Purple. There's more slide and there's some syncopation which is nice. But Dio's vocals are a little throaty to me. There's more well-constructed harmonies. I do like that Dio is true to the original lyrics, which I think were well written, so that's nice. Again keyboards are an afterthought here. There's nothing to seek out. You can even try and listen for them, but they're not really there.

Martin: It's a pretty goofy song though, right? It's like, why did he pick this song?

Peter: Yeah, well, it's the first song that's got a proper bridge on it, so that stands out and gives us a nice lift. But there's no solos. It's okay but not a standout. And obviously, they never played this live, and you really have to ask yourself why.

Martin: I wonder if Ritchie just identified with the title so much, he was blinded as to how nerdy the song actually was.

Peter: Well, and so far, this many tracks in, I have to question, at least from an outside appearance standpoint, who's in charge here? There are way more Elf elements than there are Ritchie's Deep Purple elements. So instead of it being Ritchie with members of Elf, at times it's almost Elf with Ritchie on guitar, which is a strange and awkward place to be.

Pontus: The Quatermass version, funnily enough, sounds a bit like "Bird Has Flown" from the third Deep Purple album, Mk. I; it has the same rhythm. I think they did it very well. They made sort of a production number of it. They wanted it as a single, so they drenched it in vocals—Dio is front and centre. He's very articulate and even his backing vocals seem well thought-out. Because if you listen to the original, it's quite lengthy. But they had ideas for it and I think it flows very well. I'd add that the singing on the original is not great, way less impactful than what Ronnie does with it.

Martin: But Pontus, the elephant in the room is why do this sort of ineffectual song at all?

Pontus: Yeah, I don't know why he suddenly woke up one morning and thought, this is what I want to do (laughs). Maybe he liked the melody—I don't know—because they really work on it. There's lots of guitars, lots of vocals, and the chorus, when you compare it with the rest of the album, with their own stuff that they're gonna write later, they put more effort into it. They were going to have "Sixteenth Century Greensleeves" as the B-side. What?! Who would think that? Who wouldn't think, why don't you just swap the tracks? But it's a good album track and I wonder if it's there because they put so much effort into it. I think it's succeeds, but it's not one of the best songs on the album. It's not the cornerstone of the album.

Martin: We close side one of the original vinyl with the first of two ballads.

Marco: Yes, and I'd put "Catch the Rainbow" in a certain bucket of songs with the likes of "Aqualung" and "Stairway to Heaven" and "Child in Time." It's mellow, but it builds to a crescendo. It's a little progressive, but ultimately just ends as an epic ballad; it never gets too complicated. In the eighties they might have called this a power ballad but of course it's darker than that. I love "Catch the Rainbow," although not necessarily the live version that's 15 minutes long. But here it's perfect. As for the lyrics, again, we're seeing Ronnie build this epic, timeless world of his. You've got "Ride the wind to the sun/ Sail away on ships of wonder." It's about reaching or searching for something great. In the beginning it sounds more like "Rainbow Eyes" with "Soft and warm/She'll touch my face." It sounds like a love song, but then it turns into this journey through the sky and catching rainbows and looking for something great.

Peter: I feel like this is one of the tracks that is more Blackmore-oriented. It's one of the classics and who said Dio doesn't write love songs, right? Well, there it is. Ritchie's melodic sense on this is exceptional. I think it's got a wide range of his playing abilities in it too. But again, it's a slower, more subdued track. So far we've had only one really up-tempo song and that was a cover. So you're not really sure here. It's odd because the drums are actually a little busier here, on what is a slower ballad. He's adding more fills than he played in all of "Man on the Silver Mountain," which seems backwards. And he does something else that seems odd to me. Driscoll starts the first chorus, and he's playing eighth notes, but in the middle of it, he switches to sixteenths, but then drops it and never goes back to it again. It's like, he's changing his mind. When you play really slow ballads, those eighth notes can start to drag on a bit; the sixteenths help pick it up. And I don't know if he was like, oh, wait, that. Oh, no, screw it. I'll go back. And they just left it. And I thought, okay, that's weird.

There's finally some keyboards in here that are nice. I like the chordal accompaniment underneath it. In one of the channels, you hear the strangest production choice. It's almost like a guitar that goes "waah waah" and it's distracting and annoying. He does it on another track as well. And I'm like, why did you choose to do that? It's got a weird oscillation to it and everything, and if you isolate the channel you can hear it clearly.

The song drags on a bit. There's a woman named Shoshana Feinstein who does the backing vocals on it, and very well, actually; they sound really great. Long story. She's a long-time on-and-off girlfriend of Ritchie's and they met back in '72. They were smitten with each other but Ritchie was married and they had a falling-out and they hooked up again at Cal Jam and then she was around and then they had an acrimonious breakup. So that's how she ended up on the record, because she was hanging around with them.

"Catch the Rainbow" went on to be the third most played song in their catalogue and clearly live it's a completely different animal. But for these purposes, it does drag on a bit at the end. Those "ooh-ooh" parts just repeat and repeat 'til the end; there's really nothing new to add to it. But again, these are base elements that Ritchie would take to the live stage and change them and morph them into more of a Rainbow-esque style.

Pontus: When I think of "Catch the Rainbow," I think of "Little Wing" by Jimi Hendrix. It's even down to the lyrics. "Catch the Rainbow" goes, "When evening falls, she'll run to me/Like whispered dreams your eyes can't see." "Little Wing" goes, "When I'm sad, she comes to me/With a thousand smiles she give to me free." You can hear the inspiration. Here's another thing—they wrote very good ballads when they wanted to. This is a very good song and it's one of the centrepieces of the album. It's beautiful and it has integrity. The ending sounds a bit like "Epitaph" by King Crimson, with the long fade-out. It's one of my all-time favourite Rainbow songs. Dio sings well, Ritchie plays well, good use of Mellotron. It's one of those moments, like "Children of the Sea" with Iommi and Dio, when those epic ballads come together and work. It creates something "otherwise" on what is supposed to be a hard rock album.

Matt: "Catch the Rainbow" is the first song that's totally written from the ground up by Ritchie and Ronnie together, because obviously "Black Sheep" was a cover and then "Sixteenth Century Greensleeves," Ritchie did start with a riff for that one. So this one, they're really writing together. And Ronnie has described it as a medieval blues song. And now we're getting some of that classical theming to the music. We know Ritchie has that interest himself and Ronnie proves to be open to that kind of stuff. And it suits his lyrical ambitions. This is probably the first one on the album where we hear an overt classical influence.

Song structure-wise, as Pontus alluded to, it's actually quite similar to "Little Wing" by Jimi Hendrix. The intro sounds quite a bit like that chord structure. It's fairly similar but ultimately it has a different feel than "Little Wing." It's not a total cop of it at all. I think they really do put their own stamp on it. You've got backup vocals by Shoshana, Ritchie's girlfriend, Judith Feinstein, and then the lyrics are talking about what is possibly a stable worker and some sort of courtly lady. It's quite beautiful, a really nice ballad. But rather than a ballad of a modern time period, Ronnie's telling a story that one assumes takes place in the past and so that's neat. That's something that they're going to return to quite a bit. There's very tasteful guitar. It becomes a song that is important to the band live, and you also get the name of the band in the song, which signals to you that this might be an important song to the band.

Martin: Okay, over to side two and we have "Snake Charmer," another song that could have been on *Stormbringer*, despite Ritchie's proclamation that he wasn't funky.

Marco: Yeah, and another hidden gem (laughs). I actually think Ritchie, through his guitar playing, portrays the snake charmer in this song. You often consider the drummer the heartbeat of the band, but Ritchie's the lyricist or the conceptual thing in this song as well as part of the rhythm section. Still though, you hear a lot of Elf, which makes sense on the first album, because it's basically Elf other than Ritchie. But yes, "Snake Charmer" is almost surprisingly funky given the history but also the subject matter. And it sounds like the seventies, just with the instrumentation and arrangement although that adds to its charm. Lyrically, it paints a warning picture of a being who can charm or mesmerize you and it's telling you to watch out for his magic. Like, shut your doors. I love that, "Old sparkle eyes/He never cries/One step ahead of the hounds" line. But if you read the lyrics, they are quite descriptive and visual about a guy who can take control and mesmerize you. As for him being a snake charmer, I guess we're the snakes (laughs).

Peter: Nice and tight, a driving, funky groove. There are many layers of Ritchie's multi-tracking going on here. It's like pick one, Ritchie, because he's dancing all over the place here. And there's a little wah-wah that he does in one channel with almost Nile Rodgers/Chic kind of picking, and they conflict with each other. It's the kind of playing that's an example as to why he didn't want to stay in Purple.

Martin: Like that *History in Five Songs with Martin Popoff* episode I did about all the Purple guys losing their minds in the late seventies, I'm hearing Ian Gillan Band, Paice Ashton Lord, David Coverdale *Northwinds*. So even Ritchie wasn't immune.

Peter: Yeah, absolutely (laughs). This is not something you would leave the *Stormbringer* Purple for and then say I want to play *this*. It doesn't make sense. Again, much more of an Elf vibe to it. I do like the drumming; there's some tasty fills and some good stuff going on here. Great vocals from Ronnie. The lyrics are descriptive and nice and tell a story. Beware of this mystery man, the snake charmer, who brings danger and trouble. I like that; it's easy to listen to and it makes sense. One of the best moments in the album is the solo section. I think Ritchie is just on fire here. And I love the syncopation from the band. They're doing something exciting behind him and underneath him. It's engaging and driving. And the riff that transitions back into the verse is nice. More of that on here would have really been appreciated from me. It's also a slight bit heavier. And when you get to that final verse after that section, the energy picks up a bit and it takes us to the end on a strong note. "Snake Charmer" has grown on me over the years, but it was never played live so it never had any legs beyond the record.

Pontus: "Snake Charmer" is a great side two-opener. It's one of those continuations of what he had done with "You Fool No One." Good, funky riff, lots of keyboards and I think it's Gary Driscoll's best performance. But Dio is very much in control and again, there's the confident ad-libbing at the end. And there's a good solo, plus a smart breakdown to the solo.

Matt: As Peter alluded to, there's denseness and messiness. There's a lot going on. You've got the wah-wah guitar, you've got keyboards in there, you've got a very busy bass part and the drums are quite busy as well. There are some single-line overdubbed guitar parts that Ritchie is doing that really don't add a lot. It competes for space. So sonically it's very messy. You've got a good shouting metal chorus: "Snake charmer!" That's a metal chorus. But the heaviness of the song is muted by all this messiness. So again, he's not quite embracing that heavy metal-ness that we see on the next album and that will become so influential.

I like your comment about the Ian Gillan Band. I hadn't really thought of the Ian Gillan thing, I guess, because the lyrics would be different. But yeah, that's interesting. And it's just funny, because that band breaks up and then Ian does something heavy, just like Rainbow did earlier. And also, like Marco says, Ian leaves Deep Purple and both Ian and Purple do funkier, more R&B-type things like this song. "Snake Charmer" is the kind of song you could have done with the Coverdale line-up, right? As for vocals, the vocal melody is not quite as interesting as in some of the other songs, and Ronnie gets a bit buried in the mix with all that stuff going on. So to me it's less successful than some of the other songs we will talk about in terms of creating that true new Rainbow sound.

Martin: Next we get another ballad, a sort of madrigal, perhaps.

Marco: Cool track, mellow, I love "Temple of the King," essentially medieval or renaissance music, minstrel music. The way Ronnie sings along with the melody, he makes the song hooky somehow. You can hum it in your head. But yeah, it's like a song played by an old bard in medieval times telling fairy tales or fables that are passed down, because there are allusions to the past and time and remembering and people going on journeys. I love that image, "There in the middle of the circle he stands/Searching, seeking/With just one touch of his trembling hand/The answer will be found." It's like he's talking about these kings and queens and wizardly things that have maybe altered the way we are today. Like I said, it's like a story an old bard would tell through song in an inn or a tavern, a fairy tale that we need to remember and has a lesson in it. It's clearly something Blackmore has an affinity for because it sounds like Blackmore's Night.

Peter: Ronnie's voice is exceptional; it's clean and it shows versatility even if it's not a big vocal from a power or range standpoint. It's nice and gentle and just feels good. Nice keyboard work, strings-like, but I wish, again, the keys were a little more forward in the mix. Once again, here's Driscoll and his indecision: are you playing eighth notes or sixteenths? It goes back and forth. Blackmore's solo is very delicate and gentle, and for someone who has such a reputation as an aggressive player, he sure had a soft side to him. That's on full display here, that he can put all the fireworks behind him and serve the melody. But I think it really depended on his mood, Martin, and where he was that day, whether somebody had pissed him off five minutes before he went on stage or whatever. Because that would dictate how he was going to play it or how he interpreted it that day. He's unstable from that standpoint.

Pontus: "Temple of the King" is a highlight for me. It's a great collaboration on the writing end and the acoustic guitar adds variation to the album as a whole. Dio tells an engaging and quite thorough and structured story over a beautiful folk melody. It's interesting that Ronnie was American and yet he loved the UK so much that he picked up on different things from the British Isles. This sounds very British, with him and Ritchie really being on the same page and writing well together.

Matt: "Temple of the King" is a personal favourite of mine on the album. I think this is where it comes together, this idea of a classical music-influenced hard rock band that has lyrical interests that are in the area of both sort of history and medieval fantasy. You've got the classical nylon string guitar stuff coming in, with a very low electric guitar in the mix. There's a kind of string ensemble in the middle.

It's a mellow song, but it has a really dynamic vocal. Ronnie does a tremendous job. It illustrates the way that he can get a story across through the dynamic aspects of his vocals; he doesn't just sing in one style, right? He can do something soft, and then come in with little sharp, heavy bits to put him in front, like that emphasis he puts on "fox," which has a snap to it. That's really dynamic for a mellow song. And then when he's singing these other parts, his voice in a couple places cracks a little bit. But to me it sounds like it's done in a very intentional way. It sounds like a warm, tube amp guitar, where you hit that little point where it starts to overdrive a little. That adds emotion. And then he's harmonizing with himself, which of course he does throughout his career and is very good at it. But this is an example of Rainbow early on where it's really a standout part to the vocal presentation. And he varies the rhythm of the melody, right? So it starts out with a jaunty-type thing, but then he'll stretch phrases out, with the "Searching, seeking." So for what on the surface is a lighter song, he's putting in this dynamic rhythmic variation, which I think is great.

I'll disagree a bit and say that the lyrics are more evocative. They don't so much tell a story. It's not a plot-heavy lyric. It's more about imagery and the poetry of it. "Sixteenth Century Greensleeves" is a bit more plot-heavy. But I think this fits well with it being a more mellow song, being more poetic over this lovely chord structure. You get a melodic guitar solo that's slippery and slide-y. A very successful song from my standpoint.

Martin: Then we snap back from the 1400s to the 1950s.

Marco: Yes (laughs). With "If You Don't Like Rock 'n' Roll" even what the keyboardist does is retro-rock. It's more centred around piano on *Ritchie Blackmore's Rainbow*, totally different than, say, *Rising* with "Tarot Woman" with the Minimoog and the synth and stuff. You can definitely hear that it's Elf and that they're changing their sound to conform with where Ritchie wanted to bring the band, which, again, was not that far when it comes to the first album. As for Ronnie, he was following Ritchie's lead at this point because Ronnie wasn't particularly sword and sorcery at this point and Ritchie is already there with what he likes to play on guitar. Being into classical and writing things like "Temple with the King," I think that influenced Ronnie a lot. But here they are still in Ronnie's past life, sort of thing. It's a throwaway rock 'n' roll song, even if the performances make it memorable.

Peter: I agree, because "If You Don't Like Rock 'n' Roll" is by far my least favourite song on the record, and the most Elf-sounding of the tracks. It's reminiscent of things on *Trying to Burn the Sun*, which was released not too many months earlier. So, you kill your own career, you put out an album, the whole band's gone and now you're in a different band. Not much going on there, right? (laughs). It's one of the more up-tempo songs, which is nice. Ritchie's riff is okay, but the song doesn't blend with the other tracks. Dio is aggressive and powerful but a little bit throaty, not as clean as he is on other tracks. I like the clavinet that doubles Ritchie's riff. That's a nice touch. We have our first keyboard solo, along with no solo from Ritchie. Wow. And of course it's on piano, which is of course the sound of Elf. Like Marco says, it's more piano than it is certainly organ- or synth-driven. And I don't need the handclaps; that dates it instantly. I'm not a big fan of handclaps in a rock song. Sorry, Boston. Otherwise, it's really short and just really doesn't need to be there. It seems filler to me.

Martin: It's funny; you mentioned no guitar solo and that this sounds a lot like Elf. So here and even on *Rising*, Ritchie lets his band shine. I think that's a theme on *Bent Out of Shape* as well—it's not a super-guitar type album. So there's almost an irony with this guy, how everybody talks about his big ego and prima donna tendencies, and he certainly hogs the limelight live. But it seems like on the studio albums, he is perfectly happy to let the band do their thing, right?

Peter: I do get the sense that he is truly motivated to serve whatever song it is that he is in the middle of. And that's very admirable, that he is looking to put together the best presentation for that song. And especially, like you said, in the studio, he's not looking to just throw something in to say, "Hey, look, I can throw something in." Obviously, there's a lot of bands that we can mention where that seems to be the case, where you'll have a song where the solo is so out of context, because they just want to show off and in the end it doesn't really relate, where it sounds like a separate piece that was stuck in. All of Ritchie's material here serves the song. And I want to make sure we point that out, because if he doesn't have a solo, he leaves it out. But I don't even know who decided where the songs came from on this album, because I don't know how many were pre-written, other than, I imagine "Man on the Silver Mountain" or "Sixteenth Century Greensleeves."

Pontus: "If You Don't Like Rock 'n' Roll" marks the dip in quality. It's just a rock song, a good fun track. They use a piano solo and all that. It's a bit like, we have to have more music here, what can we add to fill up the album? Compared with the highs of this record, this is lesser. It's a quickie and it works okay but it's not remarkable.

Matt: For sure; it's a really weird one on the record, a rock 'n' roll boogie song that's out of place on the album. But Ritchie and Ronnie do both have these rock 'n' roll roots in them, right? So it's not necessarily out of character for the individuals. You get the honky-tonk. Mickey Lee Soule makes it sound more like an Elf song or Coverdale/Hughes Deep Purple song. So it's another one where half the songs on this thing, Ritchie wouldn't need to create a new band to do this music. And the other half is very innovative and creating a new sound. Craig Gruber claimed that Elf had partially written some of this, including the riff, at the end of the *Trying to Burn the Sun* album sessions. I don't know that that's true; they don't get a writing credit on it.

Martin: Okay, next we're into proto-power metal classic "Sixteenth Century Greensleeves," titled to telegraph that this is meant to take us back in time yet again.

Marco: Another classic song, abundant with personality, and I love that Ronnie actually says "green sleeves" in the song, and it's actually "Green sleeves waving/Madmen raving/Through the shattered night." To me, it's the same guy who's on the silver mountain. "Man on the Silver Mountain" starts off the album and then "Sixteenth Century Greensleeves" is like, this is the conclusion or climax of the album because now that guy that's on the silver mountain, the holy wizard or whatever that's all powerful, now he's stolen the princess and locked her away. And now the knight or hero figure must come to defeat him and rescue the princess and they're coming in to fight these evil spirits and whatnot. They talk about crossbows and drawbridges and it's almost like a concept album if you think about it in those terms and include things like "Snake Charmer" and "Temple of the King" and "Self Portrait." That helps me appreciate the album more.

Actually I can talk myself into each of them being concept albums, especially *Rising*. But yeah, it feels like we're coming to the end of the wizard's reign and I like the lyrics, "Flames are getting higher/Make it leap unto the spire/Drawbridge down/Cut it to the ground,/We shall dance around the fire." So it's about like, a big battle or a war that's happening with this guy and the big tower where he locks the princess away. Makes sense that it's the man on the silver mountain to me.

Peter: "Sixteenth Century Greensleeves" is a standout track for me. I love all the elements of it. It's got the lyric content, great vocal, great riff, great bass playing, it's a really good tempo. It's got a great balance and somehow sounds more even than all the rest of the tracks on the record. It's like that odd thing where "Dream On" on the Aerosmith debut sounds like it was produced totally different than the rest of the record. Dio just sounds at home here. No one sings the words "higher" or "fire" better than Ronnie. Gene Simmons should have patented the word higher and fire together because they just work. Ritchie's solo is old-school Ritchie and one of the best from any album he's done with Purple or anybody. I think it's just a great, great solo. Again, in that one channel we've got that little thing going on where you go, "What's the point of that?" But it's well crafted and is well executed and it stands head and shoulders above the rest of the tracks on the record.

Pontus: Yes, another centrepiece and a very good rocker. The riff, the introduction to it, one could argue, why didn't they use the original "Greensleeves" as the intro? They use it live so they could have used it here. It would have made sense to add a snippet of the traditional song "Greensleeves" going into this. But yes, great production, heavy guitars. It might have made the best single choice as a rock song for American radio. I like the story. I like the descending chords after the solo, right? When they go back into the verse. And again, the ad-libbing at the end is just fantastic. I think this proved they could write together, that the partnership would work.

Matt: This one was intended to be the B-side of "Black Sheep of the Family." The origins are a little bit cloudy on it, but Ronnie said that Ritchie had the riff. I think Craig Gruber said that they were hanging out and Ritchie would have this $50 acoustic nylon-string guitar that he would bring with them without a case and that they'd play in hotel rooms and things like that. That implies that Ronnie and Craig were in the room. But in any case, it's a Ritchie riff that he comes up with. Blackmore has talked about how he wanted a song about castles and crossbows, and basically hard rock but using classical modes, right? That's his vision for what he wants to do.

And that also fits into what Ronnie is interested in doing, lyrically. So he's writing a song about some evil feudal lord who's abducted a beautiful damsel and then the population gets all upset and they revolt and they are seeking final retribution. So that one's a plot-heavy song, a medieval story to go with the classical and medieval modes in the music. You get some real Ronnie James Dio heavy metal-style singing in it, and that becomes a lot of his motif, just the way that he says words like spire and fire and higher, right? Or "Someone cries." And this dramatic heavy metal phrasing is such a good use of his voice. You've got very skillful use of the whammy bar on the guitar solo and Ritchie slips between doing slow bends and then into fast little runs and stuff, which is a signature part of his guitar style.

Martin: Okay, last one, "Still I'm Sad," which makes me sad in a number of ways—it's my least favourite on the album.

Pontus: Well, here's the thing. I think Ritchie wanted to show off. The opening riff is great. He has sped up the original "Still I'm Sad," which was a very slow, oriental-sounding ballad from The Yardbirds. Funnily enough, first time I heard it was the Boney M version. But this is a tour de force of his guitar playing. And should it have vocals? Well, maybe he was inspired by Jeff Beck, who had just done *Blow by Blow*, and he'd done a Beatles cover on that as an instrumental, "She's a Woman." Maybe he thought, if Beck can do it, I can do it. Do I like the cowbell? I don't know. It's one of those moments that if you put it away, would it work better? Maybe the cowbell helps it swing more.

Marco: Yeah, I really appreciate the jammy sort of drum performance from Gary Driscoll on this one. It's interesting that they decided to go with the lyrics on the live version but not on the studio version, where it's just an instrumental, and it's interesting that they picked that to close the album. It feels like it should go in the middle somewhere.

Peter: So yes, "Still I'm Sad" is a cover of The Yardbirds from their '65 album *Having a Rave Up* and it was originally written with lyrics, but Rainbow choose to make it an instrumental. This is finally where I think the band gets to shine. I do like the drumming on this, with some caveats. It's exactly the same cowbell part as "You Fool No One," which carries through, that double paradiddle thing. Ritchie opens with the guitar riff that he'd opened "You Fool No One" with live in Purple. That's all over *Made in Europe*. And all of a sudden Ritchie's tone gets more aggressive, more distortion, more bite. And I'm thinking, where's that been for the eight tracks (laughs) ahead of it? Because that's more the tone I'm looking for from Ritchie as a next step or an evolution from where he came from with Purple. It's by far the heaviest—or at least rowdiest—track on the record, which is ironic because Dio is not even on it.

I love when the band hits the unison machine gun section, where Ritchie just fires off. This is where he lets his technique shine and he's got all the pyro techniques and the fireworks and everything on it. Then you add the keys, which doubles the melodic line and makes it sound big. But yeah, while I love the drum pattern, Driscoll never alters it. He never breaks down or goes to a different section like Paicey does in "You Fool No One." At least Ian breaks it up when Glenn Hughes sings, and then he goes back to the pattern, which makes it easier to take where it's not just this constant cowbell thing. But I love the energy and the power on the track, even if it feels out of place, based on everything that has gone before it. This is what the album should have or could have sounded like, if they would have stuck with a heavier approach like this.

Matt: To me, what we have is an instrumental that serves as the backing for one long guitar solo—Ritchie just plays lead guitar throughout it. You've got low in the mix backup vocals from Shoshana. You get the really groovy percussion with lots of cowbell like "You Fool No One." It's got a lot of that same feel. And then later, like on *On Stage*, there are lyrics and Ronnie sings it well, so this could have been one with vocals. It's an interesting decision to do it as an instrumental with these improvised solos. I think it works, given that the album has a split personality anyway. I really don't know why it works, but it does.

Martin: Good stuff. I guess in closing, what is the legacy of this record?

Marco: Well, there weren't many that you could put in these categories, but the debut has them in a proto-progressive metal or proto-power metal space, doesn't it? Pretty unique at the time. It's quite British and sets a standard, and even, I suppose, has influence on the New Wave of British Heavy Metal, so it's predictive of that. But I like to think of it as early progressive metal, like *Sabbath Bloody Sabbath*, 1973, and *Sabotage*, which came out the same year as this, 1975. There's also *Demons and Wizards* and *The Magician's Birthday*, from Uriah Heep, which is a little closer to the sword and sorcery theme, but not so pronounced as Ronnie.

Martin: I don't know, Pontus, to me, the narrative is that he wanted to get away from certain kinds of music that they were doing on *Stormbringer* and whatnot. But yet this album is really like a mean, median, average of those final three records, *Burn*, *Stormbringer* and even *Come Taste the Band*.

Pontus: Yeah, Purple could have done "If You Don't Like Rock 'n' Roll." You can almost hear David sing that, and you can almost envision David singing something like "Sixteenth Century Greensleeves" as well, but with different lyrics. They could have done that song. And that, again, makes me wonder, where were those riffs on *Stormbringer*? Why didn't he take more control over that album? And sure, the funkiness that is apparent in "You Fool No One" is still apparent in "Still I'm Sad" because it's basically the same rhythm.

One thing that is interesting with these three albums, we're talking transitions from one major thing to the next thing, right? So I don't know; he had the mindset for Purple and now he's trying to create something new but he has to fall back on what he's done before. And he used the same producer, Martin Birch, and the same studio, Musicland. He used what he was comfortable with. Of course, it had to be a successful record. I'm sure he was nervous about leaving one of the biggest bands ever up to that point in the mid-seventies. He'd worked very hard to make Purple the way it was, taking it from this Vanilla Fudge band to the gleaming and mega hard rock band that they were.

Martin: You mention comfort. Is the idea of doing covers, like "Black Sheep of the Family" and "Still I'm Sad" so comfortable that they become a crutch?

Pontus: Yeah, that could be the case. And I understand why the other guys in Deep Purple said no. Because they weren't into covers at all. They hadn't done that since '69. Why go back and do a lousy cover when we can write something new? And I think what happened was when they write "Sixteenth Century Greensleeves" for the B-side, he realizes that he doesn't have to rely on covers with Dio. Dio is as good as Coverdale is when it comes to lyrics, even better, because he creates a different world. Remember that Ritchie is one of those people who is very interested in the occult and esoteric things. I think they had that in common. Dio could make that world for real for him. In a sense, *Ritchie Blackmore's Rainbow* is more of a follow-up to *Burn* than it is *Stormbringer*. It's more *his* album. It's odd he didn't just write a new instrumental, but then again he sure liked "Still I'm Sad" because it stayed in the set. But "Black Sheep of the Family" is gone by the wayside after it's recorded—it's just on the album.

Matt: To me, Martin, as Marco said, it's a seminal record in the genre to come of like sword and sorcery, epic-based heavy metal. We get bands whose whole careers are based on that type of music. We've had, previously, bands who were influenced by fantasy literature; *The Lord of the Rings*, J.R.R. Tolkien-type stuff, has already come up. It got popular in the sixties, but that's really like hippies and hobbits type music, right? Even the Led Zeppelin stuff is done in a pretty mellow way. Something like "Ramble On" or "The Battle of Evermore" have got the lyrics but it's not metal at all. Rush's "Rivendell" came out earlier that year but that's a mellow song. You've got Hawkwind, who is adding the Michael Moorcock influence. *Warrior on the Edge of Time* comes out that same year, but that's its own thing, right? It's not like historic fantasy heavy metal. It's more like modern sci-fi-type stuff. Very different aesthetic to it.

Martin: Plus there's wyrd folk, which, at times, you could put Syd Barrett in that box.

Matt: Yeah, and that's why I call it hippies and hobbits. It's this pastoral fairy tale-type version of the aesthetic. There's also Jethro Tull with *Songs from the Wood*. You've got bands just putting Gandalf in their name too, although that leans more psych. As Marco alluded to, Sabbath and Heep touch on it and represent the darker, heavier side. There's also going on at this time a bringing together of fantasy through Dungeons & Dragons. So Dungeons & Dragons is invented. It's not invented, but it's published in 1974. So there's an interest in aspects of the culture in this fantasy stuff that is much more like how Rainbow is treating it. And in 1975 this early Dungeons & Dragons company, TSR, produces a supplement to their book called *Blackmoor*, which sounds like Blackmore. The creators of this are not interested in hard rock music. They're all an older generation. So it's a coincidence that this is named *Blackmoor*. That name predates Dungeons & Dragons. The first campaign, when they were inventing this stuff, was called *Blackmoor*.

Martin: And sorry, what exactly is that thing?

Matt: It's a supplemental rule book that is published in 1975. I researched it. It comes out after the Rainbow album. The Rainbow album comes out in September and this book has been being worked on starting in '74. So it predates the album. Plus look (holds up book); there are similarities in the covers as well, with that castle.

Martin: Wow, that's amazing.

Matt: So again, the creators of this are not heavy metal fans, but who knows about the art? I don't know who the artist is; it's not credited at all. And this album does come out before this book gets published. So it is possible that someone picks up on the play of words, right? It's a coincidence, but some of the artists may have seen it and went, "Oh, it's a castle. This is perfect." Maybe it's a little nod to it. I'm still trying to figure that out. But this then starts off Ronnie's obsession, right? He's been quoted saying as much. He has an obsession with "mystical figures, kings and queens, angels and demons, dungeons and dragons." So that's a lyrical theme that he then carries forward in any talks about how it's suited his "epically scaled rock music that I like to perform." And then of course, later bands agreed that it's a good direction or milieu. Power metal, epic metal, traditional metal… the DNA goes straight to this album. So again, it's a very important record in terms of creating a whole new genre and aesthetic for heavy metal music.

Martin: Good stuff. Peter, any final thoughts?

Peter: Sure. We talked about production. It's dry and there are way too little keyboards—keyboards are an afterthought. Ritchie is like, "Okay, I've got keys—push them over there." Plus you compare the sound of this to something like *Toys in the Attic*. Holy smokes. It's like junior apprentice and master class. And again, from someone like Blackmore who should know better, that seems unusual. Dio's vocals are clear—he nailed it—but there's a lot of multi-tracking. There's Craig Gruber and his great bass playing on this, but Gary Driscoll is a head-scratcher. I feel like he was either told to cut it back or it's natural for him, but he's really restrained. If you listen to his playing on the Elf records, and especially the live material that he did with them, this is a very competent player. He's got a heavy feel, a great bass drum foot, very quick and Bonham-like, and he plays a lot of big, double-handed, Bill Ward kind of heavy fills at times. And none of those are here; they just are stripped away. So he feels neutered to me and I think that is to the detriment of the album, I would have loved to have heard him be more like him.

It's a confusing record. Who's the target audience here? It's not heavy enough for the hard rock or heavy metal crowd. There are too many medium- to slow-tempo songs and yet there are no pop elements to this. So he's sitting in the middle of no man's land, where it doesn't fit anywhere. This is not what you would expect from someone who just left Deep Purple.

Martin: It's almost like this is a record that could have come just before or just after *In Rock*, like a dated Deep Purple album.

Peter: Yeah, true, but of course the Purple fans embraced it because it's Ritchie. And Ronnie uses it as a nice stepping stone because clearly the evolution to the next album is immense. But it's got historic importance and there's where I think it does hold some merit. It's that stepping stone, the transition album. You say, okay, he took his first shot, and maybe he rimmed it off and lost the game in overtime. So it wasn't successful from that standpoint. But he does use the stepping stone. Come *Rising*, everybody but Ronnie gets fired and Ritchie brings in more seasoned players and the rest is history, right? The jump is maybe the biggest evolution in two albums of almost any band I can think of. How are *Ritchie Blackmore's Rainbow* and *Rising* even in the same ballpark? They're just so different.

Rainbow
Rising
RITCHIE BLACKMORE
A RAINBOW RISING...
polydor
Oyster
WORLDWIDE ON POLYDOR RECORDS AND TAPES

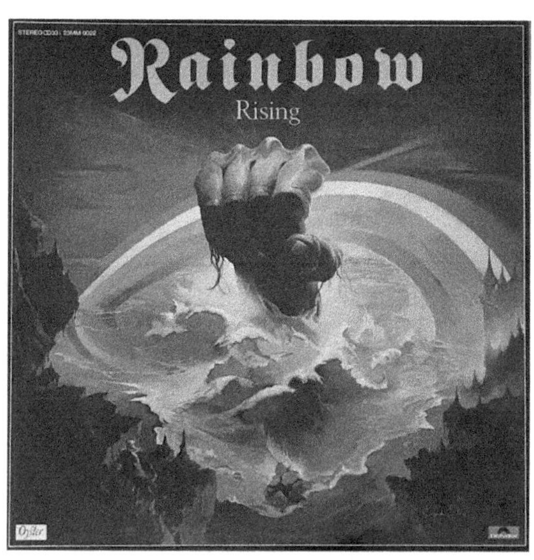

RISING

May 17, 1976
Oyster/Polydor OY-1-1601
Produced by Martin Birch
Recorded at Musicland Studios, Munich, Germany
Personnel: Ronnie James Dio – vocals, Ritchie Blackmore – guitars, Jimmy Bain – bass, Tony Carey – keyboards, Cozy Powell – drums, Munich Philharmonic Orchestra – strings

Side 1
1. Tarot Woman (Blackmore, Dio) 6:11
2. Run with the Wolf (Blackmore, Dio) 3:48
3. Starstruck (Blackmore, Dio) 4:06
4. Do You Close Your Eyes (Blackmore, Dio) 2:58

Side 2
1. Stargazer (Blackmore, Dio) 8:28
2. A Light in the Black (Blackmore, Dio) 8:12

A *Rising* Timeline

October 25, 1971. The Jeff Beck Group issue their debut album, *Rough and Ready*. On drums is Cozy Powell.

May 1, 1972. The Jeff Beck Group issue a final album, a self-titled. On drums once again is Cozy Powell.

July 1973. Bedlam issue their one and only album. Drumming is Cozy Powell, who issues a solo single pairing "Dance with the Devil" with "And Then There Was Skin" later in the year.

May 22 – July 27, 1975. Harlot play a series of shows at the Marquee in London. On bass is Jimmy Bain. Somewhere along the line, Ritchie catches a gig.

Early February 1976. Rainbow record what will be their classic *Rising* album, at Musicland in Munich, Germany, beginning and finishing in ten days, with the mix taking place back in America.

March 15, 1976. Deep Purple break up, when after a demoralizing Liverpool show (the last of five UK stops), Jon Lord, Ian Paice and David Coverdale decide to knock it on its head, unbeknownst to Tommy Bolin and Glenn Hughes. Scheduled German dates are cancelled.

May 17, 1976. Rainbow issue their second album, *Rising*, which reaches No. 11 in the UK charts and No.48 on the Billboard 200. The album certifies gold in Australia, Japan and the UK.

June 6, 1976. Rainbow plays Idaho, commencing their tour dates in support of *Rising*.

June 17, 1976. Playing the Beacon Theatre in New York, Ritchie smashes his first guitar as surly strummer for Rainbow.

July 27, 1976. "Starstruck" is issued as a single in the US, backed with "Run with the Wolf."

August 31, 1976. Rainbow play their first UK gig, at the Hippodrome in Bristol. Main support for the ensuing UK tour is Stretch. The tour begins with a minor glitch when the band's $100,000, 60-foot-long, 30-foot-high, computer-controlled electric rainbow doesn't show up in time, having travelled by sea from America.

September 7 - 9, 1976. Rainbow play the Hammersmith Odeon in London. On Sept. 7, Thin Lizzy's Scott Gorham and Colosseum II's Jon Hiseman attend the show, with some reports saying that Neil Murray and Don Airey were there as well. The following night, Jon Lord, Ian Paice, Dave Edmunds, Ian Hunter and members of Queen come to pay their respects.

September 16, 1976. When Rainbow's *Rising* tour hits London, Ritchie jams with old pal Screaming Lord Sutch.

Martin talks to Phil Aston, Marco D'Auria, Tate Davis, Nick Ermolovich and John Gaffney about *Rising*.

Martin Popoff: All right guys, lots of changes in the band, so let's break it down a bit: what does Cozy Powell bring to Rainbow that makes *Rising* so special?

Marco D'Auria: It's funny because I know Cozy is an amazing drummer and he brings a colossal sound to the live stuff, but I don't hear it as much in the studio albums. I find that he really shines on *On Stage* and *Live in Germany*. Still, Cozy brought a coherence to the band, or an adhesion, because between him and Ronnie and Ritchie, they sound like a band. After the first album they threw away all those guys and then with *Rising* and the live album and *Long Live Rock 'n' Roll*, it was like Rush to me, with three distinct personalities. And I feel like Cozy was the cohesion between Ritchie and Ronnie in terms of band politics and band presence, even if he definitely brought uncommon personality for a drummer as well.

Tate Davis: With *Rising* you get an upgrade over the greatness that you got with the debut, *Ritchie Blackmore's Rainbow*, because with *Ritchie Blackmore's Rainbow*, Ritchie is basically obligated to take on the rest of the guys from Elf into this new band that is forming. He wants to work with Ronnie and Ronnie is saying, "Okay, I'll do it but you have to take my guys with you." Ritchie is most likely going, oh, okay, and they go and they record the debut. Then he ends up firing the Elf band members, except Ronnie, and he gets Jimmy Bain, bass player, and the great Tony Carey, very underrated on keyboards.

And then at that point, he gets a pretty well-travelled veteran called Cozy Powell on drums, who was fresh off a stint with the Jeff Beck Group, the second incarnation. And then they go on and they record this album. I just read an interview Cozy did in the nineties, probably shortly before he died, where he said that most of the songs on *Rising* were recorded in one take, which explains why on subsequent reissues of *Rising*, you get all these alternate mixes instead of like alternate takes, because most of them were done in a take or two. They go to Musicland Studios in Germany to record this. And Musicland at that point was going to serve as a recording studio for Led Zeppelin *Presence*. The Rolling Stones would do some work on *Black and Blue* there shortly thereafter, and Rainbow's debut was recorded there as well.

So in summation, you get an ante-up in the personnel and you get an ante-up in the songwriting as well. Because some of the songs on the debut, like "Black Sheep of the Family" and "If You Don't Like Rock 'n' Roll" are still that sort of piano-driven, boogie woogie Elf music. But then you see glimpses of where they're gonna go with *Rising* on like "Man on the Silver Mountain," "Sixteenth Century Greensleeves" and to a lesser extent "Self Portrait."

Martin: Excellent. And Phil, you were there, boots on the ground, seeing this record happen. Tell us the story of how *Rising* was received in Britain at the time.

Phil Aston: In the UK in the mid-seventies, Ritchie Blackmore's marketing power was massive. Deep Purple were huge, although I know they were big in other territories as well. But in the UK, Blackmore was Deep Purple. Obviously we'd had the Tommy Bolin version of Deep Purple, which ground to a halt in 1976. So all the eyes are on Blackmore, and his marketing people got the poster out with the gatefold of the first Rainbow album with that classic pose that we know so well, which is obviously from Purple at the time. That first album came out and my friends were going, "It's a bit like Zeppelin and Purple." But of course, it wasn't, really. It was a mishmash. John Peel played "Man on the Silver Mountain," which is a great track. The riff is not that far removed from "Smoke on the Water," from a guitar point of view, really. And obviously "Sixteenth Century Greensleeves" was there. But the track everyone moved towards was "Still I'm Sad," which of course was a riff he'd been playing with on "You Fool No One" from the *Burn* tours and *Stormbringer* tours, etc. And that was where everyone wanted it to be. And he still didn't play live.

But I remember in the press, in *Sounds, New Musical Express,* etc., that you started seeing these posters for Rainbow *Rising.* The cover was more epic. This is the mid-seventies and there was lots of interest in King Arthur mythology, epic stuff, fantasy, sci-fi etc. I just looked at Rainbow *Rising,* with the little guy on the cliff edge, the rainbow, the fist, and without even hearing a note, you just thought, this is going to be different. So when it appeared in the shops, about May of 1976 in the UK, I remember loads of us going into Virgin Records in Birmingham and queuing up to buy it. None of us had heard a note from it. It hadn't been played anywhere. And we're looking at the pictures on the back cover thinking, we don't even know who half the people are apart from Cozy Powell, and obviously Dio. Who was Tony Carey? Who was Jimmy Bain? He'd been in a band called Harlot, but we didn't know anything about them, really. So we just thought, well, this looks cool. And I remember we're all going home, all different ways across Birmingham and thinking, there's only two tracks on side two. This must mean these are long tracks and that Ritchie Blackmore was going to let rip, perhaps.

Martin: Nice. Okay, we'll talk about those tracks shortly. Nick, how about some opening thoughts?

Nick Ermolovich: Well, I came to *Rising* a lot later than it was released and a lot later than I did the first album, as well as *Long Live Rock 'n' Roll*. So it came third and I didn't have the sort of background with it and didn't know that it was such a well-respected album with the fans. I was a huge fan of the first album, but listening to it in context, *Rising* is light years ahead, a major accomplishment. And the thing that's interesting about it to me is that Blackmore has this reputation with his ego, difficult to deal with, but on this album, he really lets his band shine. Cozy Powell's drums are punishing, and it's like Ritchie lets him do whatever he wants, whether it's ridiculous cymbal chokes or double bass or whatever. He gets the kid, Tony Carey, who introduces all these synth sounds compared to the first album, and he directs *Rising* in a proggy direction.

Jimmy Bain was buried in the mix. However, with the magic of reissue programs, we're able to hear the rough mix, which is more bass-heavy. But Jimmy is doing all sorts of interesting things on this album and in the final mix, you maybe lose some of that. In some of these rough mixes, the bass has an incredible growl. And like I say, he's doing things that I had not heard in my initial introduction to the album.

But the common theme is that Ritchie lets his band shine. Blackmore is not super-dominant on this album playing guitar. So it becomes this weird truth or fiction thing with Ritchie Blackmore, or a dichotomy. He really lets that band shine; he lets them do what they should be doing. Now maybe he sets the standards high. And you hear all these things about him. Finally, the last guy—Ronnie James Dio. Between the songwriting, carrying it in the direction that he wants to carry it in, and also just the way he sings, he's an integral part of just an incredible ensemble band performance.

So I get the accolades that are showered upon *Rising*. And it seems to be for a brief period of time, when they released this thing, this band may have been the heaviest, most hard-rocking band in the world. Scorpions, Judas Priest, UFO, American bands like Alice Cooper, Kiss and Aerosmith… this is a heavy, heavy band, where the players are just top-shelf and doing their thing and really pushing it. I guess the 800-pound gorilla in the room is, is Rainbow heavier than Black Sabbath at this point? You have *Sabotage*, an incredibly heavy album, but then *Technical Ecstasy* is sort of a step back. So during this period, '76, '77, I can't think of anybody else who would have been more aggressive.

Martin: Absolutely, we sensed that as well. I've told the story many times, but I remember *Rising* had the distinction for us as being the first album ever with no mellow music on it. Although very quickly came *Sad Wings of Destiny*, where even though there were two ballads, the rest of the album was actually all more modern and smarter and more heavy metal and thus just "heavier" than anything on *Rising*. And not to quibble too much, but we always felt that, say, the five heaviest songs from *Fly to the Rainbow*, *In Trance* and *Virgin Killer* were kinda all heavier than anything on *Rising* too, not to mention most Sabbath songs. But yes, it was the first "perfect" album as we classed it, a six out of six. Okay, Mr. Gaffney (my co-host on *Kicked in the Teeth: An AC/DC Podcast*), opening thoughts?

John Gaffney: All right, well, first of all, they get rid of the previous band and Ritchie and Ronnie move forward with a much more hard rock/heavy metal band, if you will, and the sound gets way more focused. So yeah, from the first album to the second album, I think a lot of it comes down to the change in the line-up, with Cozy, Tony and Jimmy.

I agree with the way you've always framed the origins of heavy metal but we differ a bit toward the end. *Rising*, in my opinion, is one of the early milestones in the development of heavy metal. The first big milestone for me is the big bang in 1970 with Deep Purple *In Rock*, Uriah Heep *Very 'eavy, Very 'umble* and of course Black Sabbath's first album, and if you want to throw *Paranoid* in there too, fine, because that also came out in 1970. That's how you always lay it out as well. But to me, the next heavy metal milestone marker is this album, *Rising*, in 1976. The next or third milestone for me would be 1978 with Judas Priest's *Stained Class*. So yeah, *Rising* is one of the first albums for me to really tighten the screws and get focused on the metallic sound, from the riffing through to the lyrics.

Martin: What are your thoughts on the album cover?

John: A lot of people cite this as an early power metal album or influence on power metal with epic songs like "A Light in the Black" and 'Stargazer." So the lyrical content is fantasy-related, as is the cover with the rainbow and the mountains and clouds. And you can see what looks like a little warrior guy along the side of the mountain there. It definitely sets a mood.

Tate: I think it's terrific. It shows a giant seaweed-covered hand and it's grabbing a rainbow, like it's plucking the rainbow from under the ground or the bottom of the sea. It's rising (laughs). Ken Kelly did the artwork for it, and he did *Destroyer* and *Love Gun* for Kiss around the same time. It does a great job of providing a visual aid to most of the songs on the album, particularly side two.

Nick: Yes, fantastic cover, one of the best, from the font used for Rainbow to the fist with the rainbow going through it. I just think it's imagery that if I'm a kid into hard rock in 1976 and I'm flipping through the racks at the record store, yeah, I'm grabbing that without hearing it. And as the catalogue goes on and with respect to live performance, they continued with the imagery of the rainbow itself; there's sort of endless creativity with that.

Martin: As much as I love the album, I always found the production harsh and screechy, although that also makes it lively and energy-filled, I suppose.

Tate: I really like it. Martin Birch knows what he's doing. I don't think there's an album that Martin Birch has engineered or produced that I haven't liked the sound of. This was one of his first in the production chair, along with the debut. Shortly thereafter, he would go on to work with Whitesnake, Blue Öyster Cult and then Iron Maiden throughout the eighties. And yeah, I think Martin Birch is probably my favourite producer of all time. He produced it in a way where you can hear every instrument very clearly. There's not much reverb. He produces it in a way where whatever band he's producing can go out and play the songs live in a similar arrangement to the studio versions.

Phil: It's interesting, because as the years have gone by, everyone goes, "Where's the bass player?" I have to say at the time, whether it was the primitive stereos in the mid-seventies or whatever, it just sounded fantastic. Maybe our ears were just listening to the voice, the guitar, the drums and the keyboards. Everything else was drifting in amongst the gaps. I know there are two versions, aren't there? The L.A. mix and the New York mix. Dio's voice is further back in the New York mix, the one they went with for the original album in '76. In the L.A. one, he's further forward and there's more bass.

Sure, it's somewhat flawed, but there are albums out there that have got production issues which are far more extreme than this. And to be honest, when it came out, of course there's no internet to complain on, but my friends and I, when we rung each other up and said, "What do you think?," none of us said, "Where's the bass player?" All we heard was guitars and Dio and Cozy Powell, of course. I think the lens of time has made some people compare it to other more contemporary things that have come along over the last few decades. But in 1976 it was as good as anything that was coming out production-wise, and I think it's stood the test of time, really.

Martin: Nice, and to clarify, the first mix was the L.A. mix but that wasn't used. The original vinyl used the secondary New York mix. However, the L.A. mix is used on all CD issues of the album. Phil, what do you think of this? Given it was recorded at Musicland and there's a thanks to Reinhold Mack, maybe this is the birth of the Mack sound, but in purely cleaner, analog form.

Phil: Interesting idea; yeah, I can hear that. But at least we have these mixes for variety's sake. There's no extra music. The album is so short. You wondered if there was something else waiting in the wings that they didn't have time to finish. But that is it, isn't it? There was nothing in the can. That's all there was.

John: Martin Birch did all right but not great. I don't really like the production on this record. It's totally lacking in bass, both bass, the frequency and bass, the instrument. But yes, for everybody out there, seek out the deluxe version of Rainbow *Rising*, It comes with the original L.A. mix of this record, which has way more bass, which totally changes the feel of the album. I read an interview with Jimmy Bain where he was asked about this, and he said that when they finished the L.A. mix, the record company felt it was too bass-heavy. So he says they basically took him completely out of the mix during the New York mix, which is the mix that was released to everybody.

But I would encourage people to seek out that L.A. mix because it's warmer and more pleasing on the ears. It's a shame because Jimmy has some really cool bass parts throughout this whole record that are just completely lost with the mix that came out.

Martin: Okay, past the wrapper and into the timeless journey that is *Rising*, first we hear "Tarot Woman."

Marco: First, I gotta say that *Rising* is my favourite Rainbow album and was the first one that I owned. And it would be erroneous to say that this is a solo project because, as we've discussed, Ritchie didn't have any problem allowing somebody else to take centre stage. Case in point, we hear Tony Carey's Minimoog and synths first. Those opening eerie moments brings you right into this world of Rainbow. But again, Ritchie steps aside and let's the Minimoog be the centrepiece. Tony even gets a keyboard solo in "A Light in the Black," and Ronnie and Cozy get to showcase their talents as well. In that sense, *Rising* feels like a band effort, and less like Elf featuring Ritchie Blackmore. It feels more like Rainbow.

But yes, "Tarot Woman" centres these guys and this band immediately, helped by the lyrics, which take us right into Ronnie's mystical world. It's the perfect song to open the album. I wish it opened the first album because I think it sets the mood perfectly for the whole idea of Rainbow, not to mention the Dio discography. Lyrically, it's about entering this fair and meeting a magical tarot reader who guides you into this fantasy world. Whether you want to go along or not, you'll be taken and it's too late and you're in Rainbow's world (laughs). She's going to charm you, like the snake charmer. She's going to charm you and mesmerize you and then all of a sudden you're going to be taken in—you've been tricked by this beautiful woman. "Beware of a place/A smile on a bright, shiny face." The song sets you up for sensibly seeing *Rising* as a concept album, at least loosely speaking.

Tate: "Tarot Woman," in my opinion, is the introduction to this new era of Rainbow. The moment that you put on the vinyl and you hear Tony Carey's opening keyboard motif on the synthesizer and whatnot, you're taken into this trance, and the listener is like, okay, where are we going with this here? This is obviously going to be very mysterious. And then immediately after that's over, you hear that riff and then then it becomes this gallop feel that would later influence bands like Iron Maiden. Dio comes in with a vengeance. "I don't wanna go/Something tells me no/No, no, no." It's a singer singing his passion and these lyrics about the dangers of this tarot woman who's predicting all these really pessimistic possibilities in the setting of the song. It's a great way to open up the album and it really falls in line with some of the later songs on it, particularly on side two. It's like a good companion piece to those two long songs.

Phil: I remember going home and sticking the needle down on "Tarot Woman." Like I say, this is before the internet and you can't text your friends. You can't have a listening party, at least not online. You're on your own in your room. The needle goes down. There isn't a riff. There's a keyboard intro. So there's restraint from Ritchie; he's maybe thinking his fan base is expecting a riff. Then the drums come in, then the vocals. But to begin with, it's a keyboard solo, this ethereal synthesizer sound that drifts from speaker to speaker on its own. We haven't seen that since the keyboard interlude at the start of "Speed King" back in 1970, albeit only on the long version, of course.

And then Tony fades into the background and you hear that repeating intro riff. And it's that typical Ritchie way of guitar playing, the single plectrum on a single note and a single string, and you just think, this is Ritchie Blackmore. And then everyone piles in there. Cozy piles in, the keyboards pile in, more guitars, it gets louder and we're off and running.

And "Tarot Woman," again, has all the mystique and epic imagery that you want when you're 17 years of age. We've only known Dio from the first album and some of us had seen him with Elf on the *Burn* tour, but his voice on this is so different than the first album. Before we even get to the guitar solo in "Tarot Woman," this is so different to the first Rainbow album, in its vision and its structure, and then the solo is like nothing else on the first album either. The first album is now drifting into the background before we even reach the end of that first track. But Dio has arrived. We like his ad-libs on "Man on the Silver Mountain," but on *Rising*, at the end of that first track, he's now a contender for being one of the best rock vocalists we're aware of.

The next three tracks are… they're not a letdown but they're a separate pot of tunes compared with "Tarot Woman," "Stargazer" and "A Light in the Black." Those three have an identity to themselves whereas the next three, "Run with the Wolf," "Starstruck" and "Do You Close Your Eyes," have got an almost hard rock Bad Company feel to them. But they wouldn't have fitted on the first album either.

Nick: "Tarot Woman" is a great declaration of independence. You've got that synth flourish at the beginning, neither proggy nor Gary Wright, and Ronnie is telling an interesting story. I would have loved to have heard this on the *On Stage* album. Some of those vocals sound doubled as well. So that's an interesting thing, where we're hearing multiple Ronnie James Dios. If I heard this as a kid in 1976, I'd instantly be saying, "Sign me up!"

John: All right, well, "Tarot Woman," yeah, I love that long Moog, analog synth intro. If you picture those guys from the seventies where they're standing behind these mountains of synthesizers with thousands of knobs and blinking lights on them, that's what you're getting. The intro sounds super-cool though and really sets the mood for the way it fades in. Eventually Blackmore inches his way into the sound doing the classic Blackmore pattern. Ritchie very rarely just strums or chugs away on power chords. What you hear him doing here at this intro as he fades in, it's a classic Blackmore move, where he's playing the root of the chord and then playing the octave of the chord using it as an accenting type of thing.

Then what's interesting is that the intro of the song, with the guitar fading and everything, is in the key of D, D minor, and then it changes to the key of G minor for the verse, this circle of fifths movement, which is a very classical thing. So you've got the intro in D minor, you've got the verse in G minor, and then the chorus is going to be in C minor. This is a very classical thing, to move like this; it's what they refer to as the circle of fifths. Eventually the verse comes in and now we're in G minor. I love Dio's lyrics here, where he's painting these images. Like Marco, I especially like the line, "Beware of a place/A smile on a bright shining face."

The guitar solo is awesome. Here's another classic Blackmore thing. Ritchie always played a Strat, and a Stratocaster has three pickups on it. There's a neck pickup, there's a middle pickup and there's a bridge pickup. Ritchie never plays on the middle pickup. He's always somewhere between his neck pickup and his bridge pickup. And this is a trademark of his, where in the middle of a solo, he'll switch between the two. So at the beginning of this solo, you get this plucky approach, and then you hear him flip to the neck pickup, which gives it this rounder, warmer sound. And then he goes off and he's playing these really fast runs. At this point the song has moved to D minor, again, this circle of fifths thing, very classical Ritchie. And so his picking hand is overtop of these different pickups, turning them on. And he keeps his picking the same, but there's a switch on his guitar that he flips, so that in fact, if you watch Ritchie live, you'll see him often doing this flicking his hand down motion. And what he's doing is he's very quickly flipping to just the neck pickup or just the bridge pickup. He never puts it in the middle, which blends all three of them. He's always flipping back and forth between the neck pickup and the bridge pickup. The neck pickup gives you this sort of warm, roundish sound because that pickup is closest to the neck. The bridge pickup gives you this brighter, more tinny sound because that pickup is very close to the bridge where the strings are connected, if you will.

Okay, here's another super-interesting thing about the song that I just absolutely love. The last verse and chorus of the song, coming out of the guitar solo, they modulate up two steps. So the final verse and chorus are actually two frets higher than the original verse and chorus. Now, this is not something that's never been done in hard rock before; you'll hear this sometimes. But a lot of times, artists do this with the final chorus of the song. Think "Livin' on a Prayer" by Bon Jovi, where the last chorus just modulates up three steps to make it sound brighter and like it's popping out at you. But with Rainbow, they do this here with the final verse and the final chorus, which is just really cool, that the last part of the song is two frets higher than the first part of the song. This is a similar move to what they do in "Kill the King" off of *Long Live Rock 'n' Roll*, where the final verse and the final chorus also modulate up four steps in that song. So this is a classic and rare Rainbow move. You don't see a lot of hard rock bands do that, especially at this time. Nobody was really playing around with these kinds of modulations and these key changes within songs.

Martin: Great stuff. Okay, things slow down for "Run with the Wolf," which gives me a bit of a loping, strolling "Maybe I'm a Leo" vibe.

Marco: Yes, a sort of mid-tempo straight rock song, but with magical, mystical lyrics, so the theme set with "Tarot Woman" is maintained. Perhaps once you're taken into this fantasy world, now we're running alongside the wolf who becomes our new guide. We're called to run with the wolf. Like, now we're in it. And there's magic in the skies. And if you listen to the lyrics, now we're really in this world. I like the lyric, "Like a beast in a field/He knows his fate is sealed/He runs with the wolf." So it's like we're warned on "Tarot Woman" about all this stuff that's happening in the future, and now it's like, oh, our fate is sealed, because now we're here and actually doing it. We're running with the wolf. The wolf could be its own sign of something. I don't know; maybe the band is the wolf and as fans we're running alongside Rainbow, or maybe it's Rainbow now caught up in the big, bad music industry.

Tate: I agree; "Run with the Wolf" is the second in a one-two punch of this album and it's a perfect complement to "Tarot Woman." It's almost as if the tarot woman has a pet wolf, which the listener is trying to either partner with or use it to try to escape the dangers that are prophesized by the tarot woman or something to that effect. Once again, we have a venomous vocal delivery from Ronnie.

Cozy Powell provides a swing feel with an avalanche of triplets all over the place on the drums. He does these fills that just come out of nowhere and those really add a lot to the song. Blackmore leaves a lot of space with his solo, which is something that you don't hear him do too often. But that tempo, man, it feels bouncy, or like you say, maybe walking or running. But of course you have a wolf beside you that you're either partnering with to escape danger or maybe the wolf itself is the danger and you're running from it, depending on how you read the lyrics. Yeah, that song has to be second and also right after "Tarot Woman." If you opened up the album with it, the song wouldn't have had the same effect as it does being the second track.

Phil: As I mentioned, "Run with the Wolf" is a good song but it doesn't quite join the elite group with that top three, as we see them. All the action, I think, and all the legendary praise that is poured on this record, is when you flip it over to side two.

Nick: I hear "Run with the Wolf" and picture it as a long-lost Steppenwolf album title (laughs). I like the song; it's good. Every song on this album is high quality for me. Of the six tracks, this may be the lesser of the six. But there's nothing wrong with it. It's a grinder, given that rhythmic structure. But when I stack this up with the others, it falls a hair short.

John: This is a mid-tempo one but it's got a heavy feel; it reminds me a bit of "Sixteenth Century Greensleeves," very heavy on the downbeats, somewhat plodding. Dio, as expected, sounds great on it. I love the harmonies that he adds in the chorus and I love the lyrics, especially that "There's a hole in the sky/Something evil's passing by" line, in the way Ronnie enunciates those words. And the outro of this song has a classic Ronnie thing where, as the song is fading out, he's ad-libbing and just sort of spitting out lines. Here he sings, "Like a beast in the field/He knows his fate is sealed," which is another great line. But Ronnie does this all the time. Think of the outro to "Heaven and Hell" and later on this album, "Stargazer."

Martin: What do you think Cozy's personality is as a drummer?

Nick: I hear some of Cozy's solo stuff, and some of the things when he sort of stepped out from Rainbow or Sabbath and he's maybe overplaying, but it's still phenomenal. I love Cozy Powell, muscle-y, basic, within the parameters of a hard rock song, and he is just top-shelf to me. He does a lot of cymbal chokes on this album. I think he's a phenomenal foundation and building block for any band, and in this particular album, I think he's great. When you compare him to what else was out there at the time, he's just top of the heap.

John: I love Cozy. He's from that seventies John Bonham heavy-hitting school of drummers, big toms, big fills. The production on this record, it's hard for me to get past the brightness of it. The drums are a little loud, and there's just not a lot of warmth on this record for me, but I think he sounds good. And he's not a guy that blends into the background. He's always there driving and pushing everything along.

Martin: Speaking of songs with driving drums, next is "Starstruck," basically an up-tempo heavy metal shuffle, as Kick Axe would say.

Marco: I agree; "Starstruck" is another one where Cozy is the heartbeat of the band. Ritchie's riff is a hammer-on thing, and together, he and Cozy provide the rhythmic pulse, along with Jimmy, of course. The narrative is later that Ritchie wanted to take the band in a commercial direction, but this shows Ritchie thinking that way early on. It's like a modern take on "If You Don't Like Rock 'n' Roll" and "Black Sheep of the Family" but only the next year (laughs). It's commercial and catchy and could have been a single.

Tate: Great song but it's a complete departure from "Tarot Woman" and "Run with the Wolf." Later on, Ronnie leaves the band because Ritchie wanted him to write love songs but this is about an obsessed female fan that is stalking the band, as evidenced by, "The lady's starstruck/She's nothing but bad luck/The lady's starstruck/Runnin' after me." I find it peculiar that Ronnie would even write a song like that. I don't know what was going on the band at that time, but it's even bouncier than "Run with the Wolf" because the tempo is almost twice as fast as "Run with the Wolf." I like Cozy's cymbal chokes on the crash cymbal. I hear that and I'm thinking the protagonist's head is turning left and right, trying to spot this woman who's stalking him and he's paranoid beyond belief. It's a really fun song, but it does interrupt the flow after the first two tracks. It wouldn't have sounded out of place on the Joe Lynn Turner stuff.

Martin: Except one thing, Tate. If you think about it, the music on it is just as gothic as the first two, right? It's just as European and ornate, and if it had a dragon lyric, we might not be talking about it this way. But I get what you're saying—these lyrics are pretty rock 'n' roll.

Phil: To clarify, it's about that girl that was stalking Ritchie across Europe in his Purple days. It's an okay song, but a bit boogie rock for Rainbow.

Nick: Well, I hear this and I'm thinking that you yourself, Martin, are heading for the hills because it's a shuffle and you are on record complaining about them. So I hear this and I sort of chuckle. I'm like, oh gee, Martin may not like the song but I love it because I love shuffles. It's one of those I know they do on the live album. They only play a snippet of it, but I love it. I like the pace and I like the guitars. It's odd that you have only six songs on the album and two of them have the word star in it. Like I say, I like this song because I'm a big shuffle fan. But I know it's your kryptonite. The lyrics are Ronnie talking about an aggressive fan, which isn't necessarily in his wheelhouse. That intro guitar piece is almost like a medieval jig, which perhaps serves as a little foreshadowing with Ritchie and Blackmore's Night. It's almost neoclassical but to me, that's like a medieval jig.

John: "Starstruck" has a pretty neat ascending and descending single-note guitar line in the intro, and then it drops into a swinging boogie rock feel that reminds me of "Long Live Rock 'n' Roll" and maybe hearkening back to Ronnie's previous band Elf. It might seem odd this early in his career, or on *Rising* particularly, but Ronnie will actually sing a lot about evil women. You get this in "Lady of the Lake" and you get it in Sabbath with "Lady Evil" and "Country Girl." You get it from the solo band with "Gypsy" and many, many other songs. But here we get it with lines like, "The lady's starstruck/She's nothing but bad luck." Ronnie just loves to sing about dangerous women that you should stay away from. The chorus for me is a little too sing-songy, a little too happy-sounding. There's just something about that melody that's a little too bouncy-sounding for me. But I guess it provides a little levity. You can't have everything being crushing, dark and heavy.

Martin: All right, side two closes with "Do You Close Your Eyes," which, frankly, on any lesser album, we'd be talking about like a lusty and excellent rocker—especially for 1976.

Marco: Yeah, exactly, and I don't know if you ever noticed this, but "Do You Close Your Eyes" is like a proto-"The Mob Rules." If you listen to the riff or the way the chords move, it's pretty similar.

Tate: Pretty interesting, but still, "Do You Close Your Eyes" is for me the worst song on the album. But that doesn't make it a bad song. It's got a great riff and a chunky, clunky hard rock feel, and Cozy puts in a tremendous Bonham-esque drum performance. Lyrically, it doesn't go much deeper than the concept we get from the title, namely do you close your eyes when you're making love? Not a really deep song and silly, but for some reason I think it works on here. When they would do it live on the tour to support this album, they typically extended it and I believe they would add in a solo section, which made it pretty cool. I find live versions of the song pretty interesting.

Phil: "Do You Close Your Eyes" was unusual at the time because studio-wise there was no guitar solo in it. "Our Lady" from *Who Do We Think We Are* from Deep Purple had no guitar solo in it, but of course, he was fed-up by then, on that album. But he wasn't fed-up on *Rising*. So the fact he pulled back and thought, no, I don't think we need a solo, makes it quite an unusual track. But of course, live, it took on a whole new kind of life.

Nick: Yeah, it's a little hair metal-y with respect to the lyrical fare. But you know what? That song is a real driver. I like it, it's catchy and I wish it was on the live album.

John: I see it as a straight-ahead, AC/DC-style rocker with the big open string chords at the beginning. This is another one where I don't really care for the lyrics—they're silly and throwaway and they make me cringe. The main riff reminds me of what they would do later on the *Straight Between the Eyes* album with the song "Power." It's that same type of feel. But I'm not going to deny that it's a got a catchy chorus and it's got this infectious, straight-ahead, rock 'n' roll feel.

Now I'm gonna go on a bit of a soapbox here. People will often say that, oh, the Joe Lynn Turner era of the band, they went AOR, that they went soft rock or radio rock on us. And whenever they do that, I always like to point people back to "Do You Close Your Eyes" from this album, and say, hey, there was some of this stuff going on even on the almighty *Rising*, which, everybody, when they think of *Rising*, they think of "Stargazer" and they think the whole album is like that. It isn't; you get stuff like "Do You Close Your Eyes," which, to me, could have been on a Joe Lynn Turner-era album.

Martin: Over to side two and we get what will quickly be heralded as a masterpiece.

John: Absolutely, the almighty and epic "Stargazer." At this point in time, mid-seventies, you're right; this stands head and shoulders right there next to "Kashmir" and "Stairway to Heaven" as one of the big epics of the seventies. We get one of the greatest drum intros ever here, courtesy of Cozy. The main riff of the song is totally awesome after that drum fill. Everything kicks in and it's just so cool. It's an E minor riff with this little chromatic run back up, a chromatic walk-up thing, back to the root, which is just awesome. And it has this slightly rolling, borderline plodding but circular feel to it. It goes hand in hand with these lyrics, which are about being oppressed and working for this evil wizard. Dio is in total fantasy storytelling and imagery mode here. I love the way he sings that, "There's no sun in the shadow of the wizard," line; just great stuff.

When the song moves to the part that goes, "Where is your star? Is it far, is it far?," the main verse of the song is in E minor. And when it moves to this part, we're now in what's called a mode and this is B Phrygian. And it gives it this… with the addition of the strings, which are added here by the Munich orchestra, this mode gives it a very Arabian or Middle Eastern type of sound to it, the way the strings move around. And would you like me to explain what a mode is? Or is that getting too in depth and subtle?

Martin: Sure go for it!

John: Okay, so a mode is when you're in a particular key, which, this song is in the key of E minor. But instead of emphasizing the E, you emphasize a different note in the scale. And in this particular part of the song, they're emphasizing the fifth note of the scale, which is B and inside this particular mode, you get a one fret away from the root type of thing. And so it gives it this slightly offsetting, unstable sound. And in this particular spot, the mode to it gives it this Arabian, Middle Eastern sound. Blackmore would often refer to this as his snake charmer scale, because it has that feel to it. And you add the strings on top of this, the way the strings are moving around, it gives it this total exotic feel, which is just so cool.

Then when we get into the guitar solo, it goes back to this B Phrygian. And Blackmore takes it and sort of alters some of the notes to get it to that snake charmer scale, giving it this really exotic sound. I absolutely love the part where he starts climbing up his... one of the open strings on the guitar is a B string, so this particular section is in B. So it allows Blackmore to do this sort of hammer-on and pull-off climbing up. He's jumping off his open B string, as he climbs up the neck of the string just getting higher and higher and higher, sort of spiralling around.

Much like the imagery of the song, right? The wizard is reaching for the stars. For me, when I hear this part from Blackmore's guitar line, he's just climbing up his B string, and it's spiralling and it's getting busier and busier until he lands on this note, that he just sort of hangs on and bends on. It's totally awesome. And then at the end of the solo, they land on this D chord where the guitar notes are just sort of shooting out at you from the left and the right speaker with this flange and echo effect until the main riff just totally drops back in on top of you—totally cool.

I love the way Dio wraps up the story in the last verse, especially the, "No sound as he falls instead of rising!" and right on the word rising, he emphasizes that and they put a little bit of an echo effect on it. I just love little things like that, man, because it just ties into the title of the album and everything. And then at the end of the song, we have Ronnie's trademark outro chorus thing where he's ad-libbing. I'm getting a shiver up my spine thinking about it, when he sings that line, "I see a rainbow rising." It's triumphant and epic. The strings are going, everything's going and it's just so grand and majestic. Absolutely incredible—love it.

Marco: "Stargazer" is probably my favourite Rainbow song ever, or maybe second to "Kill the King," although "Gates of Babylon" is in there too. It's hard to even compare. If you could take the feeling you get the first time you hear "Stargazer" and bottle it and listen to that feel the rest of your life, that's like a drug. It's both the epitome and peak of Rainbow. After this song ends, we're on our way down across the ensuing albums. Again, very visual lyrics. It's hard not to imagine and visualize wizards floating in the desert and slaves building a tower out of stone. It's almost like musical theatre. The whole album is like musical theatre. And that intro barrage from Cozy, he's throwing everything against the wall there. Still, although Cozy and Tony get to shine, this one is really Ritchie's. It's an eight-minute song and half of it's him, right?

Tate: Oh, man, what is there to say about the brilliance that is "Stargazer?" From the moment you hear Cozy's intro, you know that you're in for an eight-and-a-half-minute ride that's filled with genius. Dio puts in his best vocal, I think, on a studio recording ever, singing about a wizard who uses slave labour to build a stone tower to the skies that he could later jump off of, and how the slaves building said tower are doing so under the worst of conditions. They're not getting any water; they're not getting fed. Ronnie unfortunately doesn't write about any lodging or accommodations that the slaves might be receiving (laughs). I don't know; maybe the wizard doesn't have that kind of time to prepare all that. But lyrically, it's a work of genius.

Blackmore's really picking the right musicians to be able to fulfil his vision. It's really evident on this song and "A Light in the Black." Blackmore's solo on "Stargazer" is interesting because for me, it's like the wizard is climbing up the stone tower and trying to test what the whole purpose of it is. He wants to climb to the top of the tower and jump off of it and try to fly. And as you hear the crescendo up to where the rest of the band cuts out and Blackmore just lets his guitar ring, that's when he jumps, that's when he's flying. But he's flying the way that a flying squirrel or sugar glider would fly and glide. He's taking in his surroundings, he's finally saying to himself, "Yes, I'm flying, I'm fulfilling my dream."

And then, in one of the greatest-placed drum fills in the history of popular music, he falls down and dies from the fall, which brings a whole new meaning to the term, "It's not the fall that kills you. It's the landing." And Ronnie then says in the last verse, how everything that he had built, all the work that the slaves had done under these conditions, was for nought because he ended up dying and the purpose had not been fulfilled. And then going into the last part of the song where the symphony orchestra comes in and Ronnie's screaming to the heavens about seeing a rainbow rising, that really provides a great companion soundtrack to the album cover. The rainbow rising on the album cover, I think, is the one described in the song. So overall, "Stargazer" is a work of magnificent genius that influenced a lot of the clichés that we typically associate with power metal, that would come in the eighties and into the nineties.

Martin: Is the rising rainbow the wizard's soul departing?

Tate: That could definitely be a possibility; yes.

Martin: Is Ritchie out-Zeppelin-ing Zeppelin? Or does he own this space as much as Jimmy Page does anyways?

Tate: That's a good question. I think the closest Zeppelin comes to this kind of thing is "Kashmir," but this is more grandiose than "Kashmir."

Martin: Phil, what were your thoughts as you flipped the record to the second side back in 1976?

Phil: It was that side two is a different beast. It's a different animal and different band. As you look across the landscape of the mid-seventies, what can you compare this to? Where do you sit it in? Music scholars hearing "Stargazer" said, "Oh, they must have been listening to 'Kashmir' the year before." Maybe. Maybe he'd just been doodling on his cello and come up with a very simple riff and he thought, I wonder what that would sound like on guitar?

As "Stargazer" starts, with that drum intro and moving into that very dense riff, it sounds ethereal, like there are layers of wind sounds or keyboards or strings sitting in amongst it. Maybe that's the production, but you can't quite work out what's going on between the instruments, because technically, it's guitar, bass, drums and keyboards. But there's like another thing (laughs), drifting in amongst the notes. And of course, Dio's got all the right amount of reverb to sound like he really is climbing up the side of a mountain, building a tower.

But it's the simplicity of the riff that draws the listener in. It's a song about wizards. Now, none of us have ever met a wizard. They don't go shopping in their local mall. But we believe this song. There is a wizard and he's building a tower up to the sky. We just believe every word that Dio is saying. It's 1976, it's months before punk arrives and all this stuff is going to be ridiculed; they're going to try and push it away. It's been too overblown. But we believe everything at this point in time.

And I think this is probably the first place where Ritchie does that Eastern, snake charmer guitar solo. He's soloing and the notes are just pouring out like water, pouring down rocks off a waterfall coming off the top of a mountain. And he's got the perfect backing, that dense groove that just keeps going. He could just keep doing this. Again, it's got the expected instrumentation but also this other sound that's in amongst the production that gives it this huge, theatrical, cinematic feel, if you're closing your eyes and listening to this.

The other thing about "Stargazer," of course, is that it's eight minutes long, but three minutes of it is actually the ending (laughs). It's almost as if they were so amazed by Dio's ad-libs, that they thought, let's just keep the tape going. Because any normal song would have faded out way before then. It's very hypnotic. The strings come in, and that's another thing about the different mixes, the level that the strings are at. But they just keep that going and actually create or sustain a groove through strings. There's no solo or anything. It's just Dio doing these ad-libs, which he was known for. And you just feel that it could roll on forever.

Nick: That "Stargazer" intro just shows the power of Cozy and why you'd want him in your band. You really get your money's worth out of that guy. Also, like at the beginning of "Tarot Woman" where there's that synth, you get it at the beginning of the rough mix version of "Stargazer" too, same sort of air raid siren effect. Tony's got some weird sounds in there. It looks like he likes to play around with the pitch-shifter thing. It's really cool. I could listen to that synth sound all day.

But of course "Stargazer" is the opus of the album, which is underscored by the fact that they had the orchestra in there. Everything is right about that song. Eight minutes for me is pushing it to where I consider it work, but it's a great song. And I know live it was a real highlight. But I get what Nick is saying about the foundational sound in there somewhere, which adds to the underlying heaviness. Whatever synths or keyboards he's using, that effect was used well. Tony Carey earned his money on that song.

Martin: The album closes with "A Light in the Black" and it's a full-on continuation of the story, and even from the same perspective, that of one of the tower toilers, a slave.

Marco: And apparently it was a throwaway track for Ronnie in terms of the lyrics. Like, he literally just threw some lyrics together because Ritchie had a riff or whatever. But I think here's another one where the keyboard player shines. Tony's soloing is just as prominent as Ritchie's. To me, the most magical moment though is the first time you hear that "I'm coming home" line—Ronnie just kills it.

Martin: You mention Ronnie's lyrics and I know, he expressed to me himself his disdain for this song. He also told me that he doesn't enjoy writing for fast songs as much as slow, doomy songs.

Marco: And yet he quite liked "Kill the King," which is even faster. But I get what you're saying. You see that in his catalogue in the nineties up until he died. Anyway, yeah, "A Light in the Black" is a sister song to "Stargazer." The idea is that the wizard is dead and these are the people trying to put their lives back together after the wizard, who they worshipped, has gone. But looking at the positive, I feel that the song was about the slave-builder gaining back identity or power or confidence, and that the deeper message is that the listener might be inspired by the story as well. It's completing a quest or getting through a tough time and coming out the other side. Because if you read the lyrics, it's like reaching the end of the tunnel and the darkness and seeing that light out of the darkness.

To go with this concept album theme I brought up earlier, it's like returning from our journey that began with the encounter with the tarot woman. That's my vision of it. We've gone through all this, there's that light in the black when we got through it, all that darkness and magic and wizards and the wolves, and way back at the beginning, the tarot woman who tricked us. We're stronger having gone through all that. Now we're finishing this concept, putting a big red bow on the story. "A Light in the Black" and "I'm coming home" are the resolution to the story.

Tate: Agreed. "A Light in the Black" is a terrific companion piece to "Stargazer," albeit faster and more furious. What really sticks out to me in the song is maybe less about the lyrics and more about the solo section. Tony Carey really shows what he's capable of with his keyboard solo, just making as much noise as he possibly can and experimenting almost relentlessly. I don't think anybody else was doing a keyboard solo like this in 1976. And Cozy's playing under him while he's doing his thing just shows you the magic that this line-up had. Overlaying it all is Ritchie's neoclassical way of thinking.

Phil: How can you possibly follow "Stargazer?" You follow it the only way you can, with a song that's married to it, which is "A Light in the Black," arguably one of the greatest closing tracks of all time. It's a very simple riff, almost throwaway. If you isolated that riff on its own, it's a Status Quo/Chuck Berry-type riff. But then you slot it in place with the double bass drum work of Cozy Powell and Dio's absolutely epic, thundering vocal, then it takes on a totally different feel. It becomes a sort of thermonuclear proto-metal track, doesn't it? There was nothing else at that time like that, I don't think. Combine it with the cover art, the band pictures on the back and in the gatefold sleeve, plus the lyrics to only one song, "Stargazer," and everything comes together.

And "A Light in the Black," I remember thinking before I heard it, well, this is eight minutes—there's going to be a solo in it. Again, it's all about Ritchie Blackmore as a guitar hero. What's he going to do? The song is back-ended like "Highway Star," where a keyboard solo comes first. So he's going to wait in the wings for his solo. But underneath him is this barrage of double bass drums. How are you going to solo over something as frantic as that and make it anything other than just noise?

So when it comes around to Ritchie's turn to do the solo, he comes in and it's just perfect, a lesson in dynamics, light and shade. The shade is the double bass drumming from Cozy Powell (laughs) just thundering along. But Ritchie manages to put a solo in that's got, yes, hundreds of notes. Some of them are slightly off-beat, but most of them are on target. But he still manages to put melody and timing into what he's doing—it sounds constructed. I would say that Blackmore's guitar style from 1974 on, especially live on the *Burn* tour, is when he started doing these really rapid triplets on one string, or one note, between '74 and '76, '77. He continued in this style and I think it came out in his writing. He wanted to do this.

Whereas later on he held back, thinking, well, I've done the guitar hero thing but I don't want to overdo it. He wanted to overdo it now. There's something to prove. He probably thought Deep Purple have carried on without me. Who knew? But he wanted to prove something and those two songs, "Stargazer" and "A Light in the Black," definitely triumph. It comes out of that shared solo section, Tony and Ritchie, and then we reach towards the end and it just goes up and up. There's that "I'm on my way back home!" line, that scream by Dio, that one last tremolo arm bend from Ritchie Blackmore and we're done. Yeah, 32 minutes, isn't it? It's a short album but it was done.

Nick: A Light in the Black" is a phenomenal album closer. Dio really soars on it, but it chugs like a locomotive and it's eight minutes of like, hey guys, I'll see you at the end. They kick off and it's like hang on for dear life. There's a certain intensity with that song and for me, it's the quintessential Rainbow song, even if it reminds me of Scorpions' "Coming Home."

John: As discussed, "A Light in the Black" is sort of the epilogue to "Stargazer" the after-story. It's after the wizard has fallen. This is what remains afterwards, because you get lines like, "Can't believe it all/Did he really fall?/What to do now, I don't know." So they've been under the oppression of the wizard for so long that now that this guy is gone, now what do we do?

The main riff is this sort of single-note snappy line, and it shares some of the same notes as the main riff in "Stargazer." It's in the same key as the "Stargazer" main riff, which is E minor. And it's basically the same notes, but they're just sort of twisted around and played in a different order. And there's especially a little nod right at the end, which is very similar to the end of the "Stargazer" main riff. So I can't help but think that this was a conscious thing, that they took the "Stargazer" riff and played around with it and gave it like, here it is, but now in a different context.

Tempo-wise it's fast, it's frantic, it's like everyone's fleeing, everyone's escaping and their civilization has fallen apart now that the wizard is not here. You can actually hear some of the bass work in this one. Jimmy Bain has some cool little walk-down lines that pop out of this very bright mix. Here's another line that I really like—and I feel like it's directly referencing "Stargazer"—"All my life it seems/Just a crazy dream/Reaching for somebody's star."

There's an energetic and cool-sounding keyboard solo over the key of A minor. Then there's this really interesting major key section. It sort of modulates here and we get these guitar arpeggios sort of doubled by the keyboard, spreading across the fingerboard. It's uplifting and triumphant-sounding in that one part. This eventually leads to the guitar solo, which, interestingly enough, is in the same key as the guitar solo in "Stargazer." We're back in B Minor here, two steps higher than where the keyboard solo was.

Then we go back to these triumphant guitar arpeggios. Guitar arpeggios are when the guitar player's picking out the notes in the chord, just going from one note sort of ascending and descending here. And at this point now, this triumphant-sounding arpeggio part is now two steps higher than the original one. So again, we keep lifting up here. There's the keyboard solo and then it lifts up to the guitar solo and then it lifts up back to that arpeggio thing—really interesting.

Martin: John, the keyboard solo is almost like a slide guitar solo, isn't it?

John: Yeah, well, going back to these analog synth things, there's a lot of crazy note-bending and stuff, and imitating a guitar, the way a guitarist would bend notes or do crazy whammy bar things. He's doing the same thing on his keyboard with his note-bender.

Okay, so then we get the last verse in the chorus, and then there's this ascending guitar line that leads up to this big final G major chord, which is the relative major of E minor. It's sort of the major chord that goes with the minor key that we've been in at this point. It gives it this big, dramatic ending. And then Ronnie shouts out, "I found my way back home!" and everything crashes back down to E minor, and Ronnie sings, "To the sky, there in the sky. I see a star" wrapping everything up, back to the whole "Stargazer" thing. So really, the second side of this record is sort of like one thing, "A Light in the Black" serves as the closing remarks to "Stargazer," if you will.

Martin: So does the wizard experience an afterlife?

John: I don't know, maybe he sort of ascends to the stars, if you will. But now that he's left this earth, the people under his thumb are left to fend for themselves and so there's this chaos of scrambling around and not being sure what to do now.

Martin: I guess life was pretty black for these worker bees when they were building the tower, but this exciting project represented a sort of light. And now the light in the black is still there, but the definitions of both have changed.

John: You bring up an afterlife. There's the "I'm coming home!" business, and I never noticed this, but "Stargazer" has the line, "I see a rainbow rising/Look there, on the horizon." For me, I always took it as the Stargazer is building a tower to the stars, because he believes that that's his home. That's where he's meant to be when he dies. This tower that he's building will ascend him to the stars, sort of the reverse of the Egyptian underworld-type of thing where they get buried in the tombs because they believe they're going to be traveling to the underworld. Well, maybe this wizard here believes that his afterlife will be destined for the stars.

Martin: Excellent, well, whatever the case, it's an interesting story with a number of possible interpretations. Any closing comments?

Nick: Well, I'll just add that *Rising* is a very forward-looking album, whereas you could argue that the first album is almost backward-looking, I get the accolades for *Rising*; I understand it. My only criticism of the album is that I think it suffers from a tracking issue, of all crazy things. You have the two eight-minute songs on side two. For me, I'm more, "Don't bore us; get to the chorus." three or four minutes and out. We've got eight minutes of a phenomenal song with "Stargazer" and then you get "A Light in the Black," which is unusual. It's a big commitment. To propose some sort of resequencing, I don't know, I probably would have flipped two of the songs from side A, put them on side B, end side A with "Stargazer," and then end the album with "A Light in the Black."

Martin: Interesting. It boggles the mind how that would change one's perceptions of the songs. I have to confess, this is one album I can't see how to tamper with the order. I'll tell you one bloody thing though. I definitely would have liked to have seen a fifth track on the first side, because it certainly would have fit. And then I would have joined you and played all sorts of games scrambling at least those five around!

Phil: I wanted to touch on what you said about there being no soft music on this album. It's very true, isn't it? In the mid-seventies, from '70 to '76, there were bands that were called hard rock or heavy metal or whatever you want to call it. But it was almost like even if you were one of those bands, let's say Budgie, you would have your metal opening track and then you'd have a ballad. It's almost like to go rock, rock, rock, rock, was seen as being, no, you don't want to do that. Hold something back. But yes, you're right. *Rising* just left all of that off. It was just, this is what we're going to do. As you say, everything about it from the cover to the photos and the lyrics, it ticked every box, really. But those two tracks on side two, they were special then, and when you listen to them now and you look at how much time has elapsed, they still sound absolutely fantastic.

In the end, *Rising* is one of those albums where it's a classic album and everyone's got it. Everyone goes, "Oh yeah, it's in my top ranked albums list." And perhaps people that say that sometimes haven't played it for months. And it's only when you play it again, and you realize all the stuff you've been listening to in the meantime, that it's great. But this really is an island unto itself. There was nothing else like this before it or afterwards. At the time, we were all Purple freaks and we were all debating, is it as good as Purple? It was very hard then to judge that. But looking back through decades of time, you can actually see that this was a massive lift for Ritchie Blackmore's vision with respect to where he wanted to take his guitar and what he was thinking he would do.

Rainbow

On Stage Rainbow On Stage

RAINBOW'S BRITISH TOUR
31st OCTOBER — City Hall — Newcastle
1st NOVEMBER — City Hall — Newcastle
3rd NOVEMBER — Guild Hall — Preston
4th NOVEMBER — Empire — Liverpool
5th NOVEMBER — Empire — Liverpool
7th NOVEMBER — Capitol — Aberdeen
9th NOVEMBER — Apollo Theatre — Glasgow
11th NOVEMBER — Rainbow Theatre — London
12th NOVEMBER — Rainbow Theatre — London
13th NOVEMBER — Rainbow Theatre — London
16th NOVEMBER — New Theatre — Oxford
17th NOVEMBER — Granby Hall — Leicester
18th NOVEMBER — Bingley Hall — Stafford
20th NOVEMBER — Apollo Theatre — Manchester
21st NOVEMBER — Apollo Theatre — Manchester
22nd NOVEMBER — Capitol — Cardiff

Oyster

ALBUM · CASSETTE

ON STAGE

July 7, 1977
Oyster/Polydor OY-2-1801
Produced by Martin Birch
Personnel: Ronnie James Dio – vocals, Ritchie Blackmore – guitars,
Jimmy Bain – bass, Tony Carey – keyboards, Cozy Powell – drums

Side 1
Intro: Over the Rainbow (Arlen, Harburg) 0:31
1. Kill the King (Blackmore, Dio, Powell) 4:59
2. Medley: Man on the Silver Mountain (Blackmore, Dio), Blues
(Blackmore), Starstruck (Blackmore, Dio) 11:20

Side 2
1. Catch the Rainbow (Blackmore, Dio) 15:40

Side 3
1. Mistreated (Blackmore, Coverdale) 13:04

Side 4
1. Sixteenth Century Greensleeves (Blackmore, Dio) 7:35
2. Still I'm Sad (Samwell-Smith, McCarty) 11:05

Rainbow
KILL THE KING
MAN ON THE SILVER MOUNTAIN
MISTREATED
LIVE

An *On Stage* Timeline

Late May 1976. During tour rehearsals at Pirate Sound in Los Angeles, the band work out a new song called "Kill the King." Its writing is prompted after Ritchie is dissatisfied with how "Tarot Woman" is shaping up as a set-opener.

September 20 – October 18, 1976. Rainbow leave the UK for their first tour of mainland Europe, main support being AC/DC. Sept. 25 to 29, the shows are recorded for what will become the *On Stage* album, and then later, the expanded version of *On Stage* known as *Live in Germany*.

November 4 – December 16, 1976. Rainbow play ten dates in Australia, supported by legendary Aussie hard rockers Buffalo, followed by another ten shows in Japan.

July 7, 1977. Oyster/Polydor issue Rainbow's double live album *On Stage*, in the US. It's released to the public in the UK on July 15. The record charts at No.7 in the UK and No.65 on the Billboard 200. The album goes gold in Japan and silver in the UK.

August 15, 1977. Rainbow's *On Stage* is certified silver in the UK.

August 26, 1977. Polydor in the UK issue an *On Stage* three-tracker featuring A-side "Kill the King," along with "Man on the Silver Mountain" and "Mistreated." "Kill the King" reaches No.44 in the charts. After the success of the Joe Lynn Turner version of the band, the track is reissued in the UK in 1981, achieving a No.41 chart placement.

November 5, 1990. Posthumous concert album *Live in Germany* is released, through a label called Connoisseur Connection. It is widely considered the "corrected" version of *On Stage*.

DEVASTATING
Rainbow
On Stage Rainbow On Stage
NEW LIVE DOUBLE ALBUM
RECORDED ON THE
WORLD TOUR
Oyster
ALBUM · CASSETTE
polydor

Martin talks to Phil Aston, Marco D'Auria, Rich Davenport, Nick Ermolovich and Peter Jones about *On Stage.*

Martin Popoff: Okay, I was surprised as anybody seeing this come out back in 1977. Phil, what was the situation back in the home country?

Phil Aston: Well, I remember this very well, because there was a thing in your head, wasn't there? That when bands did a live album, especially in the seventies, that live album was like the pinnacle. It was an important thing. We hadn't even seen Rainbow live yet and there was news that there was going to be a live album coming out. And I thought, well, they've only done two records. There should be at least another studio album before there's a live album. Oh, well, fair enough.

And by the time it came out, we *had* seen Rainbow live. But the main part of Rainbow live when I saw them in Birmingham was "Stargazer," and they also did "A Light in the Black" on that tour. And those tracks were missing. And also, because of the constraints of two sides, four sides of vinyl, Martin Birch had to mix and match where things were. So it felt like a very mismatched album, the fact that side one was what you would expect to be side three, where there was a bit of a medley, a bit of fooling around, segueing to the blues portion and then a bit of "Starstruck." That's the thing you'd expect a live band to do about two-thirds of the way through the set. And the album starts with that, doesn't it?

Marco D'Auria: Still, I'm glad that they put out a live album. I'm glad that they have a little bit of meat on the bones with respect to the Ronnie era, because it would turn out to be brief. I'm glad it exists and I think it actually sounds really good production-wise, certainly better than *Ritchie Blackmore's Rainbow*. But for a short live album, it feels long (laughs). This record is the reason detractors say Rainbow is a Ritchie Blackmore solo project, and I don't feel that way with anything in the catalogue other than this live album. I imagine Ritchie would even admit that when they play live, that's his opportunity to shine, through improvising and jamming, essentially. I guess some of that's cool, but more so if you are there watching.

But it is a chore to listen to this version of "Catch the Rainbow."

It's a cool song—I don't need to listen to it for 15 minutes. Even Ronnie gets in on sort of improvising, melodically, and at the end of "Man on the Silver Mountain," where he does a little vocal thing with the audience that reminds me of what he'd do later on "Heaven and Hell." That's hard to unhear. But they ignored all of the coolest songs. I'm sorry. They did "Sixteenth Century Greensleeves" and "Man on the Silver Mountain," but they ignored much of *Rising*, although we get a small piece of "Starstruck." And I know they played those songs live, so I don't know why they weren't on *On Stage*.

Rich Davenport: Yes, agreed, it's a strange bunch of tracks, isn't it? Now I came to this album quite late. I got into Rainbow on *Down to Earth* into *Difficult to Cure* and then worked my way back. So yeah, it's a controversial one, partially because of the track listing. As well, it's very compressed and it sounds quite raw in places. And then on other tracks, like the new one, "Kill the King," it's all squashed in the middle, like I say, compressed; it doesn't really come out of the speakers I was listening to it on. Yeah, there's not a sense of fullness to it, I found.

Martin: What does it say about the band, putting out a live album after just two records?

Rich: It's quite a grandiose thing to do, perhaps more befitting of Ritchie Blackmore in terms of his individual status as a musician than of Rainbow as a whole. In the historical context of that timeline there, it's like, this is the great Ritchie Blackmore of Deep Purple. I suppose Cozy Powell had a bit of a name then, with his "Dance with the Devil" single. Obviously, the seventies was the golden era of live albums, but it was premature for Rainbow to be doing it. Maybe they get away with it by dint of the fact that it's Ritchie Blackmore and he's got a reputation for being an excellent live musician.

Martin: I never thought of this, but framed like that, as much as it's the messy third Rainbow album, it's also the follow-up to *Made in Japan* and *Made in Europe*.

Rich: Yeah, absolutely, because it's still Ritchie Blackmore playing a lot of guitar, and some of it not necessarily related to the song at hand. Plus he's touching on Purple by doing "Mistreated," which takes up a whole side. So it's maintaining that continuity.

Nick Ermolovich: You listen to *On Stage* and you think, now I know what the punks were rebelling against (laughs). I don't understand this. *Rising* was forward-looking. You had this dramatic shift from the first album, thinking like, wow, this band is lightyears ahead of where they were and maybe almost every other band. *On Stage* for me is just whiplash. Now, I've said to you that I'm not a fan of drawn-out live renditions, even if some of my favourite live albums have 24-minute songs (laughs). But from a hard rock band in the mid-seventies, song after song on here, 11, 15, 13 minutes... this album is work for me to get through—it's a chore. I don't get it and I'll be happy to explain myself further. But when I heard this, I'm like 1977? Oh, yeah, this is what the punks hated. Okay, now I get their point.

Martin: What do you think of the production?

Nick: I'm not a production guru but I find it pedestrian. I don't know if it's because they're in Japan for a chunk of this with different nights and then in Germany. May they boxed themselves into a corner in terms of being able to even out the sound. I found the crowd to be anaemic. It certainly is not Cheap Trick *At Budokan*. There's this half-hearted hand-clapping like they're not even sure if they should clap. I found that the performances were good, but even that gets lost in the length of the songs because you get noodling and aimlessness. I don't know if it's Martin Birch's best work. How's that? That's the best I can do.

Martin: Over to you Peter. Where does this record sit with you?

Peter Jones: *On Stage* was one of my seminal learning albums as a drummer. When I got this, it became one of my most-played albums in my entire collection, almost purely because of Cozy Powell. And Ronnie and Ritchie are fabulous on it too. But live albums can be one of three things. A live album can be a snapshot of a specific show, from a specific tour. And it says, "Here, this is what we were like at this moment." Or it can be an amalgamation of dates and different tours, like *Exit... Stage Left*. It's a collection from various different tours, and sometimes those don't sound very unified to me. Most of the times the tracks are not in concert running order and so that's a different flavour.

And then there's what this one is, a truncated version with some amalgamations of other shows. So this is a very different live record, from six different dates, three shows in September in Germany and three in December in Japan. It's like *Made in Japan* was. You have dates and they're cherry-picking tracks from those dates to put together a record. And this is an album that is edited quite a bit.

It's also incomplete from being a snapshot of where they were at the time because they're leaving out key tracks. Reviewing their set list from the shows that were recorded, there are three tracks that were played on and off, but not at all shows, that are missing. There's "Stargazer," which many Rainbow fans would just head-scratch and go, "You're kidding, right? You've left off the masterpiece." They also leave off "Do You Close Your Eyes" which, granted, is hit or miss with fans. A lot of them may pick that as their least favourite track on *Rising*. And then there's "A Light in the Black," another one which a lot of *Rising* fans would say, "You needed to have that one because that's a great, great track."

But in reality, both "Stargazer" and "A Light in the Black" were different tracks live than they were in the studio. And in all fairness, they're very difficult to reproduce and sound anything like they did on the album. You're not gonna get anywhere close. Obviously, you're not bringing strings out. And some of the shows would famously put "Man on the Silver Mountain" into "Stargazer" and then "A Light in the Black." That was their setlist. Well, as brilliant as he is, Cozy's only a human being. This was killing Cozy because he's got so much to do. He's got "Still I'm Sad" too. It's just too much. There's so much drumming; they had to break it up and they finally separated out "A Light in the Black." It falls off the setlist. "Stargazer" is only played for the Rising tour. But all of these tracks are available on bootlegs and future releases where you can go hear the full shows.

The album clocks in at about four minutes over an hour. It's a double record, but it's not very long. Queen's *Live Killers* is 90 minutes. *Double Live Gonzo!* is 85 minutes. You say it's only 20 minutes. Well, 20 minutes is a lot. Yeah, 25 minutes is a whole side. That's a lot of space to leave off. But then you ask yourself, what could they have put in to fill up the space? "Stargazer" and "A Light in the Black" were both these enormous epics that took up time. I don't know how you fit that in and have it fit with the way they were playing the songs live in sequence.

Martin: Did you dig that album cover?

Peter: I love the album cover. Let's go back to the debut for a second. I think the StratoCastle—that's what I call it—is one of their greatest album covers. Phenomenal. And if they had put the logo that shows up on *Rising* on the first album, then that's really high up on my favourite album covers of all time. And as a backdrop on stage, that castle just looks unbelievable, to have that big, towering guitar castle over the top of Cozy's head. Even though the castle isn't there for *On Stage*, it still looks great with the lights and the rainbow and the multi-coloured Rainbow logo. Plus I geeked out over all the gear that they listed for hours and hours as I was listening to this.

Martin: The album opens incredibly strong with "Kill the King." And I would think that most fans would agree that it never reaches this level of excitement ever again.

Phil: Yes (laughs). Of course the main thing that drew people in was this track called "Kill the King," which didn't exist anywhere else. It was written to be an opener. As the story goes, they felt they hadn't got something that was going to be epic enough to open the set. I've always felt that "Kill the King" off the studio album is a more cohesive and easier listen, because the solo feels more structured and there's more space between the instruments. With the live version, you felt like there's a great track in there fighting to get out amongst all the noise. Maybe it's the mix.

Marco: They came up with that song while rehearsing for the *Rising* tour dates. And given that it'll show up on *Long Live Rock 'n' Roll*, it's cool that *On Stage* turns out to encompass the entire Ronnie James Dio era, all three studio albums.

Rich: Yeah, I love "Kill the King." It doesn't come across as heavy as the studio version, with this production, but it's a great sort of thrusting live opener. Killer solo from Ritchie, great vocal melody from Ronnie, slightly different in places from what he would have eventually nailed down with the final vocal on the studio version, but you can see where he's going. What I like about it is there's great chemistry between the players. We're getting Jimmy Bain and Tony Carey playing on this. I know there's some consternation about what happened with people coming and going on *Long Live Rock 'n' Roll*, but, you hear the live chemistry of the *Rising* band here. It's so tight, and it's a shame they didn't carry that over as a whole band into the next album. Such a vibrant energy to it, which is almost fighting against the production, really, which is restrained in comparison.

Peter: We actually start with "Over the Rainbow," a pre-recorded track. I don't know how they got that. It must have been in the public domain to get that because I don't think they could have paid MGM enough money to get permission to use that music for the intro. Then they slam into big power chords and this is traditional for Purple. They almost always opened their shows with either a long intro or big power chords. And I think especially for live albums, that makes sure that all the mics are working and they've got their signals all set before they go into the song, instead of, oh wait, we missed the beginning of the tape or whatever.

Ritchie goes into this rapid-fire, machine gun-like fill, and it's just a freight train assault, powerful and aggressive. "Kill the King" is one of those songs often cited as proto-thrash, or at least proto-speed metal. Cozy is just unleashed here. Clearly it's a track that hasn't even been on a studio album yet, but they're opening their show with an up-tempo, aggressive song—that's the formula; that's the way they do it. And once Tony Carey's organ starts screaming in, I'm like, okay, this is great. There's a nice balance here. Ritchie and Tony are both there and they're equals. I love the interplay, the banter back and forth between them. And then as soon as Ronnie fires off, "Danger, danger, the Queen's about to kill," the goosebump ands hairs on the back of my head come up. Off he goes.

Here's another riff that is similar to "Man on the Silver Mountain" and all the other ones I mentioned. It's another signature riff he borrows from himself. The verses are full-on Cozy just thundering away. He's 90% on his ride. He makes use of all of his eight crashes, three on one side, five on the other, including two China cymbals, and he's just beating the bloody hell out of them. But what drives through the most is that open and enormously tight and powerful bass drum, with this bombastic snare crack as counterpoint to it. It just drives right through the song like you're busting through barricades. He's unrelenting.

I love the unison fire-off section between Carey and Blackmore. It's similar to "Highway Star" and very classical. Solo-wise, Ritchie's just going crazy, but the band kicks up the levels and we get the double bass firing underneath with the syncopations. And then they get back to another unison section. This is a band of extreme talent here. There's cohesion and unification; they're of a single mind with their playing here. And it only takes the simplest of snare drum fills from Cozy to go right back into the unison section. Ronnie's screaming away and it just sounds great. I love the energy.

This is certainly much bigger-sounding than it would be on the studio album. But the fact that Ronnie can sing over this wall of sound is insane. First time I met Vinny Appice, I asked him about Ronnie and he said, "Hey, I've played with some of the loudest guitarists in the world. When I first joined Sabbath, we were playing instrumentally; Ronnie hadn't come in and joined us yet. I thought there's no way on God's earth anybody can sing over the top of this." And he said, "He just stood there, put the mic to his mouth and blew us off stage." He says, "I just couldn't believe that somebody was capable of doing that." And that's what he's doing here. But it's a brilliant track and a great way to start off a concert.

Nick: With "Kill the King," here it is, you've got this awesome song, and I just put myself in the shoes of a German fan in the seventies going, "What the hell is this?! I've never heard it before." They come out like gangbusters, and people must have been looking around going, "Did I miss a track? Do I not have this album? What am I doing?" So there must have been that confusion, which I've also experienced, at least pre-internet, when a band opens with a song that no one has heard before. The performance itself is fantastic, but it's not necessarily a good thing having this first. It's one of the two highlights on the album for me. So you're starting off with the high point of the album and it's arguably all downhill from here, and maybe precipitously or precariously so.

Martin: Exactly; things begin to fall apart, or at least get messy. Forget the music. Typical for the rock 'n' roll business, they can't even get the naming consistent on the album. On the back, it's "Man on the Silver Mountain," "Blues" and "Starstruck." On the record label, it's "Medley: Man on the Silver Mountain, Blues, Starstruck."

Phil: Yes, and "Man on the Silver Mountain," is faster than we expect it to be. Which is good. That blues bit, or "Blues," where he goes into a solo, that's the kind of thing he was doing in "You Fool No One," just guitar on its own. But I feel that when he goes into that blues section with Tony Carey, it almost feels like a pastiche of a blues. Tony is hamming it up and Ritchie's not quite there either. It doesn't sound purist enough, I suppose. Maybe it's not supposed to be. Quite a few of my friends at the time felt that that was a missed opportunity. And why was it so early into the set? Which, of course, it wasn't, technically.

Rich: "Man on the Silver Mountain" is a classic, and from my favourite Ronnie-era album, which I suppose is quite a contrarian view. But this is a faster, heavier, more aggressive version of it. Cozy keeps the original intro drum fill as it comes in with the full band, but he really clobbers it with his typical, heavy style as it gets going. And Jimmy Bain's bass line is really cool; he's got a really punchy, heavy sound on this. Cozy really accentuates certain beats, like eighth notes with his double bass drums, which is quite a forward-reaching technique for that era. Because I know in your Judas Priest book, you talk about Simon Phillips, this sort of jazz rock player coming into Priest as a session player for *Sin After Sin* and bringing that technique into metal. But here we've got Cozy completely independently bringing that technique. So that was quite striking at that time.

"Starstruck," it's a shame they don't play the whole song. "Blues" is great until Tony Carey's hideous, farty synth solo comes in. It sounds like a drunken duck, and then there's like a duel between the two of them. He's like Ritchie Blackmore, duck-slayer. It's like, oh, man, please.

Martin: And Nick, what are your thoughts on the *Rising* band's rendition of "Man on the Silver Mountain?"

Nick: Well, it's way too fast! I think that they destroy one of the best songs in hard rock history, a song that is up there as sort of "Smoke on the Water" Jr., with its riff. I think the power of this song comes from it being played at the correct tempo. When you speed it up, one of the things I noticed is that Ronnie has to choke off notes in the verses. His vocal delivery in the studio album is so powerful and here he sounds like he's hanging on for dear life. Now in fairness, stubbornly, Rainbow play it at this same accelerated pace going forward, as does the Dio band, although I found a video recording of him around the mid-2000s where it seems like he really dialled back the speed. And I'm like, there it is—perfect. That's where he should have kept it. It's probably one of my favourite top two or three Rainbow songs, maybe even Dio songs period. But I just think that the fast version, maybe as a kid I liked it more, but I can't stand it now. I have to wear a neck brace because I get whiplash.

At the four-minute mark, out trots B.B. Blackmore and he's gonna take us into a blues thing. I don't know if this is where they played it in the set, because I'm thinking of you, Martin, going, "It's too early to take a potty break." But it's fine. You've got this chugging, way too fast, out-of-control "Man on the Silver Mountain" and then they put the brakes on and now we're in blues territory, which again, is backward-looking rather than forward-looking. Blind Lemon Blackmore doing this blues thing just seems out of place.

And then you get your neck brace out again for "Starstruck," which is only a snippet, part of "Medley." I'm not a fan of medleys. It's off the new album—play the damn thing. Especially if we look at it measured against some of the older songs in their set. I don't understand why they don't play the whole thing. And then we get back to "Man on the Silver Mountain." By the end of this, I'm like, oh, this was work. It was like 11 minutes of my life I can't get back. It's just not my thing at all.

Peter: Sure, Instantly, side one, we start to get to one of the knocks on both Deep Purple and Rainbow when we're talking about live extended jams. "Man on the Silver Mountain" is a shorter track of less than five minutes on the studio version. This one, once they've added "Blues" and one verse and chorus of "Starstruck" and some vocal ad-libbing, it clocks in at a little over 11 minutes. Ritchie fires off the riff and there's nothing reminiscent of the original other than the vocal line and the lyrics. Everything else is different. Cozy's drum fills and his drumbeat are completely different. It's much more up-tempo, with more aggression and energy.

I love what Tony Carey is doing on the keys, which is missing from the debut. But Ronnie sounds a little tired. That might be a little nitpicky thing, but when you go back and analyse where these shows came from, what was common back then is that a lot of these bands would do multiple shows in one day. You'd have an afternoon show and an evening show and they weren't truncated; they were full shows. And that allows you to get as many tickets sold across fewer dates, because you're already there. But on a musician, it's brutal and even more brutal for a vocalist. Could you imagine doing this set list twice in one day? And even from the drum standpoint, I don't know how they do it. That's youth, I guess, right? But it can cause inconsistencies. We also know that nobody was taking care of themselves back in the day. And Ronnie notoriously never warmed up; he drank, he smoked and everything. So here, he sounds a bit tired or restrained compared to the original versions.

Then Ritchie goes off into this long solo section, where they break it down into this slow blues thing. He does some back and forth with Tony Carey, who interestingly is doing it on synth and not on organ. Then he goes back to organ and a little bit of synth, but it goes on and on. If you're not a musical nerd, this is the kind of stuff you want to fast-forward through because it's not that appealing, I wouldn't think.

Ronnie kicks off "Starstruck," but it's super-short and a teaser. And I'm like, I'd rather you just leave that out. If you're gonna do it, do the song proper, because I don't like medleys, although it's a high level of playing and it's inspiring from that standpoint. But it's self-indulgent. It reminds me of what Lars Ulrich said when he was inducting Deep Purple into the Rock and Roll Hall of Fame. When he mentioned Ritchie, he said he's aloof, and that he was always bordering on the edge of electric narcissism. That's the perfect way to describe Ritchie. Because live, he does what he wants to and when he wants to do it. He will take as long as it takes to do it, even at the expense of the track and he makes no apologies. It's like, "I will go until I don't feel like I want to go anymore. And for transitions, I'll cue you and only then will we move on." But there's a strong sense of separation when you're listening to a live album as opposed to being there seeing it. If you don't see it, you feel detached from it. And now it's just this long ego thing where if you were there, you'd be thinking, maybe this is a good time to use the restroom.

Martin: Next, the guys take a heck of a long time to catch the rainbow.

Nick: Yeah, and at 15:35, I actually was able to catch a few rainbows myself, because it was so frickin' long. That's the song with the anaemic clapping I talked about earlier. The first five minutes or so are really good. This suffers from editing. I found online a review of this album, and I forget who did it, but it made me laugh out loud. Because the reviewer was so polite. What he said was, on this album, it showed that the band lacked any sense of economy. And that's so true, that there was no economy whatsoever. I assume that he thinks the template is *Made in Japan*, which has some epics on it too. If you were to compare the two, there's a certain crackling energy that comes out of that recording that is somehow missing here. But just the length of the song doesn't do it for me, whereas I might be able to get through a ten- or fifteen-minute song off of *Made in Japan*. "The Mule" is useless to me, but "Space Truckin'" is a decent investment of time. But I understand that may have been the template. But "Catch the Rainbow," he caught it, he was catching it and I caught it—whatever.

Phil: I think where the magic on this album comes from—and I do think it's well recorded—is "Catch the Rainbow," the epic from the first album, which sounded like it was paying homage towards Jimi Hendrix, specifically "Little Wing." Here it's a whole side and I think still perfect for portraying Blackmore's vision for what he wanted to do with the guitar. He didn't have to say, "Come on, Mr. Lord, it's your turn now." It was just him. Tony Carey could tinker around in the background, but this is Ritchie's show. There's lots of space for him to stretch out, and after all, this was the age of stretching out. And Ronnie obviously was his foil. So I think it's fantastic, still probably the definitive version of that track. I know there's lots of others, from the German tour and stuff. But I think it sounds great; great guitar tone—brilliant.

Rich: I bought *On Stage* second-hand on vinyl from a friend who was older than me as I was working my way back through the Rainbow albums. This would have been about 1986. And by this stage, it was like, hmm, an entire side for one song?! Similarly, some of the Deep Purple live albums, I find it a bit much when there's like three different solos within the course of the same track. But this is different. I do like this version, because it's really good ensemble playing and there's a real dynamism between the band members. I've seen Ritchie on videos conducting the band, waving his finger about to bring it back in, and I can just imagine him doing that here. There's some fantastic soloing from him, and for me, he doesn't overstay his welcome, even though it's almost 16 minutes long. It goes on, for sure, but you can tell the audience is into it because they're clapping along with the beat. It's got a nice intimate vibe. There's some excellent fast-picking from Ritchie in the way it builds up and down again. Yeah, it's quite a tour de force of ensemble playing, this one; I think it works.

Peter: We get to "Catch the Rainbow" and we have more of this strong, upbeat, heavier drumming from Cozy, which helps to pick the track up a bit. Ronnie sounds great and Ritchie's tone on here is spectacular. It's biting and edgy and cuts like a laser. And I'm like yeah, that's the Ritchie sound I like. Still, it's reserved in parts, where it comes down to almost whispers. And then we get a huge drum fill from Cozy and back they go.

The thing that is nice though, that Purple were also good at, is their use of dynamics. I do like the fact that it isn't always just slamming; it breathes, it slows down, it gets softer. And then when it comes back, when it reprises, it feels heavier again, because what was before it was softer and quieter and gentler. They get to the end and the tempo picks up and Cozy's drums sound like mortar fire. It's just heavy and crushing. And then Ronnie picks up at the end and they do a nice, ascending chordal pattern, which is just placid and pastoral. And that's how they choose to let it fade out.

Martin: Nice description; thanks for that. Okay, now we get "Mistreated," a bottom-feeder off of *Burn*. And thanks also for a whole side of it.

Rich: Yeah, not my favourite Deep Purple song either. And I know in your Rainbow book that you called it a bit of an undercooked track, which I think I would agree with. I quite like it, but I would rather have heard them play "Stargazer" or something like that. I think Ronnie sings it brilliantly. It's cool to hear Ronnie sing a David Coverdale number and he puts his own stamp on it. I figure that the Mk. III line-up of Deep Purple, from *Burn* onwards with David Coverdale and Glenn Hughes, melodically and in terms of the chord progressions, is closer to Rainbow than it is to Mk. II Deep Purple. Because the Mk. II line-up is perhaps more blues-based and sixties-sounding, with "Into the Fire" and things like that. And then as we get into the *Burn* era, it's got that darker, more European, perhaps classical influence coming in. So this is a good choice for Rainbow to play, if they're going to play a Deep Purple song. Again, you can hear the audience are interested and it brings back that continuity. There's some interesting improvisation from Ritchie. There's also a bit where it comes out of an instrumental section and there's this roaring note from Ronnie. So yes, he really does put his stamp on it.

Phil: I remember going to a rock disco somewhere, and the DJ had been given an advanced copy of *On Stage* and he played "Mistreated" from it, which obviously was a Purple track. And it starts with this style of guitar playing that Ritchie was into at this point in his career where he's literally playing on the same string as he goes up the neck and it sounded huge. But now, of course, we're in 1977 and punk has arrived in the UK. And this song was showing that there was more energy plugged into Blackmore's plectrum than there was to an entire bunch of council flats across the UK with people trying to get their first amps up the stairs. Ritchie was showing that this is what he could do. His solo, I have to say that I can look back now and think yeah, it's nice, it's a clever improvisation. At the time, being 18, a lot of us thought it was a bit boring, that he sat back and was just doodling for what seemed like a few minutes before everyone came back in. And then he raced towards the end, as you'd expect him to. But Dio takes this song, known for being one of Purple's last classics with Coverdale, into another realm—his voice on it is just perfect.

But yeah, at 13 minutes, that was a whole side, side three. And this was an expensive album, seven pounds in old money. And it was a short record overall—60 minutes and you're done. So with "Mistreated" being the whole of side three, there was a lot of dead wax there (laughs). Even without knowing much about this stuff, you think, well, they could have stuck something else on. Where's "Stargazer?" Even at eight minutes, it could have fit on this side.

Marco: I really like Ronnie's vocals on "Mistreated." And there's actually a better version of "Mistreated" live, on the Munich '77 show, which became an album, but at the time was a concert film. But it is interesting that it's such a short live album, with only six songs, and two of them are covers, of Deep Purple and The Yardbirds. I thought somewhere there was some rule where they weren't going to cover Deep Purple. But for some reason they did "Mistreated," which is written by Ritchie and David Coverdale. Now I appreciate that we have this, but Rainbow live sounded like a big, relaxed jam session, where Ritchie just played what he wanted to play, And although Ritchie was more into classical music at this point, they did do a lot of blues because it was a good framework for soloing. So that's added to the medley. Cozy, I think, sounds really good on this album and that's about the best compliment I can give it.

Nick: "Mistreated," although I love the song, I find it peculiar to stretch it out that long. Here's how I would have fixed it, in my imagination, after labouring through this thing. Chop it in half and play "Burn." Oh my God; that would have been phenomenal— "Mistreated" to "Burn?!" Come on! One of the best songs he's ever played on. But "Mistreated" is a great song, a grinding blues. Whoever's singing, whether it's Ronnie or Coverdale or whomever, it's a great song. Cozy does some interesting things as well. But stretched out to 13 minutes, I think you lose some of the power and heft. It's like, enough already.

Peter: Out of all the Purple songs, they pick "Mistreated" and you go, why? Now, I don't dislike the track, but, obviously, this was originally sung by Mr. Coverdale. And this one's even longer. Ritchie plays a heavy intro and then goes into the riff, which has some real weight to it. And as soon as Ronnie starts singing, in deference and respect to Coverdale, I have a hard time listening to the Purple version again after Ronnie's sung this. He's spoiled it for me, because I feel that this is the kind of voice the track always needed. David did a great job on the studio record, but Ronnie's got a whole different sensibility to him and it just goes up a notch. But the backing accompaniment made on this never changes. It's boring; it languishes and I find that as a listener, it's hard to stay involved.

Martin: Over to the final side, and we get a conservatively-timed stand-alone song in "Sixteenth Century Greensleeves," and as bonus, it's a song fans like.

Phil: Yes, and Ritchie plays a blinder on that little introduction when he plays "Greensleeves." And this is again heavily edited, isn't it?

Rich: Yeah, and I would have like to have heard more first album tracks, because Ritchie's tone on the actual first album is quite warm and mellow, really; it's not an aggressive, distorted tone. It's like a nice, warm overdrive, which fits with the medieval feel of that first Rainbow album. Whereas here, it's live and he's playing through a wall of amps and it's more aggressive. And you've also got the aggression from Cozy and together, they really light a fire under this song. And the sort of synchronicity between Cozy Powell and Jimmy Bain is great as well; they're so tight. The fills are really locked in, the way they play together. I suppose because it was such a short-lived line-up, as a lot of the Rainbow ones were, people don't tend to mention the great rhythm section of Jimmy Bain and Cozy Powell. But they really did lock in well together.

There are some killer fills from Cozy and a fast and fiery solo from Ritchie. I've got the DVD version of the *Live in Germany* concert, and he's really at the top of his game there in terms of improvisation. You can really hear in this late seventies stuff what all the shredder guys like Yngwie Malmsteen took from him, because of the arpeggios and the fast runs that he's playing. It's ahead of its time for a rock player. He and Uli Jon Roth were really leading the field then. And in the eighties, Ritchie seemed less inspired. But on this album, although it's not the track listing we like, there's some fine playing from him and "Sixteenth Century Greensleeves" is a good example of that.

Nick: "Sixteenth Century Greensleeves," for me, is probably the second high point of the album. Like you say, they don't stretch it out to sleep-inducing length and I think this is a better version versus the studio debut. There's phenomenal bass playing and a cool solo at the beginning and Cozy is crushing it.

Peter: "Sixteenth Century Greensleeves" is my favourite track on the record. It's only slightly longer than the studio version because of the brief intro, but once the track actually starts, it's spot-on. The feel is great, the sound is great, the solos are great and Ronnie sounds amazing. I love the energy and the intensity. You wish that the whole record was full of tracks like this, concise, to the point, yet still with plenty of showmanship, plenty of spots to reach out and show your talents. But they're easier to digest, more palatable, more accessible. And a song will always be more interesting than an extended solo, at least in my opinion.

Martin: All right, we close with another questionable choice, the Yardbirds cover from the debut. But it's fun to hear Ronnie singing it, right?

Phil: Absolutely; it's got vocals this time and it sounds great. The drum solo's taken out too; maybe in hindsight, that's probably a good thing. But it's a short album, so it could have fit.

Marco: "Still I'm Sad" and these other long songs I think point to where some of the dissension in the band originated. I know Ronnie has said in interviews that the live gigs were basically an excuse for Ritchie to show off and how he would go up and sing a verse and then stand in the back and drink a beer and basically just watch the show. So I imagine that's where some of the dissension came from. Ronnie probably started feeling his days were numbered, sitting back and watching Ritchie indulge himself in soloing while he takes longer breaks than he would have liked. I guess we're reminded that Ritchie initially called the band Ritchie Blackmore's Rainbow.

Martin: And I guess this is a seventies thing and pointedly a Deep Purple thing, to just stretch out the songs like crazy, right? This goes away in the eighties, doesn't it?

Marco: Well, certainly when Dio had his own band, you never saw that again, even if he let the guys do some solo stuff live. But obviously they took it to an extreme here. I appreciate how good the *On Stage* album sounds, but I would have appreciated more tunes. Four sides and six songs is pretty unacceptable. Give me "Run with the Wolf" or "Snake Charmer" and don't do "Still I'm Sad" at all, even though it's a cool song and now we get lyrics. I'm glad that Ronnie gets to sing on that one, because imagine if that was just an instrumental again.

Rich: Agreed, it's good to hear Ronnie singing it. Again, I'd rather have had something like "Stargazer" or something from the first album. But as a document or snapshot in time, I can enjoy the album for what it is. "Still I'm Sad" is another example of the dynamism between the members of that line-up. They've put in a lot of work and they're obviously really well drilled by this point, which you can hear in the way that there are some quite staccato stops in the middle of the song. It's just so tight the way they drop those in; it makes a real impact. And there's a brief snippet of "God Rest Ye Merry Gentlemen," the Christmas carol, from Ritchie in the solo. So yeah, overall, I like the song. It's a case of making do with what we've got, rather than what could have been.

Nick: I don't understand this cover. I'm missing something here. Maybe I'm not enough of a super-fan. It's a fair to middling Yardbirds track. It was a B-side for The Yardbirds. And this is nothing like the Yardbirds track, which is practically a Gregorian chant. We get the lyrics on it, which I think is cool, because on the first album it's instrumental. They stretch it out forever.

But I'm thinking, Blackmore, why are you giving royalties away on this one? Not only are you giving groove space and tape, but you're giving royalties away. I don't understand it. It's a fine song, but almost 50 years later, I find it perplexing why they did it. And I'm like, Ritchie, don't complain about royalties ever again, because you gave them away on that track. I sat there laughing going, why doesn't he play "Hands of Jack the Ripper" from Screaming Lord Sutch? That would have been better, as it was actually part of his history. To me it's an odd song and an odd choice, although from what I read, it wasn't their actual encore or set-ender.

Peter: I do appreciate that they decide to put the lyrics back in. So this one's nowhere near like the studio version at all, not even close. No cowbell part; it's just Cozy bashing away on his 24-inch and making a ton of noise. They break this down into a lot of different sections. Again, light and shade, loud and soft. It breaks down and we get to a really nice keyboard solo from Mr. Carey. But this version is highly edited. Cozy's drum solo is removed from the track. So after the keyboards, it goes right back into Ritchie's riff and out they go. Now, do I wish Cozy's solo was in there? Sure. I would have preferred to hear that. But if you're gonna cut Cozy's solo, why are you keeping Tony's? So that's a curious question for me, because you could have made this track more concise. And then you free up some space to maybe put another track or two on there.

Martin: Yeah, my overall impression is that Ritchie wanted to present his band on the studio albums, but put him on stage, and he's gonna play a lot of guitar, often at the expense of the songs, to the point of disrespecting them.

Phil: I think live, sure, that's the case. As you say, if we just dip back into "Stargazer," he could have easily thought that with the three-minute out-run of that song, this is time for another guitar solo, a slide solo or something. He could have easily done that but he didn't. He just kept quiet, literally for three minutes, to let the orchestra do its bit and for Ronnie James Dio to ad-lib for basically almost the length of "Run with the Wolf." So I totally agree. But on *On Stage*, it's him. This is about me, and I think that comes across. But he had the freedom. This is recorded on their first tour, wasn't it? So although it didn't come out until the summer of 1977, the actual gigs are from late '76. So Ritchie had something to prove.

I played it yesterday and I still think it has some wonderful moments on it. Would I class it as one of the top live albums of the seventies? Probably not because it's always felt a bit of a patchwork quilt, how it's been glued together. It doesn't feel like a proper gig because of the sequencing. The two-CD versions that came out later on were an improvement. You had "Kill the King" followed by "Mistreated." They followed the set. That's probably what's wrong with *On Stage*. Because if you went to see the band, the set list is back to front and sideways. It's a good performance and it captures the band, but it was probably too early. And without "Stargazer," it's lacking. It should have been a triple. But no one did those then.

Martin: Back to an original question, what is the messaging we are to receive seeing this band put out a live album so soon within the catalogue?

Nick: Maybe they're trying to defeat bootleggers, which I can imagine really ate into everything. Was this a problem with the record company? But I totally agree—it's weird. Here's another thing: they're all top-flight musicians, but you're not going to tell me that when this thing was recorded, in Germany and Japan, that they weren't still figuring each other out. They're better than 98% of the musicians on the planet, but they were not as well-oiled a unit as they could have been. Maybe if they'd waited until after the third album, you would have gotten a much different result. Although we do get to hear Tony Carey and Jimmy Bain. I have a newfound appreciation for Jimmy as a player.

Martin: Peter, any closing thoughts?

Peter: Well, I'll say this. I would listen to this at "Kill a rhino at 20 paces" volume with my headphones on in my parents' living room all the time. And that's probably one of the most prominent causes of the serious ringing that is in my ears as we speak. The drums were just so massively huge that I just listened to this over and over and over again. It's mixed feelings on the production, though. It's a little rolled off on the high end. But I say in counterpart to that, thank you. Because I'm afraid that if this had a more transparent high end, serious listener fatigue would have been a problem. The way Cozy plays and the material they were using, this could have been painful. So I'm glad that it was a little muted on the high end.

Ronnie's voice sounds great, Ritchie's guitar sounds incredible. Jimmy Bain is a very solid bass player but he's nowhere the focus on this album in terms of the mix. Plus I would have loved to have heard more Craig Gruber-style bass playing underneath all this.

But yeah, I've heard *On Stage* so many times. It'd be impossible to quantify how many times I've listened to it. It's not for everybody. It can be quite frustrating versus other bands' historic live albums that don't nearly cross into this level of self-indulgence.

Rainbow
NEW ALBUM
LONG LIVE ROCK 'N' ROLL
Rainbow
Long Live Rock 'n' Roll
LONG LIVE ROCK 'N' ROLL
LONG LIVE ROCK 'N' ROLL
LONG LIVE ROCK 'N' ROLL
LONG LIVE ROCK 'N' ROLL
polydor

LONG LIVE ROCK 'N' ROLL

April 14, 1978
Polydor PD-1-6143
Produced by Martin Birch
Personnel: Ronnie James Dio – vocals, Ritchie Blackmore – guitars, bass, Bob Daisley – bass, David Stone – keyboards, Cozy Powell – drums, Bavarian String Ensemble, Rainbow Eyes String Quartet – strings, Rudi Risavy – flute, Max Hecker – recorder

Side 1
1. Long Live Rock 'n' Roll (Blackmore, Dio) 4:25
2. Lady of the Lake (Blackmore, Dio) 3:38
3. L.A. Connection (Blackmore, Dio) 3:35
4. Gates of Babylon (Blackmore, Dio) 6:47

Side 2
1. Kill the King (Blackmore, Dio, Powell) 4:28
2. The Shed (Subtle) (Blackmore, Dio, Powell) 4:46
3. Sensitive to Light (Blackmore, Dio) 3:08
4. Rainbow Eyes (Blackmore, Dio) 7:31

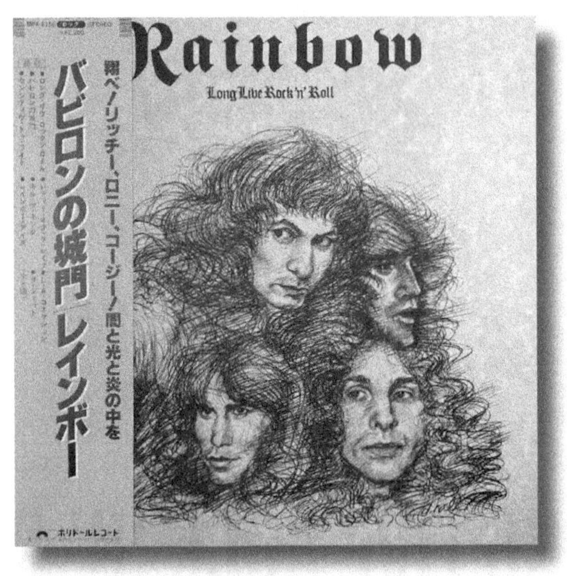

A *Long Live Rock 'n' Roll* Timeline

December 1976. Canadian progressive rockers Symphonic Slam issue their one and only album, a self-titled, on A&M Records. The keyboardist in the band is David Stone, soon on his way to Rainbow.

March 1977. Widowmaker issue their second and last album, *Too Late to Cry*. It is Bob Daisley's fifth record, and last before he joins Rainbow.

May – July 1977. Rainbow record tracks for their third studio album. Early on, Mark Clarke does the bass parts, only to have them replaced by Ritchie himself. The album is recorded in the French countryside, at The Strawberry Studio, Chateau D'Hérouville, France.

September 25 – November 22, 1977. Rainbow's Mk. IV line-up—Ritchie, Cozy, Ronnie plus David Stone and Bob Daisley—tour mainland Europe and then the UK, where Kingfish supports. Rehearsals for the tour take place the week of September 15, at Shepperton Studios. It's reported that the label had forced the band to reschedule their tour, compelling them to begin in America while the band had been all set to begin in the UK. Neither order of events happened, with Rainbow covering mainland Europe extensively first, then the UK, then Japan, then the US.

December 1977. The band return to France for a second set of recording sessions in advance of their third album.

January 11 – February 3, 1978. Rainbow execute an extensive Japanese tour.

March 24, 1978. Rainbow issue, as a single, the title track from their forthcoming *Long Live Rock 'n' Roll* album, backed with "Sensitive to Light." The single reaches No.33 on the UK charts.

April 14, 1978. Rainbow issue their third studio album, entitled *Long Live Rock 'n' Roll*. The album reaches No.7 on the UK charts and No.89 on the Billboard 200. It certifies silver in the UK.

May 9 – Early August 1978. Rainbow conduct a long US tour in support of *Long Live Rock 'n' Roll*, playing with the likes of REO Speedwagon (REO as headliner), Black Oak Arkansas, Henry Gross, Foghat (headliner), No Dice, Uriah Heep, The Godz, The Cars, Eddie Money, Max Webster, Nantucket, AC/DC and Cheap Trick (headliner). David Stone is the keyboardist of choice while Bob Daisley is handling bass duties.

September 22, 1978. "L.A. Connection" is issued as a single, backed with "Lady of the Lake." The single reaches No.40 on the UK charts.

Martin talks to Marco D'Auria, Rich Davenport, Tate Davis, Jamie Laszlo and Steven Reid about *Long Live Rock 'n' Roll.*

Martin Popoff: Okay, so lots going on as we get to the third album, including some personnel changes.

Steven Reid: Yes, as ever with Rainbow, what's normal in terms of who is in the band is whatever Ritchie feels like at the time, to some extent (laughs). Tony Carey is in the band, not in the band, being thrown out the band, being sung about on the album, about to be thrown out of the band, never actually been thrown out of the band. Because that's the way that Rainbow rolled more than anything else. You've got Bob Daisley; he's in the band, he's not in the band, Ritchie is playing some of the bass, and here comes David Stone on keyboards.

Martin: And to add to that, the bass player drawn on the front cover, you could look at that and think it's Jimmy Bain as easily as you might say it's Bob Daisley.

Steven: When I was young, to me that was Jimmy Bain, because that's who I knew. I probably couldn't have picked him out of a line-up at that stage. So when I looked at that cover, that was Jimmy Bain. Rainbow are always a confusing band, but who's in and who's not at this stage. you can be safe in the knowledge that Ritchie, Ronnie and Cozy were in the band. The rest of it was a bit open to conjecture. David Stone is there and he's pictured, but Tony Carey is possibly playing keyboards on three tracks as well, "Long Live Rock 'n' Roll, "Lady of the Lake" and "Rainbow Eyes." And David Stone does the rest. Bob plays bass on "Gates of Babylon," "Kill the King" and "Sensitive to Light" and it's Ritchie on the rest. So you've almost got two bands here, strangely, across the album.

Martin: What sort of album is it compared to *Rising*?

Steven: Much more to the point. Although musically, this is still obviously very much linked to *Rising* and *Rising* has its links with the debut, although there's a distinct difference between all three. I will say that this is much less like the debut, even though *Rising* is like the debut and this is like *Rising*. Does that make sense? Because there's definitely an evolution from one to the next to the next. But I think the shorter songs are already a sign of things to come. We're not doing those sprawling epics we get on *Rising*. Not that it's sprawling, but there's much more structured looseness on *Rising* that's not really here. We are definitely tailoring songs here and keeping them concise. It's a short album, to be fair, as albums were back then. And that's not a bad thing.

So yeah, it's not a pop record. It's not even a melodic rock record. Which is obviously where they were going. But it's not quite the intricate, semi-progressive album that *Rising* is. *Rising* is not prog; it's not progressive. Do you know what I mean? But it has a broader outlook and scope. And it definitely has a more epic feel to it. I think that's why it's held in such clear esteem. And I think to some extent, it's why this one may be viewed as slightly the lesser of the two. Whether it is or not, that's down to personal taste. I think it's viewed as the lesser of the two and I think that's because *Rising* is seen as the creative pinnacle.

Marco D'Auria: Ritchie Blackmore was changing musicians like other guys were changing shoes at that point. They didn't even have a cohesive keyboard player on this one. I've looked at the interviews and I know Tony Carey was fired and then quit and then came back and he was in another band a few times. David Stone was also in the band playing keyboards. Jimmy Bain was out and then he came back briefly and then was out again.

I don't know what was going on there. I get it that the Elf guys weren't up to snuff, but the band that they had on *Rising*, if they'd stuck around for a handful of albums, I think we would have seen more classics. It's unfortunate that they just kept switching players. That's another thing you can point to where you can say, okay, maybe Ritchie was definitely the head of the band, for sure. And for whatever reason, I think he had some Zappa-ish perfectionism in terms of how he heard the music in his head. Maybe he was just trying to jam all the players into this perfectionist vision that he had in his head, and he ended up switching these musicians around, and I think it was to Rainbow's detriment. I think you hear that on *Long Live Rock 'n' Roll*, which resembles the first album more than the second, although I think it's more cohesive than the first album. And the production's a little better, although not much.

Rich Davenport: This album is seen as a cornerstone of power metal in Europe. In fact, there was a Dio tribute album in 1999 called *Holy Dio*, and it was all those European bands like Stratovarius, Primal Fear and Blind Guardian on there. There were even two versions of "Kill the King." And it was Dio-era Rainbow, and then some Dio and Sabbath tracks as well. But it's quite surprising how many of those bands had the same instrumentation as Rainbow and how well those *Long Live Rock 'n' Roll* tracks are regarded as something of a direct blueprint, really.

Tate Davis: *Long Live Rock 'n' Roll* is a weird album, when you look at the history. I really think that Blackmore made a mistake by firing Tony Carey and Jimmy Bain because they brought a lot to the table. It's just a shame that that line-up only did *Rising* and *On Stage*, which isn't even close to the best Rainbow live album. So they end up going to the Chateau recording studio in France where Jethro Tull and Elton John recorded their stuff before and Blackmore, I think, just wanted to show complete control. So he gets Mark Clarke and David Stone and then he's having troubles with Mark Clarke. Bob Daisley comes in but Ritchie ends up playing some of the bass himself. And if that doesn't show power-hungry enough, I don't know what does. Still, the result that you get is terrific. I don't think it quite hits the mark that *Rising* does, but for me it's a close second.

Martin: Yeah, *Rising* has this interesting advantage of having that symmetry of the four songs on one side and two of equal length on the other side.

Tate: Yeah, although *Long Live Rock 'n' Roll* has good symmetry with four songs on each side. I really like albums that have eight song like that. It's perfect for vinyl in the seventies.

Jamie Laszlo: *Long Live Rock 'n' Roll*. Like you, I'm not a big fan of the album title. Rock 'n' roll is what your dad listened to. Chuck Berry, Jerry Lee Lewis, Elvis—that was rock 'n' roll. This is rock. The Who had it right when they sang "Long live rock," and they didn't put the added roll in there. This album might be more solid than Rainbow *Rising*. For starters, there's no "Do You Close Your Eyes" on this record, which really brings down *Rising*. And when I listen to this compared to Rainbow *Rising*, I'm always thinking what could have been with a less dry production on *Rising*. It's all that's on my mind. I listen to that album and I'm yearning for more beefed-up production. So instead of listening to the album I'm getting, I'm always dreaming of the album I want—the whole time. With *Long Live Rock 'n' Roll*, that thought never crosses my mind because the production fits the songs better.

Martin: What does that album cover say to you?

Marco: Oh, the album cover is cool as hell. It looks like something you would see hanging up on a church door back in medieval times. I like all three covers, but this has the most old-timey theme to it. But the *Rising* album cover's one of the most influential album covers in metal, and one where you can hear the album just by looking at it.

Rich: It's an interesting idea, and a departure from the fantasy artwork of *Rising*. It's much more basic and monotone, really. I don't like it as much, but I find it quite an interesting design.

Martin: I remember thinking, the day I got it back then as a new release, that they were emulating a classical music album cover.

Rich: Yeah, totally, with those muted colours. And yeah, Ritchie looks like a composer.

Tate: It's like they thought enough to hire an illustrator to do a beautiful and respectful drawing. There's a permanence to it. It gives off a little bit of a *The Who by Numbers* situation, right? Although that's more like a rough sketch on like a paper bag.

Martin: Aerosmith *Draw the Line* as well.

Tate: Yeah, that's true. I'm sorry. That's a much better comparison. I don't know what I'm talking about with *The Who by Numbers*. But yeah, I like it; I think it works really well. I don't really understand what that sort of drawing has to do with the title, *Long Live Rock 'n' Roll*. That's perplexing. I don't think it's as good of a cover as the *Rising* cover or even the cover of the first album, but I like it. It does its job. If you were at a record store in the seventies and you were flipping through the vinyl and you came across this, you'd think, cool, I gotta see what this is about. I really like how the text on the back is in that old-style font. I really appreciate the effort that went into the liner notes and everything like that.

Jamie: When I was a kid, I thought Ritchie Blackmore was Ronnie. You had such a fantastic album cover on the previous record where it sounded like the music; same with the debut. This looks very English and classical as well. It looks like they're all stuck in a tornado too. But I get your point; it looks like it could be the cover of some heavy classical box set.

Steven: As far as I'm concerned, the message I get from the cover is that it's a band that is tight and together. If you describe that cover to somebody, it's the five heads of the guys that are in the band and they've all got their hair intermingled. It's actually quite an effective cover. It does a good job of conveying the idea of a band that is together but there's also a mystique about it. I love the fact that nobody's really looking at the artist. Ritchie definitely isn't and I think that says a lot about him in general. He's darting off. He's thinking of something else; he's already looking a bit bored with this. Even in an illustration, Ritchie's already somewhere else. The logo's fantastic, simple enough, does the job. And yeah, I suppose it does look classical, which I'm sure Ritchie was happy with. They all look a bit like composers here. And as you would expect, although his name's not in the band title, Ritchie's very much on top.

Martin: The album opens with the title track, which I have a slight aversion to because it's a shuffle. But I'm also not a fan of that title and hence the chorus. I dunno, am I just being a complainer?

Marco: Well, I get it, because it demonstrates again that they've always had their head in more commercial material. On every album, there's a song or two that is rock 'n' rollsy. "If You Don't Like Rock 'n' Roll," "Long Live Rock 'n' Roll"… there's a connection that fits the band going back to the beginning. So it's not particularly off the beaten track. It's hooky, it's catchy, and in fact, the first time I ever heard "Long Live Rock 'n' Roll" was in the movie *Rockstar* with Mark Wahlberg, because Steel Dragon covered that song. I think it's Ritchie that gives the song personality, both riff-wise and when it comes to his solo. He can turn what might be a generic rock anthem into something special with his guitar playing.

Dio's lyrics and melody make it a sort of foot-stomper, I guess. But there's a mystical dream-like quality to them too. Is he talking about what it's like to be moved by a Rainbow concert? Can it rise to the level of ritual, sort of over and above just going to a rock show? I'd say given the subject matter, it's the song that is closest to being called the definitive Dio-era Rainbow anthem. The chorus could have been written by any big American arena band, but only Dio could do those verses, I think. But I like the idea that you've been deeply affected by this Rainbow concert that you think a spell has been cast upon you. You're not even really sure where you are or if this is even reality. At the end of it, you're back in reality and you're wondering, was that real? Did I really see Rainbow live? That's the way I envision it.

Martin: And then fittingly, the gatefold is a concert shot, right?

Marco: That too (laughs). Yeah, the famous Rush picture. "At the end of a dream/If you know where I mean/When the mist just starts to clear." That sounds like the end of the show, when you're leaving the smoke-filled hall, dazed and confused (laughs). Oddly though, it's the opening lyric to the song.

Rich: I think in some ways, "Long Live Rock 'n' Roll" is more aggressive and direct than anything from *Rising*. It just comes out and goes for the throat straightaway. Contrast "Long Live Rock 'n' Roll" as an opener with "Tarot Woman," with the great atmospheric synth intro and then Ritchie's guitar fading in. This just comes straight out with Cozy's single-stroke snare thing and the guitar and just really clobbers conclusively. Ritchie goes for the jugular with that riff and Ronnie's vocal is really quite aggressive and snarling. The keys are taking a backseat here as well; they seem to be lower in the mix. So it's much more in-your-face and aggressive.

Tate: What do I think of "Long Live Rock 'n' Roll?" I think it's awesome, and a terrific way to open the album. There's nothing more lyrically to it than rock 'n' roll is in danger of dying, and we need to make sure that it doesn't die. So we need to take pride in the music that we create and proclaim the message. Yeah, it's a great song.

Martin: Combined with the cover, Tate, the music reminds me of those debauched medieval paintings where everybody's dancing some kinda jig in the streets and swinging their bottle of booze around and groping each other.

Tate: Yeah. I have what's called the mug test, where you grab a beer stein or something like that and you're doing the Oktoberfest thing, swinging it back and forth in front of you. If you're able to do that in time with the song, that shows that the song has a good pulse to it and a good feel. So yeah, "Long Live Rock 'n' Roll" passes what I call the mug test.

Jamie: "Long Live Rock 'n' Roll;" the title actually works better in the song than it does on the album cover. I think it's a precursor to how Dio would open up his Sabbath and Dio albums. It's short, it's a rock anthem and it has the energy of "Neon Knights" and "Turn Up the Night." It also has the rock anthem lyrics of "Stand Up and Shout" and "We Rock." If you just change the production to an eighties feel, it could probably open *Holy Diver*.

Steven: It's just a hard rock anthem, isn't it? Focused and tight, but it's still lively and vibrant. And we're already seeing this more song-based direction, when you compare it to anything on *Rising*. And we're not mucking about; we're straight in there. The soloing is the Man in Black at his best, I suppose. There's a flow and a subtlety. Even though those notes are still broken down in that very Ritchie Blackmore way. When you listen to his solos, you could argue there's no flow, that it's all very staccato. He picks out the notes and he gives each note its moment. It's really quite unusual, very distinctive, and yet his flow is fantastic on this song. There's a clear space between everything he does; I really like that.

But the chorus of that song is a little repetitive. It's overused in the song, but it's also undoubtedly catchy. And it's proved to be a great sing-along live selection for the band, but also for Ronnie James Dio when he played it with Dio many, many times over the years. It was still a massive fan favourite when it was played live. Here's me being picky and this does annoy me. What's the album called? It's called *Long Live Rock 'n' Roll*. That's what it's called. Yeah, but every single time Ronnie sings it, he says rock *and* roll. Every single time. Yes, it's the most miniscule of things. It maybe says more about me than it does this song. But still, it's true.

Martin: And I always thought that chorus sounded twee and sing-songy. And let's not forget, it's just repeating the title over and over.

Steven: I don't like songs about rock 'n' roll. I love rock 'n' roll. I don't really like songs about rock 'n' roll. And I don't really know who these bands write these songs for. The fans know they like rock 'n' roll already. Doesn't matter how heavy it is, as a class, all of these "rock 'n' roll" songs sound twee. And across his whole career, I'm not the biggest Cozy Powell fan. The guy was a great drummer, but he's not one of my go-to drummers. I think that he is—and this is going to be really unkind—in places, on certain albums, he can be a bit meat-and-potatoes. He does his thing and that's what he does. I think things like Emerson, Lake & Powell was the perfect example of how he couldn't adapt to that style. And that boom, clang, boom, clang sound was just like, why are you doing that here? This is the wrong thing for that here.

It's interesting, because you can easily pick holes in this song. You can say it's repetitive; you can say it's twee. You can pick on a whole lot of things that are not right. And yet it's one of rock 'n' roll's most memorable anthems. So in that respect, you can't argue that it ticks those boxes and in a marvellously overt way. It's far too obvious and yet here we are all these years later. It clearly worked because people still want to hear it. They still talk about it and it's still played on the few rock radio stations that we have left, at least here in Scotland.

Martin: Actually, come to think of it, one of its strengths is that it has a fairly complicated and crafted pre-chorus.

Steven: Yeah, you're right. It's a shorter, concise song but it's still substantial. All the songs are reasonably substantial. We haven't taken that step into clearing away the clutter, for want of a better word. But that's where we're heading after this album. That clutter is still marvellously in place at this point. And I do mean marvellously in place—it's not in the way; it's all there for a reason.

Martin: How do you guys feel about the production?

Rich: It's less clean than *Rising*. It sounds like they're pushing the instruments slightly into the red on the desk a lot more and just going for a more direct, aggressive feel. Yeah, there's not so much polishing. The keys are not completely gone, but they're not as dominant. The keyboards are more subservient to Ritchie's guitar on this one.

Martin: I think it's interesting that all three of them are mid-rangy, but in three different ways. The first one is old and warm, the second one is harsh and bright and *Long Live Rock 'n' Roll* is sort of raucous and direct and dirty, definitely hitting hard but lacking top end. But yes, all of them are crowded around the mids.

Rich: Yeah, that's it. It's dirty. That's the exact word.

Steven: I love the production on this album; I really do. Martin Birch does a good job here. It's a tight album in terms of its sound. Everything has its place. The drums sound fantastic, where the snare fills and various things are just like hooks in themselves. You listen for all of the fills on "Kill the King" and some of the songs which we'll come to. You can't help "play" them, in inverted commas, as they come around. They're as important as anything else on the album. And it's tough, it's hard-hitting, but it's not rough around the edges. It's very focused, like I say, tight. I like what Martin Birch generally does. Not everything he did was brilliant, I have to say, but I am a fan. I think this is one of his best and I think it still stands up now. You think of remixes and remasters and all these various things out there; I'll still go back to the original old vinyl.

Martin: Next is, "Lady of the Lake," which is the second of a half-dozen songs neatly derived from "The Wanton Song" on *Physical Graffiti*. It's my favourite on the album, and yeah, one day I'm gonna do a podcast episode on all these songs with variations on that riff. Actually Ronnie's on another one of them, "Master of Insanity" from *Dehumanizer*.

Steven: Wow, yeah, you've given me a bunch of stuff to go listen to and investigate. "The Wanton Song," yeah, I can hear that in my head. It's like, why did I not think of that before? Okay, "Lady of the Lake," Tony Carey makes his presence felt before he's sent away. There's these atmospheric organ parts that bolster the coolness of the song. There's a real presence and majesty there, coming from the keyboards.

And I like Ronnie's vocals on this track. He's more relaxed, less bombastic, not that there's anything wrong when he's doing those things. It's a side of his voice that I would have like to have heard a bit more over the years, because we all know he was a phenomenal soaring singer. But what a beautiful, pure, clear voice he had. There's also this almost forgotten, eerie guitar work in the verses that also sets the tone, along with what Tony is doing. The song is almost like sighing and sorrowful, because of that undercurrent; it gives it all of the gravitas that it has. It's those beautiful little embellishments that make this album as good as it is.

The solo is quite short, but it's effective. And that, to some extent, is a phrase that works well for the album in general. You can feel the evolution. I quite like that there's not a traditional chorus on the track. We've moved from that sort of sing-along into something very different of structure. The song title's maybe sung twice in the whole song, which is quite unusual for any Rainbow song, really.

Martin: You could define that part as the chorus. But you're right, in a way, it's like a long pre-chorus, then "Lady of the lake!"—that's the chorus.

Steven: Yeah, and one of those is even right at the end—it closes the song out. So you can't really call it the chorus. It's like, "Here's the chorus. Oh, we're finished!" (laughs). And it's a traditional fantasy lyric from Ronnie. I know he got a hard time for trotting out these things. We're back in the world of King Arthur here. And if you like that kind of thing, that's great. I used to play Dungeons & Dragons and all these things when I was young. All of that stuff resonated with me when I was younger. Now they are what they are. They're still good fun and I suppose it does fit the music, to be fair. The music does have that mythical, mystical quality, so I can't really complain, in that sense. But is it twee? I don't like to use the word twee with this album. It's not a twee album, but there are a lot of twee aspects along the way. And the lyric here is one of them.

Marco: "Lady of the Lake" is cool. I don't know if Ronnie did this on purpose, but I don't know if you're familiar with the Slavic folklore of the rusalka. Ever heard of that before? It's a beautiful woman who's an undead creature in the lake, and she tricks men to come into the lake with her and she pulls them down and drowns them. This song sounds very much about that, although I don't think Ronnie wrote it about that. But I always put those two things together.

Rich: Love this one; staccato riff, quite dark-sounding in that European minor scale thing. To me, Ronnie's vocal and the general mood of the track prefigures "Lady Evil" with Sabbath. And we've got the dark, aggressive, stark verse. That gives way to a very melodic chorus or pre-chorus, quite sweeping and grand. That's a really neat trick that they pull, where it's almost like a bait and switch. It comes in with this accessible chorus after a dark, aggressive verse. It works really well. Although I hear what you guys are saying; maybe there is no chorus and it's all a set-up kind of thing, a pre-chorus with no actual chorus.

Tate: Blackmore's solo on "Lady of the Lake" leaves more space than in any other place on the album except for maybe "The Shed." I really like how Blackmore leaves this space and then the only thing that you hear under that is Cozy Powell's really solid pocket. I think that shows you that that solo was thought-out with intent when they were playing this. Not much else to say, other than it's a great rocker. I like Marco's rusalka reference, but another Lady of the Lake is Nimuë, or Viviane, from the tales of King Arthur. I wonder if Dio had been reading the King Arthur stuff and was inspired to write that lyric. And I can see that comparison to "The Wanton Song"—love it. One other thing I also want to say about "Lady of the Lake" is why did they never do this one live?

Jamie: Now I don't know if you would call this song a shuffle, but I do know it makes me shuffle and dance across the floor when I listen to it, in the same way "Temple of the King" makes me shuffle. In my mind this is a heavier and faster-paced "Temple of the King" because both songs have that dip in the music. If you take the opening lyrics to both, "There's a magical sound sliding over the ground," do you see the dips there? (laughs). "Making it shiver and shake." And there's similar dips in "Temple of the King." "One day in the year of the fox/ Came a time remembered well." I like "Lady of the Lake" a lot because "Temple of the King" is my favourite Rainbow song. I like that type of shuffle and those type of dips.

Martin: Speaking of dips, "L.A. Connection" is grinding and funky, a bit of a slog—the whole song dips.

Jamie: Yeah, fair enough. I don't know what the L.A. connection is supposed to be in the song, but I do know that it's been a comedy club in L.A. since 1977. But to me it sounds like a weekend newspaper. "The L.A. Connection comes out every Thursday!" Or it sounds like a 1970s roller skating rink where people come from all over to connect. "Are you going down to the Connection Friday night?" Whatever the case, it doesn't sound very metal and I feel like those

Elf days haunted Ronnie all the way up 'til *Mob Rules*. *Holy Diver* is where he really stripped away those less metal song titles. And why am I including *Mob Rules*? Because it has "Country Girl" on it. It still haunted him all the way up to there and it matches song titles like Elf's "Lady" and "Dixie Lee Junction."

And I should mention, we're talking about "L.A. Connection." Elf had a song called "L.A. 59." So when you see this title, you feel like you're going backwards. But thankfully, it's a really good song. It's so damn good that it breaks free of its title. It makes you forget that the title is a little corny. And he fit in a nice little Dio lyric there with, "I'm a fallen angel who's lost his wings and left out in the cold." So he fits that mysticism in there.

And what this song embodies, like a lot of the other songs on this album, is a certain earthiness. These are not acoustic songs—far from it—but the guitar tone is low and blended deep into the mix. So when I hear the notes on the guitar, I don't exactly picture bolts of lightning protruding from a guitar amp. I imagine I'm just lingering low to the ground and simmering almost beneath the music and it works. Especially on this song when you have an old-timey-sounding piano in the mix from David Stone.

Marco: I like Ronnie's lyrics on "L.A. Connection." Apparently it was written as a goof on Tony Carey, because he got fed up and quit and went home, as in, "Carry home my broken bones and lay me down to rest." I understand what you mean by the sort of low-energy music, but a track that can be seen as a throwaway I think is uplifted by the performances and the lyrics. It comes out more interesting than it should be.

Rich: "L.A. Connection" has this stomping beat and it's almost funky. The riff is simple and direct, in a bluesy vein almost like a Bad Company song, really. Still, it's not a bad fit for Ronnie. For me, this is perhaps Ritchie already edging in that more commercial direction that he wanted to go in and that he wanted to embrace more fully with Graham Bonnet on *Down to Earth*. It's arguably more of a direct single than they've ever done. And I know there's a promo film clip for this as well, which makes me think they had that in mind.

As for the story about Tony, I checked up on it in your book, and Ronnie was very—what's the word?—diplomatic about that and didn't go into a lot of details. But he hinted at that as well. And there's something about someone in the organization—he didn't say who—ringing ahead when Tony was on his way to the airport, and saying he had like a kilo of cocaine on him or something, with the idea of getting him searched. Because there's a lot of talk about these dark practical jokes and Tony mentioned that he wasn't very happy with that. So I don't know if that was an example of that. And it sounds like it was quite a fraught session, because Tony actually quit, and he put that down to the way that Ritchie was treating him. And I know you mentioned in your book, I think Ronnie and Cozy had to go and ask him to come back, because they hadn't got anybody to finish the album. And from what I remember reading about it, Tony says that Ritchie would play a lot of head games, and it was more like that than any direct confrontation, that it was a mind games thing.

Martin: Yeah, pertaining to that title, it's funny, because if you think about it, Tony Carey himself is an L.A. connection—that's where he's found. And Ritchie is living in L.A. for a little bit, isn't he? And then Ronnie makes an L.A. connection with Wendy and moves there. And then Ronnie sort of gets into Sabbath in Los Angeles. Lots of L.A. connections.

Rich: Yeah, that's right. I think he was introduced to them in L.A. I remember reading somewhere that it was actually Sharon Osbourne that introduced Tony Iommi to Ronnie, at the Rainbow. Probably not something she talks about these days, but I'm sure I read that somewhere. She was in the management organization, and I'm sure that she introduced the two of them.

Tate: "L.A. Connection" is a weird song. Dio puts in a really strong vocal performance here but it's very funky for this era of Rainbow. Blackmore puts in a good solo and he plays bass on this one as well and is very locked-in with Cozy, which is impressive. I talked about the clunky feel of "Run with the Wolf" on *Rising*; I think this has that same clunky feel. Overall, I don't think it's one of the magnum opuses of the Dio catalogue, but it's a great song for what it is and I think it earns its place on the album.

Steven: Yeah, why is it that so many bands choose one of their weakest tracks as a single? It's easy to hear why "L.A. Connection" was chosen. It's simple, it's straightforward, it has a sing-along chorus and it has the potential, I suppose, to hook in people who wouldn't necessarily have much interest in this album. It's even got a little bit of blues and honky-tonk and various things in there that don't feel like they should belong on this album and it does stand out for those reasons.

As a song, I don't know if it's just me, but I find it slow and steady and a little dull. It always feels to me like I'd like to wind it up a notch or two. The more I've heard the song over the years, the less I like it, to be honest. You can never criticize Ronnie's vocals; they're gritty, they're full of passion. But the album version rolls along at nearly five minutes and it just feels like work. And the single edit was not tidy. But it does feel like it's a couple of minutes longer than it needs to be. They do an awful lot of "whoa whoa" and "ooh ohh" and all that stuff that always makes me think that we're just padding out a song that is already spent. It's uneventful more than anything else.

Martin: Like Tate alluded to, I always framed this as a follow-up song to "Run with the Wolf." Plus it sounds like Nazareth to me.

Steven: I suppose. Yeah, you're blowing my mind here. Because this is an album that I've always held up as a cornerstone. But when you compare it, yeah, there are similarities to lots of things; that's very true.

Martin: And what is your understanding of the lyric?

Steven: Ronnie's gone out there and gone on record saying this was about Tony being encouraged to leave the band. The theory goes that nobody was ever sacked from Rainbow. They were all just hounded out slowly but surely, and it probably would have been much easier if you just said, "You know what? I don't like you; it's time for you to leave." But it was never quite as upfront as that. And yes, this is about Tony leaving the recording studio. The story that I've heard Ronnie tell is that he had all manner of illegal substances on him at the time, and that he possibly had, shall we say, borrowed some things from the studio that the band were using to record at the Chateau. And he still had all this on his person, and as he got to the airport, the band were kind enough to phone the police and inform them as Tony was trying to leave what seems to have been a really, really bad situation. And he got stopped at Charles de Gaulle Airport. And I do believe that he managed to wriggle his way through it. But that's a queer way to treat a guy you've just spent all this time with, in a band.

Martin: Rich has told the story that it was more of a prank situation.

Steven: The story that Ronnie told is that Tony had stuff on him. He puts the lyric in there about the broken bones as if he got beaten up by the police. But I guess it's vague and nuanced—was there coke or not, stolen property or not? There's that air of mystery all these years down the line. But that's the story he told. But there was definitely pranking, so who knows? The story I was aware of from many years ago is that they bricked him into his room. It crosses into being an arsehole, to be honest. It's the sort of things you read about and you go, I don't have the temperament to deal with that.

I like that until you hear the context later on about what it is or is not about, it really means very little. It's not one of those lyrics that you can read and go, well, there must have been a situation within the band and the guy is leaving the band and he's heading off and we don't know where he's going to. That's not written in the song. So it's actually true, but it's definitely written for themselves as a type of in-joke.

Martin: Picking this to be a single sounds like a record executive's idea of how a honky-tonk sort of song might go over well with radio DJs, even though that's more of a 1972 or 1973 way of thinking.

Steven: Yes, that's the idea I was getting at. It reminds me way down the line of "More Than Words" by Extreme, a sort of clinic in how not to represent an album. That's what that single is. People bought the album and said, "Who the hell are these guys?" That's not the guys strumming acoustics in these beautiful black and white videos. And to me, "L.A. Connection" is that song from Rainbow in 1978. It's a song that people would hear and then go buy the album and think, that's not these guys; these guys are not doing this stuff. What's "Gates of Babylon" got to do with "L.A. Connection?"

Martin: We close side one with what is generally considered Rainbow's second greatest song ever, "Gates of Babylon." I suppose wherever you rank it, it's a perfect microcosm of this album, i.e. still moody and mystical but somehow sharper.

Marco: Sure. "Gates of Babylon" is a colossus of a song, although it comes in at under seven minutes. It could have been on *Rising*, given those Middle Eastern tones, and it's almost as long as "Stargazer" and it's kinda like "Stargazer" part two, but it's got its own personality and it's its own beast. The lyrics are very visual and it's just abundant with amazing performances all around. There's the Minimoog synth from Dave Stone that introduces the song and it ends with some violins. Ritchie's guitar solo and Ronnie's performance and Cozy and Bob Daisley... like, everything comes together for that one. Speaking of Bob though, bass was the one thing on the album that's never really as upfront as the other musicians. It seems like everybody else got to shine except for bass players in Rainbow.

For me, it relates to side two of *Rising* given the desert imagery. I always get like an *Arabian Nights* vibe when I listen to "Gates of Babylon." It takes you on an epic musical journey and insinuates that there will be fantasies and temptations that await us. "You can see, but you're blind/Someone turned the sun around/But you can see in your mind the Gates of Babylon." Again, there's this idea of questioning reality in it—
what's actually there and what's just a dream, or in this case, a mirage?

Rich: Cool, yeah, love this track. And again, the intro recalls "Tarot Woman." I see this track very much with the scales that are being used—it's either the Phrygian or diminished scale—as quite sinister-sounding. It touches on what they used to call the devil's note or tritone that was banned in church music. It's the scale that Tony Iommi used on the main riff in "Black Sabbath." There was a series of guitar instructional videos in the eighties called *Hot Licks* and Viv Campbell from Dio did one, which I bought at the time, and he shows one of the scale patterns for the diminished scale. And he says Ritchie Blackmore used this a lot and you can really hear that here.

I see this as a sort of companion piece to "The Sails of Charon" by Scorpions. The beat is almost funky, disco in places. It also reminds me of a song on the *Jesus Christ Superstar* soundtrack, which I know obviously Ian Gillan was on it, and that's how I know the soundtrack. There's this song called "Heaven on Their Minds" and the riff is very similar. I'm not saying Ritchie nicked it, but he was obviously aware of that. And Yvonne Elliman, who's on that soundtrack, she was on Purple Records for a while and she did an album that got reissued a few years ago. They reissued some of the oddities that were on Purple Records, some really bizarre stuff. This was about five or six years ago.

But yeah, this song is tailor-made for Ronnie. It's classic

Rainbow. You've got all the drama and the different moods and the lyrics are perfect. On the chorus there's something odd, bearing in mind what happened when Ronnie joined Sabbath. There's a bit where he sings "Gates of Babylon" in time with the riff; the vocal follows that riff. Now, when Ronnie joined Sabbath, Tony Iommi said that he found it very freeing as a composer, because Ozzy always used to follow the riff. Whereas Ronnie didn't do that with Sabbath, so it brought a change. But here is Ronnie in Rainbow following the vocal with the riff, which is more of an Ozzy thing.

Tate: "Gates of Babylon" is one of the greatest songs that Rainbow ever did, in my opinion. Maybe it's their third greatest song, depending on how you rate "Stargazer" and then "A Light in the Black" in terms of like grandiose epic-ness. I don't know why they never did this one live, because it kills. All the instruments are solid and Dio turns in one of his most venomous vocal performances. He's got a really good snarl on the song, which you can hear at the tail end of that line, "I think you're ready to see the Gates of Babylon." He does what he does best with these kinds of songs.

But for me, my favourite part of the song is the bridge, with Cozy Powell being the MVP there and throughout. His fills are just so perfectly placed within the bridge. Blackmore turns in a really good solo on this one too. There's a bit of a funky feel to this song, but it's definitely not clunky. It's very tight and played with intent. I don't know if Blackmore and Powell were sitting down and working on the song and Blackmore specifically told Cozy what kinds of fills to play in that bridge section or if he just trusted Cozy, but regardless, it sounds great. Terrific song.

Jamie: The music just bubbles behind Ronnie, doesn't it? The bass, keyboards and guitar all act as one, and when Ritchie's guitar solo comes in, it feels like an extension of the keyboards and bass instead of Ritchie rising high above everything and taking control of the song. It's nice, because I appreciate textures within a song. And then the solo actually ends by blending right into a keyboard solo. So, again, they layer what they're doing and create texture.

I will say that all of this sounds very much different than a certain debut album by a certain band that came out the same year— *Van Halen*. Correct me if I'm wrong, but I just feel like before the first Van Halen album, you could do tasty little guitar solos that were further down in the mix and everything would be cool. But after that one Van Halen record, that suddenly became a little old-fashioned, where guys like Ritchie and Tony Iommi instantly became elders of heavy rock. Maybe they weren't a full generation away, but they were at least a half generation away. So if Eddie Van Halen became like, age-wise, your older brother, these guys were like your youngest uncle, that half generation older.

Martin: Nice. Yeah, I can see that. After Eddie arrived, a "guitar hero" was expected to do more. Okay, Steven, thoughts on this one.

Steven: Sure; let's start with the vocal: it's powerful, it's commanding, it's full of character. I had a little giggle to myself, because I like to go and watch the promo videos of these songs before we do this. Man oh man, Ronnie could not lip-synch (laughs). It's really, really bad. And he spends most of the video with his hands up around his mouth at the microphone. And yes, he likes to do all of these strange little movements and what he's really trying to do is hide the fact that he cannot get the lyrics in time. He just cannot do it and he's well aware of it. It's really obvious in the video, but there you go.

I love the mystical, Middle Eastern flavours that the song throws out. In the wrong hands it could feel forced and yes, a little twee. But instead the whole band absolutely go for it. I buy this hook, line and sinker. The instrumental section is overblown to verging on over-the-top. But it's all the better for it. It just fits everything that is right about that song. And credit to David Stone for the keyboards on this one; it has foundation. What he does on the song gives Ritchie the room to really go for it, not just in the solo, but in the whole song. There's little tricks and flicks that he's throwing out there, and without that basis to work from, I think that this would... not fall apart, but it wouldn't feel quite as cohesive as it does. It needs that undercurrent for it to work.

And in the end the track has a life of its own. It still retains that regalness and that impact today. You put it on and you immediately feel a bit pompous and overblown. I really, really love it. This is one of my favourite songs. And it's to do with the dangers of being seduced by evil and the devil and where it can lead. Of course, supposedly the band was dabbling in the occult back then. They often said that they summoned the spirit of Baal through a seance at the Chateau. And that led to a whole host of unsettling happenings, doors that were locked being unlocked when only one person had the key and Wendy Dio thinking that she was being pushed down the stairs by Ronnie when he was five steps behind. He had witnesses to say that he was nowhere near her and all these various things. How much of that is true? Who knows, but it makes for great stories when you're writing songs like this (laughs).

Martin: A couple of things that this just dawned on me too. "Gates of Babylon" reminds me a little bit of that Rush mentality of moving from *Hemispheres* to *Permanent Waves*, that this represents a more sober and succinct and sophisticated version of what they did on "Stargazer" and "A Light in the Black." It's like 15% more happens, but it's 15% shorter, right?

Steven: Yes, exactly. It's a more concise and pointed album overall, like *Permanent Waves*. Depending on what you want, that's maybe why *Rising* is held in great esteem. Because I don't necessarily know if people wanted that slightly more controlled and concise version of the band. It's still a remarkably uncommercial track, but it feels like a slightly more polished version of what we had before. Commercial isn't the right word, but it definitely feels like we are honing and refining what we've done before.

Martin: Like they're smarter now, or better songwriters now or something.

Steven: Yeah, but I don't necessarily know if it needed to be honed from what *Rising* was. But at the same time, why make the same record again?

Martin: Good point. All right, let's flip the original vinyl over and re-acquaint ourselves with a song we first heard on the *On Stage* live album, "Kill the King."

Marco: Yes, probably my favourite Rainbow song because it's accessible, and I never get tired of it, especially with Ronnie's performance. It's interesting that for every "Kill the King" and "Gates of Babylon," there's a song like "Sensitive to Light" or "If You Don't Like Rock 'n' Roll" or "Do You Close Your Eyes." Is it Ronnie who causes that, given that he's the last standing member from Elf still in the band? But "Kill the King" is the opposite and it's incredible, and actually Cozy gets a songwriting credit on it, as he does on "The Shed

(Subtle)." I figure that's to reward him or keep him happy because he really did become one of the prominent members of the band, which is unusual for a drummer. I don't think he did anything different on those songs than he did with any of the other songs, right? Usually you have to write some portion of the melody or lyrics to get a songwriting credit, but with "Kill the King," you can hear that the drums are prominent enough to the point where maybe some of his parts count as hooks.

"Kill the King" is as thrashy or as heavy as anything Ritchie's ever done, for sure, although Ronnie's Dio band got this heavy quite regularly, I suppose. The lyrics are based on the game of chess but I like to think of it as more literal because there are so many stories about kings being usurped or betrayed with murder and so much happens in actual, real political life that is like a chess game. But we still get fantastical elements, because it mentions spells and charms and things like that. But like I say, although they talk about pawns and kings and queens and stuff like this, I like to envision it as the story of an actual king being murdered. It's another one of theirs that revives that theme of a powerful being, like the man on the silver mountain or the Stargazer, being destroyed. Perhaps there's a political message there, that these presidents and government officials controlling us need to be taken down. Because if you listen to the lyrics, there's, "Kill the king/Tear him down/He'll rule no more/Strike him dead." Whatever your take, those are just some badass power metal lyrics (laughs).

Rich: I think with "Kill the King," you feel the benefit of the band having tried it out live before they got into the studio, because there's a lot more aggression here. The studio version actually sounds more aggressive than the live version, which is a bit strange. So maybe that's the result of having drilled it and routined it to the point of being, not perfect, but being able to take it into the studio and let rip.

Tate: I actually think it comes across a bit better on the live album. You don't have the Cozy Powell double bass during the solo section on the live album, which is really cool. But overall it's a really great, hard rockin' fast rocker. It would go on to influence a lot of power metal bands in the decades afterwards. It's a good representation of Cozy Powell's double bass drumming. You might notice I'm not going so much into the lyrical themes as I did on *Rising*. For me, *Long Live Rock 'n' Roll* is more about the music and the individual playing than the lyrics, which, to me, are comparatively less grandiose.

Jamie: "Kill the King" has a bit of a Deep Purple feel to it, particularly "Fireball." You can almost call it 1970s speed metal. I realize it's not speed metal, but it's very fast for the seventies and sometimes I hear this and I wonder that a song this fast must have blown kids' minds back in the day. And unlike a few of the previous tracks, the guitar is turned up in the mix. It almost sounds like Ritchie turned his amp up for the three heavy songs on the back half of the record. Cozy is banging the hell out of his drums and doing all sorts of licks to keep you on your toes. And "Kill the King" is a great title for a metal song. That doesn't sound like a 1970s roller rink, does it? No, sir.

Steven: No it doesn't (laughs). "Kill the King" is the crowning glory of that album. With the urgency of the thing, it's maybe my favourite Cozy Powell performance of all time. The snare and tom fills are as important as anything Ritchie's doing on the song or anything that Ronnie is singing on the song. It might be my favourite Rainbow song of all time. What I like about the production is it's not tempered, it's not watered down. It would be easy to apply bells and whistles to this song and make it something else. And it's not; the production is quite simple and straightforward. You can't say that Martin did this and Martin did that and he brought in this and we've got an orchestra over here. He's just got a group of guys here that know what they're doing and doing it bloody well, and he's letting them get on with it. This song is almost breathless. It's got such power and energy. But Ronnie sure isn't breathless; it's powerful, full-throated singing, but he makes it sound so damn easy, doesn't he? He makes it sound simple and off-the-cuff. And it obviously never was, because it's just glorious. But it's one of those songs where everyone is just ripping it up.

There's that last furious guitar solo from Ritchie, but it still sings and dances. It's not what the guitarists that he would go on to inspire across the next couple of decades thought Ritchie was doing. They wanted him to throw a million notes at everything and arpeggios all over the place and show all of his classical inspiration. That's not what he does. That's never what he was about. How that became the interpretation of who he was through other people has always confused me. Because you listen to this and it's urgent and it's vibrant but it's controlled. It's obviously showy because the guy knows he's fantastic; there's no doubt about that. But he doesn't necessarily need to shove it down your throat. He's playing for the song; it's still all about the song.

David Stone is brilliant here, Bob Daisley is holding the whole thing together because those drum breaks are all over the place. The guitars are darting here and there. If you don't have Bob there, then that song doesn't happen. And I think this is one of those songs that when they got to the end and they finished it and they played it back, they must have looked at each other and said, "We have something here." This is one of those lightning in a bottle moments. It's the pinnacle. And as Marco has explained, it's inspired by the game of chess. The queen's going out to checkmate, which is not necessarily what you pull from the song as you're listening to it. But when you read the lyrics, you go yeah, I see that. Pawns are referenced and various things like that. But that lyric feels much more violent and dangerous.

Martin: Just generally speaking, what are your thoughts on Cozy as a drummer?

Tate: I like everything that he's played on. He's one of my favourite drummers of all time. For me, maybe the best thing he's played on is *Jeff Beck Group*, the last album they did, particularly the song "Ice Cream Cakes.' Cozy was getting his proper professional start in that group. I think he puts on a phenomenal performance throughout that entire album. Generally though, I find him to be very musical, playing with intent and I appreciate how he ends fills. There's a lot of single-stroke snare stuff and he often ends that with a sort of John Bonham-like sweeping thing. You hear that on the Jeff Beck stuff as well as in Rainbow. A great example of that sort of thing is in the *On Stage* version of "Sixteenth Century Greensleeves." That's one of my favourite individual performances of his. That's an unbelievable, historic performance.

Rich: What I like about Cozy is that he's very balanced, I find. You can certainly tell it's him. He hits really hard but he's not without finesse. He doesn't have the sort of lightness of touch of Ian Paice or his immediate replacement in Rainbow, Bobby Rondinelli, who's a similar player but has more lightness of touch. Whereas with Cozy, it's more about the power. He can put in some impressive and dexterous drum fills. I don't know; maybe he's got the flash of Ian Paice but he's rock-solid like John Bonham.

Martin: All right, moving on, we have "The Shed (Subtle)," which is anything but.

Marco: This is another hidden gem of a song. I never get tired of the lyric on this one. It's probably one of their heaviest songs, other than "Kill the King," which has the advantage of speed. This is stomping or plodding or marching, kind of simplistic. The lyrics are sort of like a precursor to the Black Sabbath song "I" from *Dehumanizer*, which of course is also Ronnie. "I'm steel/So come and try to bend me." What a cool, badass lyric. Like, come and test me, come and fight me, I'm gonna crush you, I'm gonna roll over you. It's a song about confidence generally but I like to equate it to Ronnie boasting about his band, Rainbow. I don't know; it's got the reputation as a lesser song or throwaway. In my opinion, it doesn't get the credit it deserves.

Rich: There's this one-minute guitar solo intro, with heavy delay, which is quite effective. The delay effect probably came from an Echoplex, back then. The riff's a little bit like "Stargazer." It's okay. Not my favourite track on the album. A bit ho-hum.

Tate: For me, "The Shed" is all about the riff, as well as the space Blackmore leaves when it comes time to solo, which is slide-y and slippery and not particularly note-dense. But that's one of the nastiest riffs Blackmore ever came up with in his recording career. It's just a great, straightforward rocker for this era of Rainbow.

Jamie: Of all the songs in this album, this has a riff that's closest to something like "Man on the Silver Mountain" or "Smoke on the Water." Ronnie sounds angry on this song. He's getting very close to that angrier style he displays on "The Mob Rules." The lyrical content is about a man with powers of invincibility so it has that mystical aspect. But if you didn't know any better listening to the song, you would think it was called "Street Walking." Which again, sounds a little old-fashioned. I'm glad that they didn't go with that and instead with this little weird title, "The Shed (Subtle)," with the part in parentheses adding a little bit of mystery to the song.

Steven: Is this the forgotten song on that album? Not to say there's anything wrong with it. I suppose it's solid and unflashy. It's an album track, is what I would suggest. It's one of those that provides the glue that holds the more exuberant songs together. Which is not a bad thing. It's got a great groove and some real nods to Deep Purple, in some of the guitar phrasing here. And that's not always something that you got from Ritchie at this stage, because he was trying to make it clear that he thinks differently between one and the other. Personally, I don't necessarily listen to much Rainbow and think, "That's the Deep Purple guy." It clearly can't be anybody else—Ritchie plays as Ritchie plays—but some of the phrasing in this one makes me think, oh, that's definitely the Deep Purple guitarist.

And much like "L.A. Connection," I think "The Shed" suffers from having too much good material around about it. So you forget the material like this that is solid and just doing the job of holding its own. It's just not one of the songs where you're going to walk away from that album still playing it in your head. I suppose it's like any great live show, where it's about pacing, where you build to those little crescendos as you go through the live set. This album does that too. "The Shed" is a bit of a breather before we head on to something else that's really good.

Martin: Next we have "Sensitive to Light," which I always put in that widdly Ritchie riff box, along with the likes of "Burn," "Lady Double Dealer," "No Time to Lose," "Can't Happen Here," "Rock Fever" and "Make Your Move."

Rich: Yes, exactly; it's a circular riff. It's almost playing a 3/4 over a 4/4 rhythm, a triplet thing, and repeating that over again to make it fit within like a bar of 4/4 music. And on this one, the construction is not exactly a 12-bar blues but it's borrowing from that. Yeah, I was trying to think of the Deep Purple track that riff reminded me of, and it is "Lady Double Dealer," as well as "Lay Down, Stay Down." And in the verse, with that octave-jumping, it's also a bit like "Black Sheep of the Family" on the first Rainbow album, and also just by the mood of the track. Good solo, quite brief. So, yeah, with this great list of songs that go to this place, it's like a stock Ritchie feel. It's something that he's known for doing. It's not filler exactly, but there's more interesting tracks on the album, I think.

Marco: "Sensitive to Light" could've been a single. It's catchy but maybe a bit too fast and heavy. I like the way Ronnie says "light-a," which is sort of that thing people say about James Hetfield all the time, right? But it's cool how little inflections like that can make a song memorable.

Tate: "Sensitive to Light" is a good, up-tempo song. It evokes the image of the popular girl in high school where she's a bright and shining star and attracting all the attention of the jocks and everything like that. And the protagonist says, "But I just must be sensitive to light," meaning that he's doesn't really understand why all of these jocks are attracted to this really pretty girl. He's sort of saying that the light is too bright. Good solo, great, energetic drumming from Cozy, a good way to close out the hard-driving rockers on the album. It's also probably a good precursor to the types of songs that he would do on *Down to Earth* and later on after that.

Jamie: They pack so much into a three-minute song. It comes on like a barnburner, then they find a riffy guitar piece and then it builds up and goes right back into the in-your-face rock energy. If you wanted to give someone with a short attention span—which is about 95% of people on Earth—a quick idea of what Rainbow is all about, I'd probably play "Sensitive to Light" for them. In three minutes you get it all, the big riffs rocking chorus, great vocals and a little moody guitar, all wrapped up in a bit of mysticism. In fact, this song could have been called "The Rainbow CliffsNotes Song."

Steven: Again, there's real cohesion here. This sounds like a band operating at a high level. And that's why it's fascinating that we do have people coming and going during this album. It doesn't feel like that at all. I never think, well, here's one keyboard player, here's another and oh, Ritchie must have played bass on this one. If you really analyse it, you can't actually tell who's playing bass. And the keyboard sounds as well, I suppose more than the actual playing, but it sounds like a band there too. It's focused and driven. And actually, I suppose the guitar tone supports such a strong connection from song to song. You could almost believe that you are listening to really good live sessions. "Sensitive to Light" sounds like a band playing live. And that, to me, is the sign of a good producer. It doesn't sound like this part was done and that part was done next and then we added this on top of it.

But yeah, I really like "Sensitive to Light." There's a funky underbelly in the verse that isn't really on show anywhere else on the album, save maybe for "L.A. Connection," but that's at a different speed. And the chorus, same again, it's another one without a chorus. It's a line or two of vocals; you blink and you miss it. What more does it need?

Martin: But again, just like "Lady of the Lake" you can debate whether the whole section there is the chorus. But I see what you are getting at. I'm 50/50 on it. You could call the whole thing a chorus or you could call it 95% pre-chorus and then, like you say, "blink and you miss it," where the 5% tail of it, "I just must be sensitive to light" is the only piece that qualifies as chorus!

Steven: Yes, that's a good way of putting it (laughs). Also, interestingly, the drum breaks, Cozy is beginning to kinda repeat what has been used elsewhere. You can hear exactly the same drum breaks in "Kill the King." In "Sensitive to Light," maybe it's not quite as good or exciting because we've heard them before. It's a quick, in-and-out three-minute song that still somehow leaves you singing that non-existent chorus. I find that I end up at the point where that "I just must be sensitive to light" line just sticks in my head. It's such a great hook; it works. And the lyrics; was Ronnie a great lyricist? Not particularly. That might be controversial for some, I suppose, and not for others. When we're talking about bright, dazzling women who are maybe too much or too dangerous to handle, everyone's done that, haven't they? But it's a good song; I really like it.

The production and the sound and the approach on this album is not that of a melodic rock album, but you listen to a song like this, and you see it as a step between *Rising* and a couple albums down the line. It's interesting listening to albums like this against ones from the Graham Bonnet or Joe Lynn Turner eras. They're not as different as you think, and yet they are remarkably different. But they're not as different as you think (laughs). The constituent parts remain in place, right the way through them. I've actually enjoyed coming back and listening to these albums and thinking specifically about the songs. You go from this to *Difficult to Cure* to *Stranger in Us All* and you go, these are remarkably similar albums that we all talk about as if they're such different beasts. They have no connection whatsoever. And then you listen to them and you think, yeah, they do (laughs).

Martin: Nice, very true. Okay, the album closes with its lone ballad, "Rainbow Eyes," decisively a ballad, very quiet. What's funny, is that it's the first ballad we've heard from Rainbow since 15 songs ago!

Marco: Yeah, and this is probably the only song across the first three albums that I'm not a huge fan of. And it's not because I don't appreciate the performances and the musicality. It's that to me it's

"Catch the Rainbow" part two, and it doesn't reach the highs that "Catch the Rainbow" does. "Catch the Rainbow" is epic. It has the crescendo—it builds up to something that's powerful. "Rainbow Eyes" just stays even-keel with that mellowness. There's flutes and recorders and strings and no drums, no bass and very little guitar. And Ronnie's voice is a little bit different. But other than that, it's basically "Catch the Rainbow" part two and the first one's always better than the sequel, right? And even with the band's other mellow songs, like "Temple of the King," there's more differentiation of arrangement and melody. But this doesn't go anywhere, despite it being seven-and-a-half minutes long.

Lyrically, it's a love song. There's actually some pretty poignant and poetic lyrics. I envision it being about a mystical woman who casts a spell or mesmerizes with her eyes. It turns out to represent a suitable ending to the Dio era of the band, if you think about "Tarot Woman" representing entry into this mystical world. And then in this song we find out that perhaps it's only a dream, even if we're never the same after. I like the lyric, "Summer nights are colder now/ They've taken down the fair/And the lights have all died somehow/Or were they ever there?"

So it's a call-back to when we entered the fair with the tarot woman and he's talking about this beautiful woman and her eyes. She's got rainbow eyes. Like maybe we were mystified the whole time. And now all of a sudden, we're just leaving the fair and it's like, wait, were we ever even here? Like, did we ever even talk to the tarot woman? Did we ever actually run with the wolf? Were we ever actually enslaved by a wizard in the desert? (laughs).

Tate: "Rainbow Eyes" is obviously an uncharacteristic song to put on the album. I really like it, but a lot of people that I know hate it. They're like, why would you even include this on the album? I admit it does drag on, because it's essentially Ronnie and an orchestra, for the most part. As Marco says, it's a love song, talking about a girl that's pretty and has rainbow eyes. It's a great song to listen to if you want to relax. It's a break from the hard rockers that came before. I would go back to my earlier point about how the sequencing of this album was done with intent. Placing a long ballad at the end is a sombre way to end the album. Funny thing is, if you put a rocker like "Sensitive to Light" at the end, I bet less people would complain about "Rainbow Eyes." Putting it here makes it seem like an afterthought or a bad bonus track.

Jamie: At first glance, you see the seven-minute runtime and you get a bit excited. But it's not as epic as anyone wants it to be. It could have been their "Stairway to Heaven." It could have been. It could have started off the way it starts off and then build in intensity, add a little percussion, add a few guitar licks and then end it with a big sweeping guitar solo. But no, none of that happens for seven minutes. It's fine as it is, but it makes one think that it's a great blueprint for a more epic song that doesn't exist.

Steven: As I've said, I'm a sucker for Ronnie singing like this. Yes, he can bite and he can snarl and he can get you to commit murder and all that stuff. But I love it when he just sings beautifully over some wonderfully nice guitars, flute, recorder, strings. Recorders were one of those instruments… I don't know if you guys had this. At school, we were all made to play the recorder.

Martin: Yes, absolutely! That is so funny. Here you are in Scotland telling me this, and I was across the Atlantic and on the far side of Canada and it was the same damn thing!

Steven: Oh man, the whole class was given this thing that you blow into and you can get no tune from whatsoever. So even now, reading the word "recorder" in the credits of an album makes me cringe. And then you go and listen and you go wow, how good is that?! (laughs). See, it does work. Someone knows what they're doing.

But what an unexpected vehicle on a fantastic and otherwise rocking album. I really like the juxtaposition between everything that's come before, all that incredible guitar work, all those massive drum beats, and then we get to the last song and it's, yeah, we're not gonna do any of that at all. It's just about emotion and you can't help but get caught up in the whole thing. It's one of those songs that is so well realized that it makes me a little bit sad when it finishes.

What a melancholy way for this line-up to end. You go from "Long Live Rock 'n' Roll" to this. It's a journey across the whole album. And it's sad, now looking back and thinking, well, that was the end of it. But it doesn't cop out in any way. Most bands would cop out and get to the end and you would suddenly get some snare-bashing and riff-torn rock anthem and you would punch the air as the album finishes. There's none of that here. Yeah, we don't need to do that at all. You just think, you know what? This is actually fabulous. This is one of the best things on the whole album. That's one of the best things this line-up has done. So let's just leave it as it is and put it at the end. I could listen to it all day, to be honest with you.

Martin: Interesting. I did not expect that enthusiasm for "Rainbow Eyes." Good stuff—that's why we talk it through. Rich, any closing thoughts?

Rich: Yes, well, "Rainbow Eyes" is a nice ballad, and I don't mean nice in an insulting way. There's a little bit of repetition here, in that there's a fill on the intro that's very similar to "Catch the Rainbow" and there's a very strong Hendrix influence on this as well, which is unusual for someone of Ritchie's vintage as a player. Because he was established before Hendrix. Or he was certainly on the scene as a musician making his living and is more of a contemporary of Hendrix. But I'm sure I've read somewhere that he quite graciously did acknowledge Hendrix as an influence.

I remember an interview with David Coverdale. There's a song that he did on his first solo album in the nineties, the one that didn't get a lot of attention. And there was a track on that that had a very Hendrix-y opening lick. And he apparently played it to Jimmy Page during the Coverdale Page period, and Jimmy Page said something to the effect of, "I'm not playing that. I'm Jimmy Page. That's too much like Jimi Hendrix." He didn't want to sound derivative of another guitar player. Whereas Ritchie has been quite happy to acknowledge his Hendrix influence.

And even if he doesn't acknowledge it, it's very similar to "Little Wing" on the sort of rundowns, the descending runs that Jimi does on "Little Wing," and in a more bluesy way on "Hey Joe." So you can hear it, whether he would admit it or not. It's very conspicuous. But in the end, "Rainbow Eyes" is not as effective as "Catch the Rainbow," because it doesn't have the dynamics. It's very one mood and reminds me a little bit of the Moody Blues, really, with that flute in the background. It's okay. Maybe this indicates why Ritchie felt he needed to shake the formula up a little bit with the next album. Because we're getting that little hint of repetition on this record's last two tracks.

RAINBOW AT A DOWN TO EARTH PRICE.
RAINBOW
DOWN TO EARTH
Down to Earth, the new album by Ritchie Blackmore's Rainbow, which includes Cozy Powell, Roger Glover, Don Airey and Graham Bonnet in the line up, has been brought down at all HMV Shops. It's £1 off list price, NOW.
And at the HMV Shop every week: The HMV Shop Top Albums up to £1.50 off list price. The HMV Shop Top Cassettes at 70p off list price.
Valid until August 25th. Subject to availability
the HMV shop
363 Oxford Street, London W.1. (next to Bond Street tube)
Bedford
Birmingham
Bradford
Brighton
Bristol
Coventry
Derby
Edinburgh
Enfield
Exeter
Glasgow
Gloucester
Gravesend
Holloway
Hull
Kingston
Leeds
Leicester
Lewisham
Liverpool
Luton
Manchester
Newcastle
Nottingham
Notting Hill Gate
Plymouth
Portsmouth
Southampton
Stockton
Stratford
Sunderland
Sutton
Swansea
Wolverhampton
Singles at 80p until August 25th Singles at 80p un t 25th Singles at 80p until August 25th Singles at 8 August 25th Singles at 80p until August 25th Singl until August 25th Singles at 80p until August 25th
STOP PRESS: SPECIAL ZEPPELIN OFFERS AT ALL HMV SHOPS NOW!

DOWN TO EARTH

July 28, 1979
Polydor PD-1-6221
Produced by Roger Glover
Engineered by Gary Edwards; assisted by Michael Palmer and Leigh Mantle
Personnel: Graham Bonnet – vocals, Ritchie Blackmore – guitars, Roger Glover – bass, Don Airey – keyboards, Cozy Powell – drums

Side 1
1. All Night Long (Blackmore, Glover) 3:49
2. Eyes of the World (Blackmore, Glover) 6:36
3. No Time to Lose (Blackmore, Glover) 3:41
4. Makin' Love (Blackmore, Glover) 4:36

Side 2
1. Since You Been Gone (Ballard) 3:10
2. Love's No Friend (Blackmore, Glover) 4:52
3. Danger Zone (Blackmore, Glover) 4:30
4. Lost in Hollywood (Blackmore, Glover, Powell) 4:51

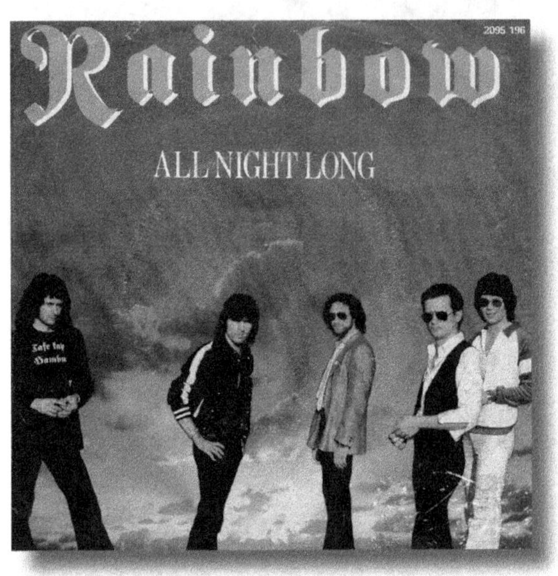

A *Down to Earth* Timeline

December 1978 – March 1979. Ronnie James Dio leaves Rainbow, the official announcement coming in January of '79. The band is in a fluid state, with Ritchie and Cozy left as the core members. Keyboardist Don Airey joins in December, and for a short while, Jeff Beck's bassist Clive Chamen is in the band. Jack Green is also touted as bassist. Peter Goalby was considered for the vacant vocal slot as was Marc Storace of Krokus fame.

December 27, 1978. Ritchie Blackmore joins Gillan on stage during one of the band's Marquee dates. Prior to this, Ritchie had shown up unannounced at Ian Gillan's house and after a few drinks together asks him to join Rainbow. Ian says no and then asks Ritchie to join Gillan. No reunion results, save for this on-stage visit.

March 1979. Graham Bonnet joins Rainbow and work accelerates on what would become *Down to Earth*. Bonnet, 31 years old at this point, is ex-Marbles, but most recently had issued a self-titled solo album in '77 and a follow-up called *No Bad Habits* in '78, both on Mercury. The studios are Château Pelly de Cornfeld in France, and Kingdom Sound Studios, Long Island, New York, for the vocals.

August 3, 1979. Rainbow issue *Down to Earth*. The album reaches No.6 in the UK and No.66 on the Billboard 200.

August 31, 1979. Rainbow issue as a single, the band's cover of Russ Ballard's "Since You Been Gone." Ballard had previously recorded it for his 1976 solo album *Winning*, with another popular version being Head East's, recorded for their self-titled album from 1978. Two months later, Rainbow's rendition of the track receives silver certification in the UK. The single sells quickly, no doubt aided by the fact that the B-side was a non-LP track called "Bad Girl." "Since You Been Gone" reaches No.6 in the UK and No.57 in the US. It certifies gold in the UK.

September 20 – December 20, 1979. Rainbow "Mk. V" tours America in support of *Down to Earth*. Most of September and October, Rainbow find themselves supporting Blue Öyster Cult. November and December, with the mighty BÖC having departed for the UK, Rainbow play with the likes of Gamma, Scorpions and Randy Hansen's Machine Gun.

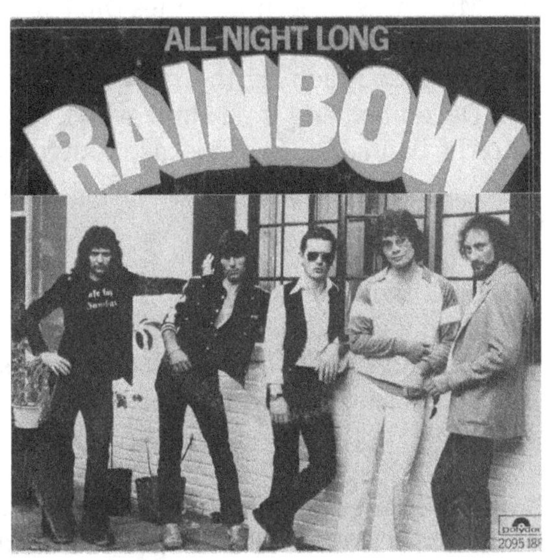

ALL NIGHT LONG
RAINBOW
Polydor
2095 188

B面
LP未収録
DPQ6160 STEREO
¥600
Polydor
シンス・ユー・ビーン・ゴーン
SINCE YOU BEEN GONE
レインボー
RAINBOW
Side B
BAD GIRLS

November 19, 1979. *Down to Earth* certifies gold in the UK.

January 16, 1980. Rainbow reconvene in Sweden after the Christmas break to rehearse for their European tour. Cozy Powell takes advantage of the break to do press for his solo album, *Over the Top*. Produced by Martin Birch, the album also includes among its ranks Bernie Marsden and Don Airey.

January 17 – March 8, 1980. Rainbow conduct an extensive European tour in support of *Down to Earth*.

February 1980. "All Night Long" is issued as the second single from *Down to Earth*. The B-side in the UK is an instrumental called "Weiss Heim." America gets "Danger Zone" and the Dutch get "No Time to Lose." "All Night Long" reaches No.110 on the Billboard charts and No.5 on the UK charts, The single also goes silver in the UK.

March 1, 1980. *Sounds* issue their Readers Poll, summing up results for 1979. Rainbow take the No.5 slot for top band, with *Down to Earth* achieving the same rank in the album category. "Since You Been Gone" makes No.4 in the single department.

March 10, 1980. Ritchie Blackmore guests on stage during the encore at Gillan's Rainbow (the venue) gig in London. Roger Glover was at the show as well but wouldn't go on stage.

May 8 – May 19, 1980. Rainbow tour Japan, playing multiple dates in Tokyo and Osaka.

Mid-1980. RCA recording act Fandango issue their fourth and last album, *Cadillac*. It is Joe Lynn Turner's one and only recording band before he joins Rainbow a few months later.

Rainbow
DOWN TO EARTH
at least
£1 off
R.R.P.
Album and Cassette
at these stores
Friday 3rd and Saturday 4th August.

FOREST ~ VORST
NATIONA(A)L
AU DUOLOIS
FOREST/BRUSSELS
VENDREDI 1 FEVRIER 20h30
VRIJDAG FEBRUARI
ICO ICW LION CONCERTS LTD PRESENTS
RITCHIE BLACKMORE'S
RAINBOW
RUDY'S MUSIC SHOP
antwerpen · gent · oostende · sint niklaas

Martin talks to Tate Davis, Nick Ermolovich, Luis Nasser and Pontus Norshammar about *Down to Earth.*

Martin Popoff: Okay, well let's see how this goes. I'm on record all over the place calling *Down to Earth* my favourite Rainbow album and have had to defend that seven ways to Sunday. What do you guys think of it? Or actually first, maybe set the scene. What changes have taken place within the band?

Tate Davis: Well, they get a different singer, obviously. Blackmore is very influenced by Foreigner and all the success that they're having and asks Dio, "Hey, can you write some, like, love songs?" And Dio is like, "Hell no, I can't and I'm not going to." So he leaves and they get Graham Bonnet from The Marbles. And Bob Daisley's eventually let go and Don Airey eventually comes in on keyboards and then Roger Glover produces this album and then ends up playing bass after they couldn't find a bass player. And immediately from the first note, you understand that you're in for a different ride with the first song "All Night Long." But that doesn't make it any less great. It's a really good, radio-friendly, hard rocker.

Martin: I'll correct you on one thing. You say first note, but the interesting thing about this song is that the beginning is quite heavy, as is the chorus. But I know that you meant the song in general, and yes, the verse is shockingly poppy compared to anything the band has ever done. I totally agree with that.

Tate: Okay, that's my bad. My apologies about that. But no, it's a great album, if you want to listen to really good late seventies/early eighties radio-friendly hard rock. I think Blackmore got what he wanted. And then he sees maybe they've attracted a new fan base with this album, even if they alienated a lot of the old fan base when Dio left. And so it was almost like an experiment. How is this gonna go? They're taking a big risk with this. That's what I get. It's a good experiment with this new direction that Blackmore wants to pursue.

Nick Ermolovich: Well, I love *Down to Earth*. I don't come to this album as having been a fan in the seventies. I was younger, so I wasn't offended that Dio's gone and we're losing the lyrical imagery that he provided and it's a different band. I didn't have those kinds of thoughts, whether it was a bias or not. I came to this as a blank slate. And from the moment I heard this album, which would have been about the mid-eighties, I loved everything about it.

At the outset, we've got a different band, evolved away from Dio. But here are the keys to this album for me. Roger Glover is an underappreciated producer. He is very good and it's surprising how many albums I have of his that I think are really great, whether it's *Razamanaz* or *Calling Card* by Rory Gallagher, who generally didn't work with outside producers. There's *Perfect Strangers* and his later work with Rainbow. He's a great producer and an underappreciated producer. And as a bass player, I don't know if he gets enough accolades either. So I think he's key to this album's success.

Secondly is Don Airey. Even though I like Tony Carey and David Stone on *Long Live Rock 'n' Roll*, I just like Don Airey. You get piano on here, you get B3 and you get synthesizers and I think he's just so tasteful. And when you start listening and breaking down these tracks, I'm like, "Oh, Don Airey!," "Oh, Don Airey!" He's a secret weapon in this band, not unlike other good secret weapons like Paul Raymond in UFO. So he's someone else that I think is a part of the success of the album.

The last secret ingredient is Graham Bonnet. He's a unique guy. Graham Bonnet sounds like he looks. Doesn't necessarily quite fit, peculiar, but at the same time you do not forget him and you do not forget his vocal approach. Nobody sounds like him. And he's sort of that last ingredient that really makes this thing shine. Now that's also Graham Bonnet in a studio setting. That is not necessarily Graham Bonnet live. But Graham Bonnet in the studio and on this album really, for me, brings it home.

The songs, I like the three or four minutes, "Don't bore us; get to the chorus." I like the change of direction of the band—I get it. And I think this album is a lot heavier than people may think it is, or give it credit for. You hear, "Oh, they want to become Foreigner." This is a lot heavier than Foreigner. I understand that comparison; I understand what he was going for. But this is a heavy band and I would have liked to have seen this band together and do something else after it.

Luis Nasser: *Down to Earth*, to me, is a strange record. I should like it a lot more than I do. You look at the personnel, Don Airey on keyboards, tremendous, Cozy Powell, Roger Glover, of course, Ritchie Blackmore, and we have Graham Bonnet. And I think that Graham

Bonnet is a wonderful singer. The only issue I have with that record is that it can't seem to make up its mind what it wants to be. It's just been very difficult for me to connect with it through the years for that reason.

Pontus Norshammar: This is a transition album. One of Ritchie's major bad decisions was to let Dio go. Ronnie enhanced that band; Ritchie had the best thing he could ever have gotten with Ronnie. If he had stayed on, they probably would have made a few more albums that might have been classics. But what happens is—and I'm only half joking—he was inspired by a certain band. And he always said he was a fan of that band. Behind this band is a woman and it's a blonde woman. And there's a brunette as well, but the blonde woman is the major asset and she was a great singer. And she was in a band like Fleetwood Mac, a family band. And I think he got informed by their music and her appearance—many were. Enter Agnetha Fältskog from Abba. I think he got very much intrigued by the whole thing that you could have songs that, as he said in an interview, "the postman could sing." Or could whistle. He was intrigued with that.

I think he wanted to get back to America. He had left America behind him, which was very hard to break with Rainbow. So he decides he wants to be more commercial. And that's a big beef with Dio. Let's just have a fun look at this. This record is called *Down to Earth*, right? And Dio's next project is called *Heaven and Hell*. Isn't it funny that Ritchie wants to go down to Earth, and Dio is up here and down there? It shows the mindset of these two guys. Ronnie is saying I want to expand, whereas Ritchie wants to be in the mainstream.

What also happens is that he contacts Roger Glover and brings him back, both as producer and as a writer. He acknowledges that he has made a mistake by firing him. And the funny thing with that is that Roger and Ritchie work together until 1993. When there's a break, when Purple Mk. II breaks up, Roger is his partner from 1979 until 1993. He sticks with him through thick and thin. He's the one who's a constant member from now on in Rainbow. He's also a great organizer and I think Ritchie wanted that. It also harkens back to the Purple days, right? Here's a person I know. I wrote *Machine Head* with him; he knows how to produce things.

And I think for Roger, it was very much like, "Oh, I'm gonna do this, but you're gonna give me a day job. You owe me this." Right? And so Roger is on board and now there was stability for Ritchie because everybody else is leaving. And he brings Graham Bonnet in.

Sometimes I think he wanted a Lou Gramm. I think Graham is very close to that. He had been in The Marbles with "Only One Woman." So he gets another singer who has a strong voice. And he also gets Don Airey to do the Jon Lord bit. There was a rumour, and I don't know if it came from Jon Lord himself, who said that he was invited about nine times to join Rainbow and said no.

So he gets the next best thing; he gets Don Airey, who will end up in Purple later. So that is the line-up. And now we're going to make an album. And I do think that the major sort of blueprint for this record is the *Boston* record. Because I think he wanted to go into that area, but slightly rockier-sounding. He wants to go forward but he wants to be conservative as well. So he doesn't want to go full-on Journey.

And this is a funny thing with this record. It's very schizophrenic. It has moments where he wants to go back and do another sort of slightly lesser version of "Gates of Babylon," with "Eyes of the World" and "Danger Zone." But he still wants to do "Since You Been Gone, "Makin' Love" and "All Night Long." So it's a transition, because when we hit *Difficult to Cure*, it's even more in that commercial direction, with "I Surrender."

But this is a fun record; it's a party record. When we open, we have the guitar in the centre. It's a very dense production. It's almost like mono. It's not widespread but also everything is very clear. And Ritchie is front and centre here. And you've got Graham Bonnet coming in and doing more rock, rather than Gillan or Dio. He's very much like a crooner. And he has his mannerisms that I personally sometimes think is too much. I think he reaches too hard sometimes, but it works.

Martin: What do you think of the album cover?

Tate: I really like it. I think it's better than the last one. The colours on the rainbow really pop with the black space background.

Nick: I love it. You get the rainbow imagery coming in there, you've got the name of the album, the background. I don't know if it evokes what the band's about. It's not as good as *Rising*; let's put it that way.

Martin: It's a bit disco!

Nick: Yeah, well, I was just gonna say, the one negative is it might be perceived as a little light (laughs). But I see the darkness too, and with that swirling rainbow, there's an imagery of speed there.

Luis: As a physicist it annoys me, because how can you get a rainbow in outer space? I'm looking at that and I'm thinking, all right, that's dumb. That's my first impression. Also, it doesn't look like the old stuff. There's a rainbow. It's an odd cover, and like you say, disco, like a Donna Summer record.

Martin: Okay, how about the production?

Tate: Like Nick says, Roger Glover does a terrific job with it. The production is well suited to the direction that Blackmore wanted to go. I might like the production of the Dio albums better, but everything sounds really good. Cozy's drums perhaps have a bit more reverb on them because you're getting into the eighties.

Luis: By that point, Cozy Powell had a pretty strong voice in terms of how he wanted his drums to sound. The guitars sound good, although I think they're a little too polished. The vocals are a bit overwrought, maybe. But it doesn't sound like it was recorded in a tin can. I don't mind the production. It's possibly trying too hard for its own good.

Martin: I've asked this of previous speakers, but what's the personality of Cozy Powell as a drummer?

Luis: Well, that's a tough question, isn't it? Cozy Powell was one of those guys who was like a chameleon. That guy played with Rainbow, he played with Jeff Beck, played with Sabbath, Emerson and Lake, and yet he always managed to sound like him. But he also sounds like the band. He was also with Michael Schenker. I never met him; I never talked to him. I'm not sure if this is his most comfortable record. It seems like he was told to bring it down. It has less of his previous flamboyance and over-the-top power. There's only the one song that he co-wrote, "Lost in Hollywood," and that's up-tempo and percussive. The rest of the album, he's calmer. So yeah, it's not a Cozy Powell showcase; I'll say that.

Martin: The other big thing about Cozy, Luis, is that he was very opinionated. And he was a natural leader, or co-leader. He was an outspoken, loud guy in a band, right? He helped set and shift the direction of any band he was in. He would always give you his point of view.

Luis: Actually, I've never been in a band where the drummers don't do that. And I think that's a good thing. The drummer has a unique perspective on the quality of the songs. A drummer will rarely weigh in on the harmony part of the song, like the chord structure, but they will always weigh in on these accents, the one-and-a-half and the four, this song, that song, can we shift it? These are the sort of things that you may not be thinking about as you're writing and it really helps with the finished product. I've always welcomed that. I love it when drummers talk because they have interesting things to say.

People normally disrespect them because they don't know any music theory or whatever, but who cares? They're musicians and they're smart. And they say good things 90% of the time, in my experience. But Cozy, the guy needs no introduction. That to me was always what I loved about Rainbow, that the drums were at the front. And the drums with Cozy Powell, you can think of them as a timekeeping thing, but there's also this sense of orchestration, right? It's like, "All right, you played that; I'm going to play this back to you." And it's like they're running a race—let's go.

Pontus: I feel like Cozy had to restrain himself a bit on this album. He's quite solid throughout, but as you say, he has a stompy style of playing. One could say it rescues it from being too poppy, that the record has a good solid beat to it. But he also seems restricted. In "All Night Long," he's not really making that song swing, but I think for "Love's No Friend," it actually works, because it's a slower song. But then on other songs he lets loose.

Martin: All right, time to get into the songs. *Down to Earth* opens with "All Night Long." Are you on board or not? There's some pretty sugary singing in there.

Tate: It's a great way to open up the album and like you said, now that I think about it, it almost sounds like a *Long Live Rock 'n' Roll* song. And I love Cozy Powell, but I have no idea why he would go to the toms for the chorus. For me, he just needs to stick with the high-hat or go to the ride cymbal for that chorus. It sounds like really tribal and I don't understand why he would do that. Maybe Blackmore told him to; that could have been Blackmore saying I want toms on the chorus here. Because in Rainbow, whatever Blackmore said went. Cozy would know better than to challenge him on that.

Graham puts on a phenomenal vocal here, but I think it sounds very Las Vegas-y. "I wanna love you all night long," all that thing, plus the pre-chorus thing with all that seduction stuff like Wayne Newton would do. So I found that really interesting. I think the song comes across better live than in the studio, especially where Bonnet plays with the audience.

Luis: "All Night Long" is a perfectly functional rocker, good opener, but I'm just not convinced that it's a good Rainbow opener. I see what you mean about the stomping chorus but the poppy verse. There's light and shade there; it's sitting in two different worlds. Which is part of the problem. You just nailed it. That's true for pretty much the whole record. What is this? Is it a hard rock album or a pop album? It's pretty difficult to be both and sell. I've never really heard anybody who is both. It's too heavy to be successful commercially, but not heavy enough to be a legendary Rainbow album.

Martin: The other thing that has always bothered me about "All Night Long" is that at the rhythm end it's a thick, noisy slog, basically four-on-the-floor. Not that I really want this, but it would be interesting to hear a bouncy, pert, pop performance, arrangement and mix of this song.

Luis: Yeah, and that's exactly what I was trying to express before. As a drummer yourself, you know this as well as anybody, and I'm on record as saying this as well: a band is only as good as their drummer. That's the bottom line. You can have a phenomenal singer, great guitars, whatever, but if the drums are not gluing it all together and propelling it, the music just doesn't flow. And I don't think that Cozy Powell was allowed to do his thing with the songs as much as he was on his previous two Rainbow albums. It's like he was told to curb it. As a result, it's more polished, but it's not as good. And not what we as Rainbow fans had come to expect.

Nick: But the vocals—holy mackerel. It's a great singalong. You've got all sorts of cool stuff in there. You've got handclaps that are the best handclaps this side of like Joan Jett and Slade. There's some bass work on there that's really cool, with Roger hitting some odd notes.

Put your headphones on and you'll hear some interesting things going on. Like "Tarot Woman" on *Rising*, this is a good declaration of independence. "This is who we are, this is where we're going, come on and join us." And from a vocal standpoint, I'm gonna focus on the uniqueness and the phrasing of Graham Bonnet as opposed to what he's actually saying. I'm always sitting there pretty much amazed about what he's doing. If you're a hard rock fan, what's not to like about this song? It's heavy enough—go listen to it.

Pontus: Two key things about "All Night Long" is that it has a classic Ritchie riff and there's this cool bridge where they drop down to half time. And there's the Boston thing, with the handclaps and the repeated refrain and lots of backing vocals, answering back. Plus it's a short and sweet song. Oddly, it was not released as a single until 1980, so six months after the original album.

And I feel your pain when it comes to the metre and rhythm of the thing. Because that's Cozy Powell, right? He can't really swing the way the song really needs to be swung. But as hard as he fights it, those melodies work as a single. It's the most commercial track Ritchie had done certainly since the debut and maybe back to Deep Purple. I'm trying to think of a Purple song that mirrors it, but I can't find one. But yes, it's distinguished by those handclaps.

Martin: But they're not handclaps at a party or a concert. They're more like handclaps in a prison yard.

Pontus: Yeah (laughs). Could it be that we want to do this but we don't know how to do this? Could that be the case? We want it desperately, but we're Englishmen. We're not Americans. We don't understand, really, why you should do this. It's a second-guessing, perhaps, of what they should do. If they'd had Ted Templeman producing the album, he would have strategized that. He would have said, 'No, do it faster and cut down on those vocals." Plus he would have made it less noisy. This is an English interpretation of what American rock sounds like.

Martin: Plus it's Cozy just banging the hell out of it, and heavy on the four-on-the-floor.

Pontus: Yeah, it's almost a mock disco sort of thing. It's a funny concoction of a song.

Martin: Next is "Eyes of the World," a top five Rainbow classic, even if a large chunk of the fanbase forgets that it exists.

Tate: Absolutely, and yeah, for me the best song on the album. It's unbelievable. It sounds like it could have come off of *Long Live Rock 'n' Roll*. Don Airey does this great keyboard intro and Bonnet really brings forth the message of the song, as he does all over this record. He sings about how evil is all around us and how humanity is really naïve. And Blackmore's solo somehow reinforces that point. You could see this song as the second cousin of "Tarot Woman." I don't know if you agree with that or not. Plus I could also imagine Gary Moore covering the song on like on *Corridors of Power* or *Victims of the Future*. I listened to it the other day and for some reason I thought, man, Gary Moore should sing this song.

Luis: With "Eyes of the World" you get more of an old Rainbow vibe. The slow, building intro, the harmonic minor scales—it's all the things that Ritchie Blackmore mastered and incorporated into hard rock; they're all there. Sure, there's less drama to it versus songs this epic from Dio, but it still works.

Nick: It's six minutes but it goes by fast. It's a regal sound. You've got this really cool B3 in there. Again, Glover is like the master of octaves on the bass. He doesn't just chug on an A or an E. He's gonna give you that octave switch. Even though I'm a weekend warrior bass player, it's a style that I enjoy. It's a style that I employ a lot in the different bands I've played in and it gives a certain texture to bass playing that suggests movement and heaviness. You don't have to do crazy licks and riffs and play bass chords à la Billy Sheehan to be a heavy bass player. Just listen to Roger Glover with his octaves. It's a great song. There's even grand piano in it. Love it.

Pontus: With "Eyes of the World" you get a bit of "Mars: Bringer of War," that sort of motif on the keyboards. Here's another thing I wanted to say. I know you and Pete Pardo did a *Sea of Tranquility* video on front-loaded albums a few years ago, but I must say this album is back-loaded. I truly think that side two is better than side one. Side one is not bad, but side two harkens back to the more progressive stuff like "Gates of Babylon," even though it's more condensed into sort of straight rockers. But it still has those sort of Moroccan motifs going. And here's the other influence; if you listen to the piano solo, you get the sort of Benny Andersson chords like in "Dancing Queen," right? Those big, showy, Vegas-like piano chords. It's a very good song, but it was hell live because they couldn't do the backing vocals. No wonder he later worked with those girl singers, because the band couldn't sing backups. I've heard bootlegs of it and it's funny in its own way.

Martin: Strength to strength, next is "No Time to Lose," which, as discussed last chapter, is part of a family of songs featuring a certain type of circuitous single-note riffing from Ritchie.

Pontus: Yeah, absolutely. And you can actually go back even to the chorus in "Space Truckin'" to hear that thought process played out; like you say, circular but also commercial. And we get the first organ solo on the album, right? I think it's the only one, pretty much, because the others are with normal keyboards. It's altogether a good mid-paced rock song. I like that syncopated triplet bit in it and I like that there's a bit of backing vocals. Still, it's not as cluttered as some of these pieces are. It's in that "If You Don't Like Rock 'n' Roll" space but done in more of a worked-out way, on a much better song altogether.

Nick: On "No Time to Lose," you've got some rippin' bass in the middle solo section. You've got guitar followed by organ. It's a driving song, and good luck playing that riff. As a bass player myself, I like that it's syncopated, where Roger has to play what Ritchie is playing. I kept thinking that there's a Monty Python skit that employs that phrase, "No time to lose" where they keep saying it over and over again. But no, that song is a ripper. What's not to like about it? As for your analysis of the circular nature of the riff, I can hear that. I actually picture him wandering around the fretboard searching for something, because that's his job—he has to find riffs (laughs). Maybe it's my level of fandom, but I don't find it that derivative. I thought it fit well with everything else going on in the song.

Tate: This might sound odd, but for me, this is like a first cousin to "Rock and Roll" by Led Zeppelin. I'm not like a huge fan of the song; I think it's fine. I'm not a huge fan of "Rock and Roll" either. I picture a scenario where I'm driving in rush hour traffic in L.A. with Graham Bonnet and Blackmore in the car with me. Bonnet is in the front seat like we're filming like an MTV video or something. And he's sticking his head out the window and singing the lyrics to the song in an attempt to get the traffic moving. And in effect it's Graham creating the traffic jam, because who's this guy in sunglasses sticking his head or his body out the window trying to sing this song? And he really emphasizes the "No time to lose" because we're in rush hour and we want to get to where we're going as quickly as possible.

Martin: Sweet. For some reason I picture Ritchie in the back seat not giving a damn, finding the whole thing funny. If we're late, we're late. Luis, your thoughts on this one?

Luis: Well, with "No Time to Lose," you start getting into these songs that are basically saying, "We can't take ourselves too seriously," where we're just a rock band that wants some success and wants to chart. It's your standard three-chord song in A minor, right? And the words are exactly what you would expect them to be over that riff. The chorus is basically an A minor to a D major, A minor to a D major. Somehow it doesn't bring anything new to the Rainbow catalogue, right? It's a song that I think had they come up with it earlier, it would have never seen the light of day. It would have been considered a weaker track. The most interesting part of the song is the solo, which is basically D minor, A minor, major C, major G, repeat, right? "Since You Been Gone" is a song where I can at least hear interesting things happening in the songcraft. In this one, I don't hear that at all. Plus I hear a clichéd lyric and I don't even know if Graham is selling it.

Martin: Side one closes with "Makin' Love," a ballad, but I'm on board with it, given that it's got a full band arrangement and some sophisticated chords, not to mention a brief but heavy break section.

Tate: Yeah, this is an interesting one. I feel like the sort of secondary riff in "Perfect Strangers" riff was somewhat inspired by this song. It's a bit funky and Cozy puts it in a great pocket. I don't think Blackmore's solo is long enough. As for the sex lyrics, I just don't think they fit with this band. With "Perfect Strangers," you're talking about ex-lovers and after all this stuff happened throughout the relationship, they're just best remaining perfect strangers, not talking to each other anymore. But a song about making love with this funky background, I don't know, it just doesn't compute with my brain.

Nick: With that staccato picking, I also thought this sort of foreshadows "Perfect Strangers." That string effect on the guitar is really cool. There's a nice harmony solo and tons of Cozy cymbal chokes in this song, which is cool for the drummers. There's a harpsichord sound, there's a synth sound, all this stuff and it's well blended—it's a nice production number. Maybe not the strongest song lyrically, but it's fine for what it is.

Luis: I love Ritchie's little classical intro to this, and the music is happening, but the lyrics are not really my thing. I understand that this is a "me" thing. I've never understood why a band would not match the effort of the creation of the music with a similar effort to the creation of the words. That's something Rush was so good at. I'm not gonna say they were infallible—nobody is—but they really put a lot of effort into every aspect of what they did. The quality was just so high across the board. Whether or not we agree with Neil Peart's vision about the world, this is irrelevant. It was very well-put-together. And these are just rock 'n' roll clichés. So it's all right, but we've heard this a dozen times, and now we're hearing it from a new guy.

Pontus: "Makin' Love" to me is the turkey of the album. It's an attempt at a ballad, but it doesn't really knows where it's going. I also hear "Perfect Strangers" in that galloping riff. The best bit is the middle eight, that percussive heavy part where Graham goes, "Don't believe that I'm a liar." Otherwise I think it sags. My notes say "Verse, bridge—average. Chorus—great. Disco rhythm." There's that slight suggestion of disco to it, and it doesn't work well.

Martin: I find that tambourine whack in it amusing, because it's only on the one of every second 4/4 bar. Also, what I like about it is it fits the narrative of Ritchie being a proponent of "goth-lite." Like Michael Schenker, there's an overtly commercial melodic aspect he can locate while also being European or Teutonic.

Pontus: True, but I'm still not buying it. I don't know why this is on here, especially when they had "Bad Girl," which I think could have ended the side much better. I would have swapped "Bad Girl" out as the B-side for "Since You Been Gone" and put "Makin' Love" as the B-side of that single instead. Or if they wanted a slow song, why not "Weiss Heim?" Which was an instrumental recorded at the same time.

Martin: Speaking of "Since You Been Gone," Rainbow's swell cover of that song opens side two. It also puts into a tailspin much of the Rainbow fanbase, who instantly begin to debate what has happened to their band.

Pontus: Yes, this is Rainbow's Boston moment. We have Russ Ballard, who was in Argent, writing this very good slice of American pop played by Englishmen. It's like "More Than a Feeling" part two and very poppy. The fact that it was not their song is very clear. Ritchie couldn't write this; it's a different way of thinking, melodically, a different context. But it worked creatively and became a hit, so it served its purpose as well. It's a good way to open side two. It's both a rocker and, subsequently, a radio hit. One can wonder why they didn't swap the tracks, but I suppose they thought that "All Night Long" was a better opener for the whole album.

Luis: "Since You Been Gone" would have never happened with Ronnie in the band. I remember being a little bit disappointed with it as a kid. And as I get older, that impression hasn't really shifted too much. If anything, the details of how they're trying to make themselves commercially viable just seems more transparent and that puts me off. Another thing I don't like about it—and I know this is something that's my thing and most people don't care—I think some of the lyrics are just terrible. Musically though, "Since You Been Gone" is redeemable and also a bit of a mystery. It's so obviously not written by somebody in the band. But Russ Ballard is a very competent songwriter and the song has a lot of very interesting chord movement; it's more than a three-chord song.

However, I've watched some live videos of Rainbow doing it, and it's a little bit painful to watch them go through it, because it seems to me that it's not something that they're really into. Especially Cozy, right? You're hearing these upbeat and almost syrupy harmonies and these chord progressions and the vocal melody and I feel like Graham Bonnet is the only guy who's really comfortable doing that song. Cozy Powell is wearing these leather bracelets with spikes and he's playing at about 10% of his usual speed and power. Roger is the consummate professional on bass; so he's playing exactly what the song requires. But it feels like you're given a Ferrari and you're stuck in a 55-mile-per-hour zone.

The song was commercially successful for them to some degree, although I don't know if it achieved the success that Ritchie

Blackmore hoped for. I can respect the song for the songcraft that went into writing it and then Rainbow arranging and performing it. Like I say, it has interesting chord movements, even though it may seem like there isn't. There are nice little variants and it resolves. And the little arpeggios Ritchie play, they're always shifting. He's not just playing a shape over and over. There's lots of little things that you might miss because the overarching envelope for the song is a very direct melody.

Martin: I get what you mean. It's a smart cookie. The verse chords are pretty upscale, it's got an almost classical or proggy pre-chorus, and then the big payoff is the chorus, which has got these hummable, dependable "Louie Louie" chords, as I like to call them.

Luis: Yeah, so again, I think it suits the album, because that's the vibe of the album. There's a little bit of classic Rainbow in this weird blend with this new commercial side. And then there are parts where you scratch your head and think, what is *this* doing here?! "Since You Been Gone" has all of that. As a Rainbow fan and as a rock guy, I'm not feeling that song very much. I tried.

Tate: People under the age of 40 might know the song from *Guardians of the Galaxy Vol. 3*. It does the job of lead single and I think it's great. They add to the arrangement by doing the key change right before the fade-out with Blackmore's solo. It's probably the best version of the song there is. I know that a lot of hardcore Rainbow fans hated it, but I think it's well done. It's the first Rainbow song I ever heard.

Nick: There's dozens of versions of this out there, most notably besides Rainbow, by Head East the previous year. I understand your criticism of those Midwest bands. They're one of those bands where I find their albums for two bucks. I've got them built up in my mind, but I don't think I've heard even one (laughs). I've got *Flat as a Pancake*. You get all these albums and they've got the one good song and that's the band. I'd forgotten about the Cherie Currie and her sister version that I listened to, prepping for this thing, which is also very strong. I just think this is the definitive version. There's things in here that I pick up on almost every time I hear it. I think it's pop rock perfection. There's so much going on. You've got a classic interlude in the middle of this with a guitar and vocals. You've got handclaps, you've got piano driving it, you've got synth.

I know this may sound strange, but when Graham does that descending vocal line, it reminds me of "All the Young Dudes." And the one thing it does that no modern rock or pop song does anymore, there's a key change in it, a modulation. That's another sign of a great song masterfully crafted by Ballard, and Rainbow execute it perfectly. It's a dying trick that no one does anymore, but I'm always up for more of that.

It's funny, prepping for this, I looked at the algorithm to see which songs are most played, and I'm like, what?! I know Rainbow means different things to different people in different parts of the world. But I can guarantee you, Martin, I have never heard "I Surrender" on the radio. Never! I discovered this band in the early eighties and it was a weird time for me because I was heavy into Ritchie Blackmore. I'm discovering Deep Purple and all the old Rainbow albums. "Stone Cold" is everywhere on rock radio and then right after that, "Street of Dreams" is everywhere on rock radio. At that same time period, I'm discovering "Man on the Silver Mountain." But in that period—and granted, I learned about Rainbow a year or two after "I Surrender"—I have never heard that song on the radio once, not then and not since. So it's interesting seeing what songs the world gravitates towards.

Martin: Good stuff. Okay, next we have "Love's No Friend," a big, bruising blues, Rainbow's own "Mistreated," for better or worse.

Tate: Ah yes, "Love's No Friend," unlike "Makin' Love," is a good platform for the song's relationship-themed message. Through his sort of actorly vocal performance, Graham makes you believe that love is not a friend to anyone, that you shouldn't try, that you should be very wary of who you date.

I really love that little triplet hiccup after Don Airey's brief keyboard feature. It's an example of these little details, these fills coming out of nowhere, expertly placed. Then we're into Ritchie's solo. That little triplet transition, with Cozy just accenting it on high-hat, there's like a revelation to it, where it makes me think the characters realize that they will be lovers and that they are wrong about turning away or resisting love. And then Blackmore's solo adds to the soundtrack of the story in the lyrics, like additional drama, maybe a betrayal. We're back to, "I don't think I can trust another person again." Yeah, "Love's No Friend" is a great song. And we're back to the Vegas-type vocals on this, where Graham Bonnet sings from the gut, again, really thespian, especially on the chorus. Maybe it's not as much of a Wayne Newton-type of thing as you get on the pre-chorus of "All Night Long," but you get a little bit of that here.

Nick: "Love's No Friend," like you say, is "Mistreated" Jr., a heavy grinding blues track. I could see Coverdale singing this, I could see Ronnie James Dio singing this, but Bonnet does a phenomenal job. When he sings, "That's all right," he soars! And then when he sings, "Love's no friend of mine," It's a powerful Graham Bonnet piece. People might find this song plodding, but I like it. It highlights Bonnet's voice well. I doubt he could sing it now.

Luis: "Love's No Friend" has a good lyric for a heavy blues. It's a blues in G minor, but with a sharp five, which is a very Blackmore thing. He loves what are called harmonic minor scales, which give you that Arabic flavour. As I've said, *Down to Earth* doesn't know what it wants to be. It's a band trying to be commercially more successful, but at the same time, it doesn't really have the tools to do those things on their own. So they need to get a lot of external help, which they don't solicit. The tune itself, I do always pay attention to the lyrics, which may not be the wisest move when it comes to Rainbow. The lyrics are what you would expect. The weary protagonist has been chewed up a few too many times by life. You could say it's clichéd, but that's not fair, because one would be forgetting that Blackmore was one of the guys who perfected this particular style of song.

Martin: I'm more concerned that the music is clichéd.

Luis: Yes, but he's the guy that basically invented that particular blues song. He's referencing his own work. An interesting part of the song, which Tate has explained, is that peculiar little triplet tease before we get to the solo. It's completely different and it's the only time they break from the previous structures. You think, well, this is gonna go somewhere interesting. And then he just plays a blues solo, right? (laughs). So that's emblematic, where they mix the familiar with some new flourishes. So it does have those little details. It even has these sort of gospel backing vocals over the solo, which, to my knowledge, there aren't many Rainbow songs that do that.

Don Airey is finally given a little bit of room at the end to give us a taste of what that man can do. Otherwise, it's quite a Ritchie

Blackmore-centric album. A lot of the main melodies and leads are all Ritchie, which is a shame because Don Airey is a monster player, as we know, right? But it's a nice song; I like it a lot. If anything, I'm thinking it's a bit of a missed opportunity in the sense that it could have been made even better with more of those little teasers and diversions. Because then it becomes more than just a blues song.

Pontus: I think "Love's No Friend" is Bonnet's best performance on the album. It has a good riff, a good vocal. He was an R&B guy from start, so he can really work that skill on a song like this. He can really be the R&B guy and inject a bit of emotion into it.

Martin: All right, next we have "Danger Zone," which despite its over-used and not very Rainbow title, it's pretty much a top five Rainbow song for me and a big contributor to why *Down to Earth* is my favourite album of theirs.

Tate: Wow, really? But you're right, it's a great, great song. The riff definitely evokes danger. It really does sound like the listener is entering a zone with a high probability that something dangerous might happen. If you want to hear Bonnet screaming, this is the song for you, along with "Assault Attack" from his MSG album. There's also a great solo section that provides a guiding light to exit the danger zone. And Cozy Powell creates a solid pocket. One of the highlights of the album for me.

Luis: "Danger Zone" is a great tune, but the words, to me, they're just alphabet soup. Seriously, the very first line is, "Shaking off the thresholds of a long-forgotten dream." No idea what that means. So weird. I don't know, it seems like a record where they didn't want to be taken too seriously. But then when people in fact didn't take them seriously, it bothered Ritchie. Otherwise, this song retains most of the DNA of the original Ronnie James Dio-era Rainbow.

Nick: This makes me think—and it's not—but is this Rainbow doing disco? Because it's heavy octaves on the bass, and actually with that guitar riff too. You have this heavy song, "Danger Zone." Oh, what do we need? More octave-jumping (laughs). But it's a great performance and there's a lot going on here.

Pontus: We've got those patented Middle Eastern melodies again, amidst good ensemble playing. For the first time we hear each member of the band shining or stretching out. Don Airey solos extensively and everybody seems to be in a very good place. It's very much traditional older Rainbow.

Martin: But the difference is that you get the proto-hair metal chorus.

Pontus: Yeah, but it works because it still makes it a good song. But, you're right; that's new. Once again, we're trying to do something we don't know how to do, really, like a square peg in a round hole. We want it to fit so we make it fit. It's still one of a couple highlights for me on the album, and you hear Cozy letting loose a bit.

Martin: Speaking of highlights, you all know I rant and rave about how "Lost in Hollywood" is Rainbow's best song. If "Gates of Babylon" is a more compact "Stargazer," I figure this is the next step again. It's got everything except a good title, and arguably, a lesser lyric.

Pontus: Yes, of course, the best is saved for last. "Lost in Hollywood" has got to be one of the best Rainbow songs. Here it actually goes together, the love song motif and old Rainbow. You've got classical overtones, a magnificent solo section, great drumming, AOR backing vocals but it's gothic, it's up-tempo and it ends on a triumphant note. It's the whole album condensed into this one song, really? It's where all the pieces of the puzzle meet.

Tate: "Lost in Hollywood" is Cozy Powell's shining moment, not only on this album, but probably across the whole Rainbow catalogue. This one and "Stargazer." Lyrically, the protagonist is lost in a city that he's never been to before and he's trying to find a way home. And then it almost seems like the solo section represents him finding a shortcut and he thinks that he's going the right way. And then later, with Blackmore's like unaccompanied solo at the end, when everything else drops out, he thinks that he's finally found his way out of the city, and then it's, oh crap, I'm still lost.

Martin: I like that (laughs). That guitar solo section with the punchy music behind it, it sounds like maybe he's getting chased by a gang or something, right? Maybe there's a second similarly themed video to go with your "No Time to Lose" clip!

Tate: Yeah, being chased would have fit well, filmed like an eighties action movie, sort of thing (laughs). Bonnet puts in another great vocal performance here. The song would take on another life of its own live when they would extend it out live. But what a professional and upscale way to finish off the album.

Nick: Masterful song, and I think this one really benefits from Roger Glover's no-nonsense production, because there's a lot competing for your attention. It's frenetic of pace and yet tight—there's no looseness and the band is firing on all cylinders. There's synthesizer, there's a guitar solo that incorporates the keyboards in it and Cozy might have set a world record for cymbal chokes He's everywhere on this song. Lyrically, there's a nice juxtaposition of the words whiskey and rainbow, which of course, that's two clubs in Hollywood. Otherwise, sure, it's not some mythical Ronnie James Dio tale.

Luis: I have a soft spot for "Lost in Hollywood," only because when I was a kid and listening to this record, I remember thinking that those lyrics are full of rock 'n' roll clichés but they're very believable, about a guy who's essentially had too much to drink, too much of everything, and he's just trying to find his way back home. Outside of the words, it's 100% quintessential Rainbow. There's no doubt that's a Rainbow song. It's my favourite from this album.

Martin: Now there are a couple of B-sides from this era, later used as bonus tracks. What do you think of "Bad Girl" and "Weiss Heim?"

Nick: Yes, when you get the deluxe version of *Down to Earth* now, they throw in "Bad Girl" and "Weiss Heim." I love "Bad Girl," which was the B-side to "Since You Been Gone." The bass is so driving, which I appreciate as a bassist myself. It's like a throwback to "Black Night," from Deep Purple. Lyrically, it's pretty much moronic. It would have made a good stripper song. But the riff is great, it's heavy, there's cowbell. I just love that song.

And "Weiss Heim," the instrumental, I like the guitar harmonies in this song. It's a simple song. Ritchie doesn't overplay, not that he's an over-player. I don't know if it would have fit in with the rest of the album. There's a weird and sort of connected thing with Cozy at this time. October of '79, so two months after *Down to Earth*, he put out a solo album called *Over the Top*, which had this famous song "The Loner" on it, which Gary Moore did years later. And that album was produced by Martin Birch and Don Airey plays keys on it. So Martin Birch is over here with Cozy doing an instrumental that came out around this time and like how did he fit all this in? He does "The Loner" and then "Weiss Heim" is the same sort of slow instrumental ballad. Very similar.

Martin: Yes, you're right, although both of them put me to sleep. Geez. All right; let's wrap this up. Any final parting shots? Points you wanted to make?

Tate: Well, let's remember that Graham Bonnet would go on to do better things. After he was let go from Rainbow, we'd get *Assault Attack* from The Michael Schenker Group. It's a shame that Michael didn't work more with him around that time because holy cow, that is a great album and it's even got better vocals, not to mention the fact that Graham is now writing lyrics, which he didn't do on *Down to Earth*—that's all Roger Glover. "Samurai" on that album; oh, my God, it's so good, as well as the title track. Anyway, I'm getting sidetracked but I just wanted to make the point that this was just the beginning for Graham, because of MSG and then Alcatrazz.

Nick: I'll just add that for me, *Down to Earth* achieves what they were going for. It's the perfect balance of old and new. It's still really quite heavy, definitely heavier than its reputation would have it. What's interesting too, compared with, let's say, *Rising*, where I'm like, "Where's Jimmy? I can't hear Jimmy" I put on my Beats headphones and boy, even though this was recorded in 1979, every instrument is well defined. I can hear everything and can pick everything out. It's a triumph in that department. So whether it's in the production or the mixing or whatever, it's really pleasing to the ear through headphones.

And in terms of the performances, it's a band effort. Ritchie lets the band shine. I know that he's had problems with line-ups, but on this record, he lets them do their thing. And they're not noodling, like they do onstage. They're not off meandering. We don't have drum solos and things. There's this really phenomenal foundation with Cozy's drumming and Roger's bass playing. You've got Don Airey playing tastefully and with versatility. And Blackmore's right in there, but he's not super-dominant. I feel like if I had been there experiencing *Down to Earth* in the fall of 1979, I would not have been turning up my nose at this album.

Martin: Yeah, it's funny, for all this talk about Foreigner, it really doesn't go too far in that direction at all, certainly not far enough to get it on radio.

Nick: That's a very good point. Yeah, he describes it as Foreigner but it's not really Foreigner. You could throw some other bands in there too. Still, I feel like there was a niche for this, and they tried to explore that more during the next phase.

Martin: Yeah, "Stone Cold" and "Street of Dreams" are much further along.

Nick: That's exactly it. They went and inhabited that bandwidth. It's not like he did another right turn and went back to the Dio days. This is sort of where he stayed. And maybe that's a problem, as if he wasn't forward-looking enough.

Pontus: In the end, I see *Down to Earth* as a good party album, and a good follow-up to *Long Live Rock 'n' Roll*. You wonder what would have happened if they'd changed the name of the group. Would it have been easier to go through the transition if this was framed as a new band? Then again, he had worked so hard with the Rainbow moniker. But the font on the cover is different; it's no longer gothic. And it's called *Down to Earth*, for a more down to earth album.

And things were looking up. "Since You Been Gone" was a hit, at least in Europe, or at least in England. It went gold in the UK—100,000 copies in the UK is really good. When I grew up in the eighties here in Sweden, this album was readily available in stores and so were all the other Rainbow records, especially the Joe Lynn Turner ones. They were big sellers in Sweden. The guys from the band Europe absolutely listened to this album. There's a story about Ian Haugland auditioning for Yngwie Malmsteen way back when Yngwie was living in Stockholm. And Yngwie and Marcel Jacob and Ian, they played "Lost in Hollywood." That music mattered to a lot of people. It was a record that sold to all the rockers. I don't know how many Abba fans bought it.

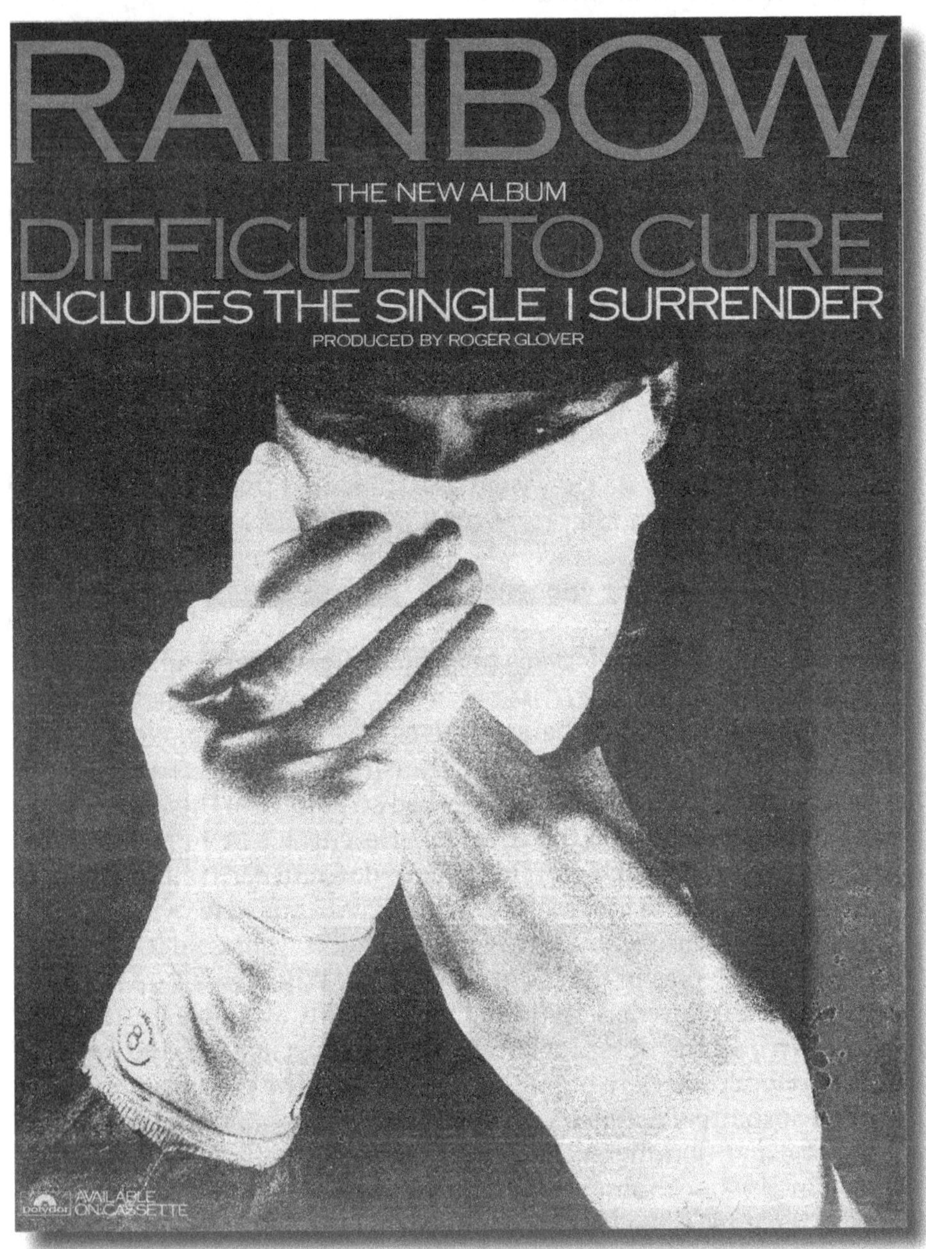
RAINBOW
THE NEW ALBUM
DIFFICULT TO CURE
INCLUDES THE SINGLE I SURRENDER
PRODUCED BY ROGER GLOVER
polydor
AVAILABLE ON CASSETTE

Beacon Theatre, New York, New York, November 12, 1975.

© Frank White
© Frank White
© Frank White

Empire Theatre, Liverpool, UK, November 4, 1977.

The master, 1977.

Newcastle City Hall, Newcastle, UK, February 19, 1980.

© Alan Perry Concert Photography

Tour Book 1978.

Louie's Rock Concert City, Baileys Crossroads, VA, February 22, 1981.

Japanese "All Night Long" single, with "Weiss Heim" as the B-side.

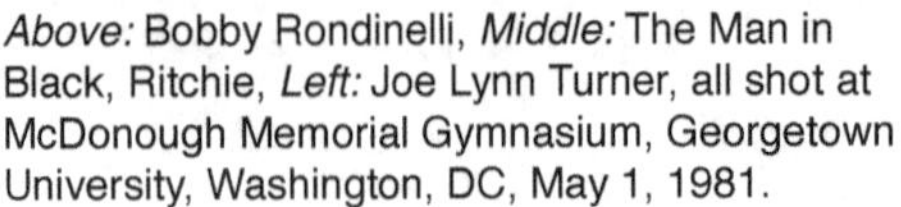

Above: Bobby Rondinelli, *Middle:* The Man in Black, Ritchie, *Left:* Joe Lynn Turner, all shot at McDonough Memorial Gymnasium, Georgetown University, Washington, DC, May 1, 1981.

Capitol Centre, Landover, MD, July 20, 1982. Supporting was Krokus.

Baltimore Civic Centre, Baltimore, MD,
November 8, 1983.

Palalido, Lilan, Italy,
October 28, 1995.

GET INTO "SHAPE"
GET RAINBOW
AT OUR PRICE
ONLY £4.79
ALBUM OR CASSETTE
RAINBOW — "BENT OUT OF SHAPE"
MUSIC, SERVICE, SELECTION - THINK OUR PRICE
COMING SOON   BOB DYLAN   SHAKATAK   GARY NUMAN   UB40   PUBLIC IMAGE   JO BOXERS
OUR PRICE
Records
ADDRESSES
NOW OPEN!!
A NEW OUR PRICE
RECORD SHOP IN
THE PARADE SWINDON
& KING'S MALL HAMMERSMITH

45RPM   12INCH   45RPM   12INCH   45RPM
R   V1200
RAINBOW
CAN'T LET
YOU GO

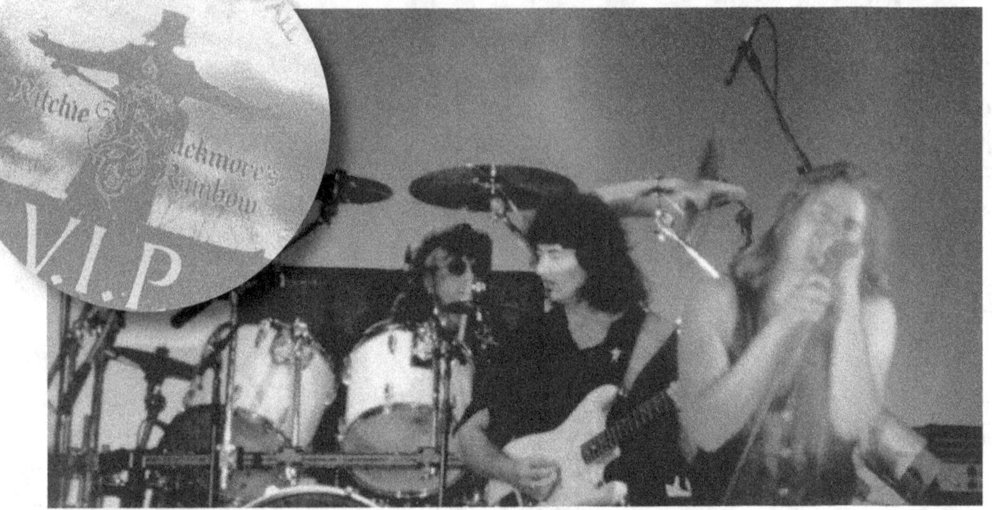

Insert: Stranger in Us All backstage pass.
Below: Ritchie on the cover of the venerable Japanese heavy metal magazine, *Burrn!,* 1995.

© Jerry Bloom / Wymer Collection

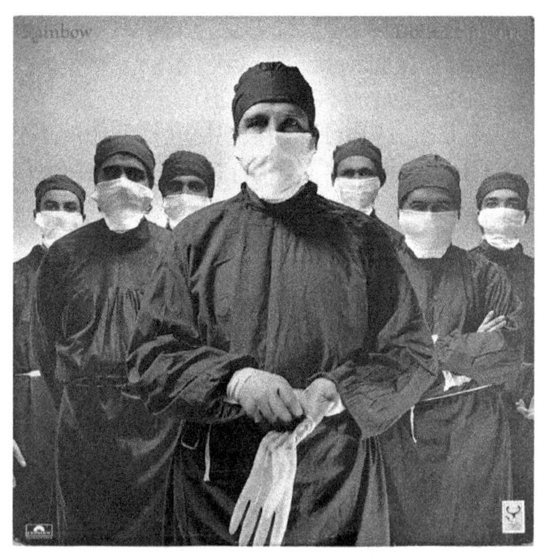

DIFFICULT TO CURE

February 3, 1981
Polydor PD-1-6316
Produced by Roger Glover
Engineered by Flemming Rasmussen; assisted by Clay Hutchinson
and Thomas Brekling
Personnel: Joe Lynn Turner – vocals, Ritchie Blackmore – guitars,
Roger Glover – bass, Don Airey – keyboards, Bobby Rondinelli –
drums

Side 1
1. I Surrender (Ballard) 4:01
2. Spotlight Kid (Blackmore, Glover) 4:52
3. No Release (Blackmore, Glover, Airey) 5:20
4. Magic (Moran) 4:05
5. Vielleicht Das Nachster Zeit (Maybe Next Time) (Blackmore, Airey)
3:20

Side 2
1. Can't Happen Here (Blackmore, Glover) 4:55
2. Freedom Fighter (Blackmore, Glover, Turner) 4:20
3. Midtown Tunnel Vision (Blackmore, Glover, Turner) 4:31
4. Difficult to Cure (Beethoven's Ninth) (Beethoven; arr. by Blackmore, Glover, Airey) 5:55

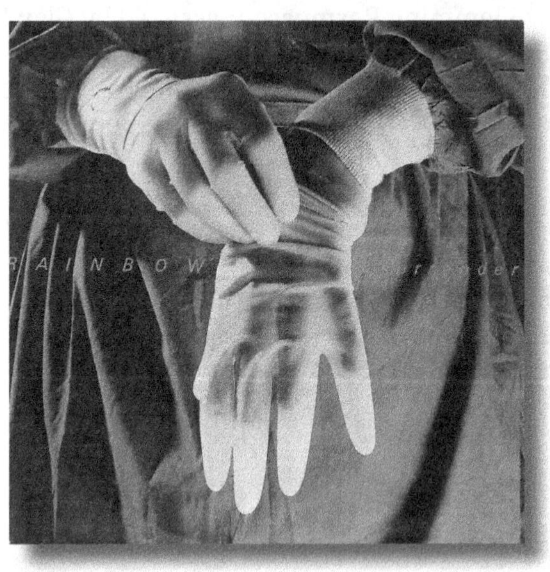

A *Difficult to Cure* Timeline

August 8 – August 16, 1980. Rainbow play a handful of European dates, culminating in the very first Monsters of Rock, which is held at Castle Donington racetrack. The European dates were somewhat considered Donington warm-up dates, the stakes being raised because Rainbow was intending to issue their Monsters of Rock set as a new double live album (this never happened). The line-up for the festival features Touch, Riot, Saxon, April Wine, Scorpions, Judas Priest and Rainbow as headliner. A commemorative album is issued. This would be the last Rainbow shows with Graham Bonnet and Cozy Powell as part of the line-up. Cozy actually quits Rainbow the day of the show, although he does in fact play the gig. His replacement, Bobby Rondinelli is in attendance at the show.

September 1980. Graham Bonnet quits Rainbow.

October 1980. Polydor (Rainbow's label) issue *Monsters of Rock*, commemorating the festival of the same name. Rainbow is represented with "Stargazer" and "All Night Long," both, of course, with Graham Bonnet on vocals. Roger Glover gets an Executive Producer credit on the album.

January 23, 1981. "I Surrender" is issued as the first single from *Difficult to Cure*, backed with "Vielleicht Das Nachster Zeit (Maybe Next Time)." The Russ Ballard-penned tune would become the band's most successful ever UK single, achieving a No.3 placement on the UK charts, as well as certifying silver.

February 3, 1981. Rainbow issue *Difficult to Cure*, the band's first album to feature Joe Lynn Turner as vocalist. The album is tracked at Sweet Silence Studios, Copenhagen, Denmark and Kingdom Sound Studios, Long Island, New York. It reaches No.3 on the UK charts, No.13 in Germany and No.50 in the US.

February 21 – May 12, 1981. Rainbow tour America promoting *Difficult to Cure*, supporting or co-headlining with The Pat Travers Band. Krokus is included on some dates as well.

February 24, 1981. *Difficult to Cure* is certified gold in the UK. It also goes gold in Japan.

May 16, 1981. Ritchie Blackmore marries for a third time, to Amy Rothman.

June 1981. "Can't Happen Here" is issued as a single, backed with the non-LP "Jealous Lover," which is recorded on a day off amidst US tour dates, using a mobile studio in Minneapolis, Minnesota. Japan picks "Magic" to issue as a single, backed with "Freedom Fighter."

June 3 – July 27, 1981. Rainbow tour extensively in the UK and mainland Europe in support of *Difficult to Cure*. The European leg includes dates with UFO but mostly with Def Leppard supporting. In the UK, support comes from Rose Tattoo.

August 18 – August 28, 1981. The band conduct Japanese tour dates in support of their fifth album. Don Airey decides to quit the band after a show in Hawaii on the way home, after unknowingly being left on stage while the rest of the band were already on their way back to the hotel.

October 19, 1981. Polydor issue a 12" EP in the US, featuring "Jealous Lover," along with "Weiss Heim, "Can't Happen Here" and "I Surrender." It reaches No.147 on the Billboard 200.

November 1981. UK compilation *The Best of Rainbow* is issued.

November 28, 1981. Don Airey officially quits Rainbow.

November 9, 1982. Rainbow play the Deutschlandhalle in Berlin. A picture of Ritchie sitting on the edge of the stage shot by Ross Halfin is used four years later on the cover of the *Finyl Vinyl* compilation.

Martin talks to Rich Davenport, John Gaffney, Jamie Laszlo and Steven Reid about *Difficult to Cure*.

Martin Popoff: So we arrive at the Joe Lynn Turner era. What kind of first album do we get out of this new configuration of the band?

Rich Davenport: Well, Rainbow were huge in Britain, certainly at this point, and I'm sure across Europe, and they were obviously making some inroads in America. For context, Rainbow were one of the second wave offshoot Deep Purple bands that benefited from the New Wave of British Heavy Metal. They weren't part of it, but they had been slogging away for a few years like Whitesnake. There was this influx of younger rock and metal fans, and both bands benefitted, as did Gillan and Black Sabbath. When they were reinvented with Joe Lynn Turner, younger metalheads embraced that.

I remember I did an interview with John Gallagher from Raven a couple of years ago and I asked him, "In terms of the fans that you were seeing at your gigs, for this new breed, New Wave of British Heavy Metal band, was there any sort of differentiation in the fans that you would see with a Purple offshoot band that you were supporting?" He said, "No, you got a lot of the same audience. The younger kids didn't see the older bands as old farts or anything. I don't quite know how the more established rock fans would have viewed the younger bands, but the young rock fans just thought it was great."

That was where my friends and I got into Rainbow, because we'd missed it first time round. And just to show how big they were in Britain at the time, I was nine years old in 1981 and I knew who they were. I was at primary school, elementary school, and it was so big that it wasn't just through people's older brothers. There was a kids TV show called *Tiswas*, which stood for *Today is Saturday: Watch and Smile*, and it was insane, quite subversive humour. This was a kids program that ran for three hours on a Saturday morning and they would have Lemmy from Motörhead as a guest. So you've got cartoons like *Bugs Bunny* and then, "Look, here's Lemmy, kids" and they interviewed Lemmy and showed "Ace of Spades." And I think that's where I first heard "I Surrender." And I remember they had Graham Bonnet on as a solo artist around the same time, talking about why he left Rainbow. So as a nine-year-old kid, I knew who Rainbow were and I was seeing this on TV and I knew the song. As soon as I had enough money to buy albums, this was the one I aimed for.

Martin: Could they sell a lot of tickets? Could they get 5000 people out?

Rich: Probably. I believe they were playing Wembley Arena around that time, because there was some sort of incident, I believe, either at the end of the *Down to Earth* tour or the start of the next one. And they'd already headlined Monsters of Rock, the first one, and they played Wembley Arena at that point. They experienced a huge crossover effect with this because the album got to No.3 on the pop charts. And that's back when you had to sell bucketloads of albums to get that high in the mainstream pop charts in Britain. This is the biggest they ever got in terms of certainly chart placings and it could have all gone wrong, because people knew that Graham Bonnet was out by then. That was very, very public, but people still stayed with the band.

Martin: Interesting; thanks for painting that picture. John, what was your perspective, being in America?

John Gaffney: Rainbow had begun this movement towards radio rock, if you will, the more commercial side, with *Down to Earth*. But here they're taking another step towards. This is the first album with Joe Lynn Turner, with his clean, smooth, unoffensive type of voice. There isn't really any edge or anything to Joe's voice. He has a natural high tenor, almost like a crooner. He has a nice rounded sound to his voice, no real distortion. Imagine if Frank Sinatra was a heavy metal/ hard rock singer (laughs), he might have a voice like Joe Lynn Turner. It's very in control but he has a ton of range. It's almost deceiving because his tone is so round-sounding and so even and bassy, not necessarily bassy-sounding but just warm-sounding. When he sings in his upper range, it never sound shrill or high-pitched or anything.

But I'm going to challenge people. This album is heavier than they think it is. When you really sit down and you start adding it up, putting these songs in the plus and minus columns here, there's a lot more heavier things than people might realize on this album. I particularly love Blackmore's playing on this album. Some of these songs were apparently started when Graham Bonnet was still in the band and then finished off when Joe Lynn Turner came in. So some of these songs—and Joe has admitted this—didn't quite sit in the key that he would have sang them in had he been there from the start. Graham Bonnet has this insane voice, where he could just sing super-high. So some of the songs don't exactly sit in Joe's money zone. But he still pulls it off very competently.

Jamie Laszlo: I guested on a show on your *Contrarians* YouTube channel and I called *Difficult to Cure* the worst Rainbow album. But the question is, did I exaggerate my thoughts in order to make video content? Or is it really that bad? Well, let's find out. But before we get into the song, I'd ask is it 100%? bad? No. But none of the songs are 100% good—not a single one of them, in my opinion.

Steven Reid: With *Difficult to Cure*, we get a step further, is what we get. We are clearly in commercial rock territory now, although it really didn't blow the world apart in terms of sales and success. Still, it reached No.3 in the UK, and remains the band's highest-charting album. It's the best Ritchie ever did outside of Deep Purple. There is actually some vindication there. They got it right, if that's what they were looking for. But in terms of worldwide success, this is a non-event. All of this evolution into what we class as commercial rock, how commercial is that? I don't know; that's a separate question entirely.

But yeah, it's smooth, the songs are short, it's all about the chorus. I like Joe Lynn Turner; I always have. He does what he does and he's very good at it. And to be fair, I think he was perfect for the band at this stage. People don't like this album. I can see why. I don't have a great problem with it. I have an ability or a belief that bands go through certain points. I don't need them to change the name, but a lot of people out there go, oh, if Ritchie called it something else, that would be much better. He's earned the right to call it whatever he wants. Because you build up a success, you build up a fan base, and even though you evolve, you will take some of those people with you. So why should you then go call it something else? Who's this? I don't need to know that. You don't need to re-educate the public to the fact that Ritchie Blackmore is playing. This is Rainbow. Then you take your choice as to whether you want to stay on board or not.

For some it was a step too far; there's no two ways about it. The production from Roger Glover is clean, it's precise, it's poppy. But that's what was required here. That's what this whole thing was going for. Flemming Rasmussen was the engineer, which is a nice little quirk because his career took a different trajectory after this, finding significant fame through his work with Metallica. As you would expect in Rainbow, we've got band member changes. We have Joe Lynn Turner on board but we've also got Bobby Rondinelli on drums, joining the core of Blackmore, Airey and Glover.

So there are links to the past, but we will continue moving forward. There's the interesting dynamic between Blackmore and Glover, considering how Deep Purple evolved and how their relationships evolved, how Roger came back into Ritchie's fold and ended up the producer. How he then ends up the architect of this era, that's a strange dynamic. Ritchie goes from telling Roger, "I totally don't want you part of what I do" to actually "You can steer the ship." It's a strange journey but it works here for what the band mission was. As John explains, the album was written initially with Graham Bonnet in mind. Joe Lynn Turner took over, but an awful lot of it was already constructed. So some of it doesn't quite suit his voice, I would suggest, in the way that you would hope. But I too think he does a good job of it.

Martin: What do you think of the album cover?

John: The cover art is famously a Hipgnosis design that was originally pitched to Black Sabbath for their *Never Say Die* album. I think the world was better off that this landed on *Difficult to Cure* and that Black Sabbath got their *Never Say Die* cover. It matches up better with the title, *Difficult to Cure*.

Steven: I like the album cover, even though it's not one of the better ones. I agree with John that it goes better with this title. I can understand why somebody at Hipgnosis would go, "Hmm, we've got something here that might work for you guys." It doesn't have much to do with the music though. It doesn't convey what's going to be inside. It feels much more like a prog rock album cover.

Martin: I see that the photo is badly cropped on the UK version and that the typestyle is different. I like the detail of the little surgical instrument pictures, one on the front and one on the back, plus the slash through the descender on Rainbow so it looks like Rx, the sort of drug sign.

Steven: The typeface on mine is very boring. My CD version of this credits Joe Lynn Turner as Jolyn. When I was younger, I did wonder if those doctors were actually the band members dressed-up.

Martin: And what are your thoughts on Roger Glover's production?

Rich: I think it's great. You can hear everything clearly, on things like "Spotlight Kid" and on "Difficult to Cure" itself, the title track. You can hear the roots of earlier Rainbow tracks like "Kill the King" on the upbeat, faster tracks like that. The classical arrangements are more polished, but it's not completely blunted the impact of the band. There came a point in the eighties where a lot of rock bands lost their edge because everything was covered in that horrible reverb. We talked about this for your Blue Öyster Cult panel book with *Club Ninja*. That album and a lot of the Southern rock bands just got destroyed by eighties production techniques. But Roger executes a commercial production here that's kept enough of the band's essential identity. You can still tell it's Rainbow. He's polished it to the point where it's radio-friendly but not gone too far with it. And I like the way he's produced the harmonies too.

John: Maybe I'm being influenced by the album cover, but to me, the production feels cold and sterile. It sounds like these doctors on the album cover, bright, not very warm, a little clunky. You can hear everything but it's clinical. When you get into *Straight Between the Eyes* and *Bent Out of Shape*, it's still that way, although I wouldn't say that about *Down to Earth*.

Martin: All right, like the great Samson album with Bruce Dickinson that would come out three months later, we open with a Russ Ballard cover.

Rich: Yes, that's right (laughs). Only "I Surrender" is not as rockin' as "Riding with the Angels." Still, I love it. I really liked "Since You Been Gone," but this is almost as though it was tailor-made for Rainbow, given the classical feel to it in some of the chord progressions. That section where the twin guitar harmony comes in and there's the descending bit and the melodic counterpoint from Roger's bass, that's almost like Baroque pop, isn't it?

Martin: Yes, it plays to this narrative I've always felt about Rainbow, that they were a nice blend between old-school classical-based European metal and pop or pomp rock or proto-hair metal.

Rich: Absolutely, and in that respect, it's just such a good fit for Rainbow. And the arrangement and Ritchie's solo... I've interviewed Ritchie once, and I know he improvises a lot and thrives on that, and he was saying that he never plays the same thing twice. And I think once he's inspired, it sounds great. We were interviewing for Blackmore's Night, and I phrased it diplomatically, but I said that on some of the Blackmore's Night stuff, for me as a guitar player, I can hear when he sounds inspired, because he's playing so fiery. But I've seen live videos of Deep Purple in the nineties, and it's like he's just checked out. You can tell he doesn't want to be there, that he's not fired-up. Whereas on some of the Blackmore's Night stuff, he seems more into it, more connected with the track in terms of his lead playing than he does with some of the later Deep Purple stuff. And I think in this period of Rainbow, you can tell he's enjoying it and he's inspired, because the solo on "I Surrender" is fantastic.

John: I guess they figured covering Russ Ballard worked so well last time, let's do it again. This was the first single from the record. I like this song. It has interesting chordal movement to it, the sort of ascending and descending rolling chords. There's a lot of chords in this and it keeps moving up and down and back and forth. Joe's voice is soaring here. It's slightly too high of a key for Joe but he still pulls it off. It doesn't sound like he's straining.

The chorus of the song is radio-friendly but also catchy. I'm a sucker for melodic, catchy songs. I love "Since You Been Gone" and to me, "I Surrender" has a chorus that is very much like the one in "Since You Been Gone." You hear it once and you can't get it out of your head. The lyrics are also safe and radio-friendly. Ritchie loves melody and he loves to play over these types of chord progressions. They are almost classical-sounding. I made reference to this when we talked about "Tarot Woman." This circle of fifths classical thing where you're moving from... the next chord is five notes lower, the next chord is five notes lower, the next chord... it creates this rolling effect. In "I Surrender," we're in G minor, and playing over these types of keys allows Ritchie to play melodically. And this melodic guitar line that he plays, it returns throughout the song.

Jamie: The way I see it, they're starting the album off with an average Russ Ballard song, and maybe that's not the best strategy when introducing a new lead singer. Plus Head East just covered this the year before, and it's not good when they did it either. But Joe Lynn Turner sounds great; he's in good voice and he's always gonna sound decent. But right off the bat, the band is very eighties-sounding with kinds of pop hooks, right down to the way it's constructed. It's not hair metal and it's not quite in the style of bands like Loverboy and Sammy Hagar. If anything, we are right into Foreigner territory with this song. There's some nice guitar passages throughout the song. But you're bound to have that with Ritchie. The chorus is supposed to be catchy, but I find it amateurish from a songwriting perspective. It's flat and annoying. But Ritchie's guitars behind the chorus save it from being a complete disaster.

Steven: With the album reaching No.3 in the UK, if you didn't know Rainbow, this is the Rainbow song that you're liable to know, the highest charting single for them anywhere, coincidentally also getting to No.3. And it's easy to hear why. It opens up with this regal, full-band bluster, and during it, you get this little sweep of what sounds like grand piano. And then you get quite a spectacular and stratospheric vocal from Joe Lynn Turner. You're either gonna love that or you're gonna hate it, but I tell you what, it's an unforgettable entrance. That's the way to say, "Hi, I'm the new guy in the band."

As I say, some of these other songs were supposedly written with Graham Bonnet in mind. It's difficult to imagine him doing this one. I know it's a cover. Russ Ballard is one of the best pet writers for other people. It's interesting that as Ritchie steers this ship towards sort of Foreigner territory, his guitar work still retains that classical feel. There's a strange contradiction when you really sit and listen to this album. Because yes, it's much more melodic. We are edging into pop territory rather than rock, or classic rock as we now call it. And yet his personal evolution is much slower. The songs' evolution is quite fast; his evolution is slower. He's still bringing the Ritchie Blackmore that we know from Deep Purple to all of this. I don't know how thought-through that was, if he decided that he could make these mainstream hits that did and still do get radio play, while at the same time not compromise on what created his legend. Is that the right move? I don't really know, to be honest with you. The solo fits the song— we've always known it as that. But I don't know if I was to hear it with fresh ears all these years later, if I would go, "Well, that's the guitar solo you would expect to hear on this song."

Martin: Let's focus on Joe for a moment. What's your assessment on him and his fit for the band?

Rich: I think he's a great fit. And ironically, I've interviewed Joe a couple of times and actually spoke to him about this. I know Ritchie expressed in interviews the admiration he had for Foreigner, and I think that comes into play more on the later Joe Lynn Turner albums, with tracks like "Stone Cold" more so than the *Difficult to Cure* songs. Joe said that Ritchie asked him to sing in a slightly smoother style, not to copy Lou Gramm, but in that style, because they were aiming for FM radio airplay in America.

And I remember hearing one of Joe's first solo albums afterward, in the mid-nineties, after Deep Purple, a record called *Nothing's Changed*. There's a lot more brashness and throatiness in his vocals and I was quite surprised by that. And I think that was more naturally how he sings, although it does come through a little bit here. So he's got power and personality and he's really belting. He described himself to me as a blues rock singer. So I think he's got polish, but he can still bring that edge and grit, although not as much as Graham Bonnet. If anything, he's more versatile than Graham.

Jamie: Joe is very New York, very Italian. A bit of a cheeseball. I love his voice. I don't know if I could hang out with the dude. We probably wouldn't get along, certainly not politically. But yeah, he's a definite cheeseball. And a lot of this music he's singing with Rainbow, some people call it cheesy. So it fits. Some of it's less cheesy than others.

Steven: He's strong right through the whole album. But he's an "all about the chorus" kind of singer. He did a more power metal album recently, which was a sideways step. Up until then, he's a guy that writes hooks, sings hooks, sings choruses, does it very, very well.

Martin: And what school does he come from? Who would you compare him to?

Steven: Fandango was a completely different beast entirely. When he was singing with them, you would imagine he came from a pure pop background. He's got a sense of showmanship about him, a "stage show" feel to what he does. You could imagine him treading the boards in a musical, in that sense. And that is also where we've moved vocally. Graham Bonnet was a hard rock screamer, a shouter even, at points, which is oddly not his background either. Joe takes us a step further. We never get… well we do get occasional gritty vocals and they don't work, to be fair. When he tries to step up to something a bit tougher, a bit more street, for want of a better phrase, it comes off as really disingenuous. But if you give him something quite dayglo to sing, if you get what I mean, he can sell that. It's all about the melody and the hook; he'll deliver that for you every single time. It's not to everyone's taste.

Martin: Is he like Paul Rodgers or Lou Gramm?

Steven: I don't think he's got that bottom end that Foreigner have. If you think of "Hot Blooded," I don't quite know if Joe could bring you that dirt. I don't find much dirt in what Joe Lynn Turner does. Further down the line, yeah, but his voice is older then. But at this point, there's no dirt there; he's a very clean singer. You imagine him, how you see him at this stage. He looks young, he's good-looking, he's remarkably clean-shaven. There's not a hair on his face. And with hindsight we know there's a medical issue there. But he's a really clean-cut guy and he sings like a really clean-cut guy. He sounds well-to-do. He doesn't sound like he's had to fight to get here. And that's total conjecture, not actual projection of what his life has been. That's just how he sounds. "Yeah, it's all gone well for me, and I sing all these happy songs for you!" (laughs).

Martin: Things pick right up with "Spotlight Kid." Actually, they didn't have one of these "OTT" (over-the-top) barnstormers on the last album.

John: No, and I love the energy on this one. It's a Blackmore/Glover composition, and sure, maybe "Kill the King" but safer (laughs). Don't kill the king; just send him an eviction notice or something, or send him a warning. This was their concert-opener for many years and you can totally understand why. I love the intro to this. There's a sort of swing feel or Southern rock lick and then it straightens itself out.

It's this weird, bluesy guitar piece. I haven't mentioned this yet, but another thing that makes Ritchie unique with his rhythm playing is that Ritchie almost never just chugs away on standard heavy metal Black Sabbath-style power chords. He does this thing where he plays dyads, two notes. In a typical power chord, you have the lowest note which is the root, you have a middle note which is the fifth and then you have a top note which is the octave, which is the same note as the bottom note of the chord. And what Ritchie does is he takes the bottom note out and he just plays the top two notes of a power chord and it allows him to play really snappy, fast lines, little patterns like you hear in the intro of the song here.

Okay, so I love the lyrics too in this song. "They love you/But you're in love with the spotlight." I can't help but think that Roger might have been referring to Ritchie, because Ritchie is notoriously cold with the fans. So maybe this is a reference to Ritchie. He's a guy that doesn't particularly like the "jokers and women" knocking at your door, like it says in the lyrics. But he loves to be in the spotlight. The first part of the solo is in B minor and we get this classical thing. On the first part, Ritchie is going crazy here and then it changes to C sharp minor and we get this classical line that Ritchie plays, this single-note line, like a Bach or Beethoven thing. It's interesting because it's two frets higher than where he was soloing before this; it modulates up.

And then it modulates up another two frets to E flat, a totally un-rock 'n' roll guitar key. Nobody likes to play in E flat because you don't have any open strings there. But this is over the keyboard solo. And it has this weird diminished sound to it, a very dissonant sound, where Don Airey is playing all these crazy, out-there, weird notes. And then it drops back to the original key, which is B minor, and they go back into that classical Beethoven lick thing here with the guitar and the keyboard doubling each other. This harkens back to the Deep Purple days when Jon Lord and Ritchie would both solo, and then they would double a line with each other. It's cool and creative, the way this has moved now, cycling through unrelated keys, and we manage to land back into the original key here.

Rich: Yeah, killer riff, and quite an interesting intro, like you say, almost like a Southern rock lick, before he goes into the riff itself. You're like, where's this going to go? That sounds quite jolly and happy and upbeat. But then it sounds like he's bringing that vibe from "Burn" and "Kill the King" into the eighties. It's not as heavy, but it's still got teeth. There's places where Joe Lynn Turner lets a bit of that bluesy rasp come through.

Bobby Rondinelli's double bass drums are really good, really propulsive. This is not a criticism of Cozy, but Bobby's got a more deft touch behind the kit, a lighter touch than Cozy, which works really well. And there's that classical-sounding riff again, which comes in the middle of it, which almost sounds like a polka. There's a bit where you can imagine Joe doing the Cossack dance (laughs).

As for the lyric, it's interesting to conjecture if that's about Ritchie. It's crazy to look back now. These guys were probably only in their 30s. At the time, we probably thought of them as relatively old guys, right? They'd been around the block because they started so young. And that lyric, it's not exactly a cynical, jaded viewpoint. It's more a case of this is the danger of what can happen. Maybe it's an observation of the kinds of people they've seen in the music business. That's what I took from it. But it could be about Ritchie, yeah.

Jamie: I wasn't buying rock albums in 1981. I was still too busy playing with *Star Wars* figures. But I'm assuming there were Rainbow fans who wanted the Dio era sound back when *Difficult to Cure* came out. And 1981 is only three years removed from *Long Live Rock 'n' Roll*. And there was only one album released since—*Down to Earth*. So some people who missed Dio might have thought that *Down the Earth* was a small hiccup.

So when you come to this album and you get to track two and you hear "Spotlight Kid," maybe this song gave some people some hope, because I could totally picture Ronnie singing this song. All you've got to do is take out the vocal track and put in Ronnie and it could be on any of the previous albums. I can actually picture the parts where Ronnie would do the double horns. It's got great keyboard work from Don Airey and the guitar solos sounds like something that would be played at a renaissance fair. It might be a heavy metal renaissance fair, but still, people shouldn't be so surprised when Ritchie formed Blackmore's Night in 1997 because the clues were there all along. But yeah, in the end, "Spotlight Kid" is like a hard-rocking version of "Jukebox Hero" or "Shooting Star" by Bad Company. It's probably my favourite song on the album.

Steven: Yeah, I love "Spotlight Kid" too. This was to me proof that Rainbow could kind move away from that traditional rock arena and make it work. Ritchie and Don Airey are soloing and they're riffing off each other in the verses to such good effect. And that allows Joe Lynn Turner to do what he's here to do, and that's hitting the mark in the choruses.

But "Spotlight Kid" is really about the solos. That whole song, even though it's got ample pop hooks, that is just a vehicle for the solos. It's an underrated masterclass from Ritchie. You get your trademark sound, then we go to some Beethoven, because well, that's what we're going to do. And there's even a considerable amount of eighties pop in the keyboards. Don Airey, every step of the way, his playing is excellent. Some of the actual technology, the sounds, in hindsight we don't love all of them, but there you go. And yeah, that whole solo section is stolen by Joe Lynn Turner going, "Hey!" That is simply genius (laughs).

Martin: Next is "No Release," which is a swirling cauldron of Euro-metal mixed with up-tempo blues styles, really pretty much emanating from the band's new lead singer. Quite an under-rated track, no?

Rich: Absolutely, and I'll tell you, I remember reading in an old copy of *Kerrang!* from around the time of *Straight Between the Eyes*, and Ritchie was talking about what a great fit Joe was for the band. And he flagged this track up. He said that they tried it with Graham Bonnet when he was still in the band. And the quote from Ritchie was, "I won't tell you what Graham said." And they said that Joe came in and made that whole breakdown section in the middle and that was all Joe. Ritchie would ask, "What have you got in your magic bag?" Because Joe could just pull ideas out like that. And Joe, this is where he told me he started off as a blues rock singer, and that this was a very comfortable fit for him, this track, just to bring that in.

So yeah, I really like the track. It's quite moody and atmospheric from the sort of string bends with the delay on in the beginning, and then it builds up into that riff. We're almost in the same territory as "Jealous Lover," that kind of feel. There's an interesting sort of syncopation when the drums and the riff actually come in. They come in at an odd point, midway through the riff almost. And the harmonies are great. They're stacked but it's not as opulent as somebody like Queen or Boston might do. But the harmonies are polished behind Joe. Ritchie's solo is really good, there's some nice rhythmic phrasing and then I just love that breakdown with the handclaps and the bass drum going underneath. Odd to say this, but it's almost gospel and disco at the same time, the way Joe's background vocals are worked into that.

John: "No Release" is a Blackmore/Glover/Airey tune. Bluesy intro; it's got this down and dirty voodoo blues vibe to it, with Ritchie sliding and bending the notes into the open strings. The very first few notes of it always remind me of Hendrix's "Hey Joe," because

Jimi does a similar thing where he's bending notes into open strings; that's basically what Ritchie's doing here. Plus there's some echo and delay on it.

And then when the main riff kicks in, it's heavy but funky, maybe like something you would have heard on *Burn*, with Glenn Hughes and David Coverdale, where they were mixing blues with hard rock. Ritchie's almost playing a "Back in the Saddle"-type of Aerosmith riff there, for the verses, with Bobby Rondinelli being particularly groovy but also driving.

Not sure what the lyrics mean, but I do like the lines, "Through the smoke the dancers move/Demonic, dirty, downtown groove." I think that's a pretty cool line. I'd have to say I don't appreciate the part where everything sort of drops down for those handclaps and there's this chanting thing going on. To me, it sounds corny. They're trying to go for this dark voodoo vibe and it just doesn't work for me. But the double time at the end of the song adds a lot of energy and it takes it out on a high note.

Jamie: "No Release" reminds me of a Whitesnake song. That line, "I can't get no release" just has not aged well for me. I probably wouldn't be bothered by it as much if they didn't have that breakdown in the middle where they keep repeating it. And I counted, Martin; if you include the backup singers, they say, "I can't get no release" 15 times within a very short break. It's funny how something like that can get stuck in your brain one day, and it just ruins the whole song for the rest of your life. So yeah, cringe-worthy lyrics.

Steven: I suppose the only place this record can go for me after "Spotlight Kid" is to something that's a bit pulled back, more restrained. "No Release" has a great groove spiralling around another great guitar line. It's classic Ritchie, and it sounds like he's fully on board here. A lot of people I know don't like this album. For a lot of them, it's their least favourite Rainbow album. I listen to the spirit in Ritchie's playing, and I don't get the impression it's his least favourite Rainbow album. He sounds totally invested in this in a way that I would argue isn't the case on all of *Straight Between the Eyes* and most of *Bent Out of Shape*. I think with *Bent Out of Shape* he sounds disinterested, whether it's a better album or not. That's open to question.

You got another good if not quite great guitar solo. In fairness, though, I agree with John and Jamie—I could do without the breakdown with the handclaps and the chanted vocals. You're in pure stage show territory there. This is playing to Joe Lynn Turner's strengths and it's a big gang vocal. But you can imagine that horrible scene out for a night of live theatre where they're all crouching towards each other with their shoulders down and clapping their hands. We're in really kitschy *West Side Story* territory here. And that is how tight a line this album walks. I can understand why people feel that it falls off the edge at certain points. It *does* fall off the edge, but Ritchie rescues it with another great solo at the end. But the damage is done. There is a cringe level there.

Martin: "Magic" seems something of a squandered opportunity. They take one of the few pop shots they'd be allowed on the album, and yet it's another cover and it's not particularly instantly appealing. To add to that, it wasn't even issued as a single, except in Japan.

Rich: Yeah, this is an odd one. I quite like it but it's very poppy, quite simple, melodic. The vocal is overtly poppy, which is possibly the main reason why they get abuse for it. Then again it's both classy and a bit classical-tinged, isn't it? With that intro motif, that is used later too. It makes me wonder why they would have done this. Was it with a view to it possibly being a single? I can't see a need to bring in an outside writer, unless they were short of material. But it just seems odd to have brought in something from an outside writer if they were not going to use it for a single.

John: Oh, boy, "Magic." As Rich says, here's another outside songwriter, Brian Moran and man, this might be my least favourite song in the entire Rainbow catalogue. You'd think it's a deliberate attempt to get on FM radio or even AM radio, but yeah, they didn't even put it out as a single. I absolutely hate the Disney-sounding keyboards at the beginning of it. It's way too soft and melodic for me and I'm a person that loves melodic, sort of over-the-top catchy things. But these lyrics are just absolute cringe. Nope, negative. And the song flopped; it didn't do anything. "I Surrender" is very melodic and radio-friendly, but to me, it still has some heaviness to it. There's some interesting chordal things going on like I mentioned earlier, and the lyrics are somewhat interesting. This is just total fluff, a throwaway. I have no idea why they would even put this on here.

Jamie: I hate being down on this album, because I don't want to sound like a hater, but "Magic" makes me dance a certain way. Can't dance in a book, so for people asking, "What kind of dance?" it's the kind of dance The Pips would do behind Gladys Knight (laughs). That's what this makes me do. And that's not good. Another idea I came across in my brain, if Rainbow appeared on a 1981 TV variety show that had the demographics of everyone's parents and grandparents at the time, this song would go over well if they performed it on there. And that's not a compliment. Grandma would be there tapping her toe. This song is goofy; it's goofier than the Olivia Newton John song "Magic" that came out the year before. And other than Ritchie's solo, it barely feels like a Rainbow song. To me anyway.

Steven: Yes, this is by a songwriter by the name of Brian Moran. I believe Ritchie was jamming with this guy, and whoever his band was at this time. And "Magic" was a song that they would play that Ritchie basically said, "I would love to do that. Can I take it away and put it on the album?" It's performed with an underplayed bombast that runs throughout, and Joe sounds really committed here. It's interesting that on the songs that are written by other people, Joe Lynn Turner sounds right on the money, maybe more so than the ones that were written within the band at certain points. It's not a standout, but it moves along nicely. As discussed, it was not a hit. But it does have a few high-end hooks, the high-register vocals of "I Surrender." You also get a "Whoa," with the end result being that it comes across as another showtune. With Joe, I imagine him stepping straight out of a West End musical into this band and not really missing a beat.

Martin: Side one of the original vinyl closes with "Vielleicht Das Nachster Zeit (Maybe Next Time)," an instrumental that is pretty much a classical music ballad with a bit of noise.

Rich: Yeah, I love this track. I remember as a kid taking this to a guitar lesson and asking my teacher to work this one out for me (laughs). Very subtle. There's a video called *Live Between the Eyes* and I think they play a snippet of this on it. And Ritchie is actually playing slide guitar here. It's hard to tell because he plays it very subtly. So he's a good slide player. He doesn't play a lot of it, but when he does, he uses it a little bit differently. It's not the sort of

Duane Allman-style bluesy slide. He uses it to get a smoothness in the melody, perhaps in the way that a classical musician would use a bow on a violin; maybe that's what he's aiming for. This is co-written between him and Don Airey, and the interplay and the chemistry between the two of them is great, especially in the middle section, where it builds toward a symphonic classical feel. And then Ritchie's solo is just pure classical; he plays around with the main melody of the track to begin the solo, and then just goes off into this really blistering bluesy run with some minor scale notes in there as well. Quite a few Ritchie signature licks by the end of it.

John: Agreed; there's some beautiful melodic playing from Ritchie here. It's interesting. I'm going to mention this when we do *Bent Out of Shape*, that when Ritchie has a chance to do an instrumental, he doesn't just go for shredding. Ritchie tends to go for melody and melodic lines. As Rich explained, another unique aspect of Ritchie's playing is his use of the slide. For those who don't know, a slide is a little metal tube that you slide up and down on the guitar neck. You can slide in and out of notes and it gives it a vocal quality. Other people use it in rock but nobody uses it the way Ritchie does. Ritchie uses it to play melodies.

And the chord progression in it is fantastic also, with the classical overtones to it. The main part of the song is in A minor and there's just this beautiful part where the A minor chord changes to an A major chord which sets up this D minor section with these beautiful, haunting keyboard lines from Don Airey. It reminds me a little bit of "Mr. Crowley," where he's sort of climbing up the keyboard line. It's the same key as "Mr. Crowley;" maybe that's why it reminds me of that. But I just love that part, that A major chord that sends us to that D minor section, and when Don Airey takes over with that keyboard line. It sort of takes it into a dark and epic feel in that one section. And then we modulate back to A minor and Ritchie takes it out again.

So this is why I love Ritchie Blackmore. Ritchie can shred with the best of them. Obviously there's tons of guys out there that can shred now. At this time in history, there weren't many people that shredded like Ritchie. So Ritchie can shred, but what very few people can do is play as melodic as Ritchie does in this particular song.

Jamie: With "Maybe Next Time," normally I would say a guitar piece like this is just a little interlude between tracks. I'd say it's a moment for the listener to take a breath, compose themselves and prepare for the next song, while also enjoying and appreciating the guitar techniques on display. But for this album, it's a highlight. So instead of being a breather between highlights, it becomes a highlight unto itself. If I had to rank all the songs on this album, it would probably be third or fourth. But it's cool in a way that it sounds like it belongs on a better album. There I go hating again. I know, I know; fans of this album are gonna be mad at me, but I have to be honest. But pacing-wise, I'm not so sure. After "Magic," I need a pick-me-up big time. But what we get is a laid-back guitar instrumental where the keyboards and guitar are melting into one another. There are some interesting guitar parts in the second half, but it's not what I needed after "Magic," particularly.

Steven: As was Ritchie's wont around this time, this is one of two guitar-led instrumentals on the album. And I'd say he sounds really invested in it. I do wonder, there are strange contradictions at this point, because we are trying to write a pop album. We're unabashed about that that. Ritchie stated at a time that he was moving the band into this realm. He'd changed the line-up and he was heading in a specific direction. And this is the album's non-ballad ballad. There's heart and soul in the playing from Ritchie, but I think it pinpoints a lack of understanding of exactly what the mission was. We seem to have missed what the actual picture was.

"Maybe Next Time" is serious; it's austere. It's almost lost among all of those big choruses and handclaps that we've got elsewhere. We're moving into something else entirely. It's not that it feels half-cocked. Not the song. But the album construction does. They'll do the same on *Bent Out of Shape*, where we have two guitar instrumentals as well, which are questionable in themselves. But you just wonder, why were these dropped in at these points on the album? I don't dislike it, but it doesn't make much sense to me. And this is how we choose to close out what has been a really upbeat and up-tempo side of music. Let's sing all these songs together and let's have a party, and yet they go out on what is a serious and conservative note.

Martin: You're right, Steven. Pretty funny. For an album that is a deliberate commercial play, there's not a single conventional ballad on it, with vocals. Like there's no proto-power ballad, right?

Steven: Yeah, absolutely. And they've got the right singer for that. But what we do is we replace that idea or slot with a song that has no singer at all. And that's a regular thing for Ritchie. He's done it consistently throughout Rainbow's catalogue, where he brings in guys that turn out to be top-rated singers and he doesn't let them sing on all the songs. Is it his territory being marked? I don't know. You can look for a deeper meaning, but either way, sometimes it works and this is one of those times where I don't think it does, necessarily.

Martin: Or maybe he's promoting the idea that serious virtuosos must have instrumentals on their albums.

Steven: But the serious virtuosos don't release "I Surrender" as a single. I don't think you can have both. I think if you're going to have a solo album, you can say, you know what? I'm going to cover all the bases. It's going to be out there and it's going to be this is who I am. I love this and I love that and I love this and I love that. That's fine. But *Difficult to Cure* is supposed to be the product of a band. The ethos here is catchy numbers, hooks a' plenty, big choruses. And then you go, "But I'm also a virtuoso." Well, I'm not really worried whether you are or not.

Martin: Excellent, Steven. I think that gets to the heart of what's wonky about this record. Side two opens with "Can't Happen Here," which, to my mind, represents the most cohesive song on the album, not to mention the fact that I can enjoy it without thinking about which base is being covered or which box is being ticked.

Jamie: "Can't Happen Here" is a nice bright spot on this album. It opens with a great riff and has a decent chorus. When you listen to these albums and you start to dissect them, you start to notice things you never noticed before. I talked earlier about how Ritchie's guitars sometimes blend into the keyboards to form one sound. But with this song, the keyboards are a piano or at least sound like a piano. So the guitar is much more prominent because they've created that sense of separation. Often Ritchie's guitar tone is in the same vicinity as the organ or synth sound. I swear he plays the guitar a lot like Jon Lord played the keyboards, or maybe it was vice versa. You really hear this on something like "Space Truckin'." And he brought that technique into Rainbow and whoever was playing the organ at that time. So that was a bit of an epiphany moment with this song, that I could be comfortable hearing both of them distinctly. I'll add this as well:

"Can't Happen Here" sounds like Bad Company, because it's rock 'n' rollsy but also because Joe can sound like Paul Rodgers at times.

Rich: I'd suggest that "Can't Happen Here" is also in that family of songs that utilize those "Burn"-type riffs. And there's a track on the Doogie White album, *Stranger in Us All*, called "Too Late for Tears," which I know Doogie flagged up to Ritchie and said, "Hang on, this sounds a bit like 'Can't Happen Here.'" And Ritchie said something like, "Well, that was one of mine anyway."

Again, as an indication of how big Rainbow were at the time, the big pop station in Britain at the time was Radio One, and I remember during the summer holidays going on a day trip somewhere with me parents, sat in the backseat of the car, and in amongst whatever was in the charts at the time, "Can't Happen Here" was played on daytime radio. Even though it's got enough of that old-school Deep Purple and old-school Rainbow vibe to it, Roger's produced it with the harmonies and the strong melodies and just the general overall polish that it could fit on daytime radio. And quite clever lyric as well, with the "contaminated fish and microchips" wordplay from Roger. Quite different for a band in that era, and certainly for Rainbow. They also did a proper video for "Can't Happen Here." It's quite political, with live performance mixed in with news and current events clips, quite a fast-moving jump-cut sort of vibe, which helped illustrate the lyrics.

As for the guitars, this is something which I think weakens some of the tracks. Because he plays like between… on "Long Live Rock 'n' Roll" he does it too. It's this rhythm technique where he doesn't play the full chord. He plays like between the low and high octave. And he's doing a faster version of that here. Sometimes you just wish he'd play a power chord, like the full chord and fill it out more. Because it sounds a little thin. It doesn't undermine this track particularly, but I think it does more so on "Kill the King." If you listen to the version that Steel Dragon did for the soundtrack of *Rock Star*, it's got a lot more bite to it. That riff is great, but under the verse it would have more power if he didn't revert to that single note thing.

John: "Can't Happen Here" is a Blackmore/Glover number with a "Long Live Rock 'n' Roll" feel to it, a bluesy shuffle vibe, although fairly straight. As Rich explained, we get the classic Blackmore thing in the verse, where he's playing the root in the octave, accenting the notes, hitting single notes. "People out of work, but there's people on the moon/Looking for the future." There are lines here that are funny but also dark. I like the arpeggios that bring the guitar solo in, which is nice and bluesy. It's just a fun one for me. It seems like Ritchie always likes to have sort of a shuffly, bluesy rock number on his records, and this occupies that space.

Steven: Talking about album construction, we opened side one with a big, unforgettable blast and we repeat the process on side two. What a chorus. This is a proper, live singalong. I love the urgency. It just flies along at full pelt. There's no mucking about here. The drums are a little more restrained, with fewer fills, but that economy works. It allows the song to pack a real punch. It's quite simple stuff but it sticks in your mind. I suppose it's worth commenting on the lyrics of this song. Not all the lyrics on this album are profound or overly exciting, but this is ahead of its time, really. We're covering pollution, we're covering corporate greed, wealth being hidden in certain places and being held by certain individuals and not enough for the people. There's inequality, the arms race, conflicts in general. It's quite galling to think this was written in the eighties because it's as relevant today as it was forty-odd years ago. That's depressing in itself. But it's really insightful, and Rainbow isn't necessarily renowned for that.

Martin: There's a lot of Deep Purple barroom chemistry to this song. It sounds like an Ian Gillan-era Deep Purple song, right?

Steven: It even sounds like an Ian Gillan lyric, in that sense too. I quite like it when you get that contradiction or dichotomy. It's a great upbeat song, and then we're all going to go "Can't happen here!" It's a good-time, drinking, sort of rock 'n' roll song and we're all upbeat and we're smiling, but if you read the lyric, it's not that at all. That's a juxtaposition I like, personally.

Martin: I pointed to the cohesiveness of "Can't Happen Here," although after that cool explanation from you focussing on the lyrics, I guess it's more pointedly a cohesion of the music. But the next one, "Freedom Fighter," has always bothered me for its wild mood swing between its sort of pomp rock verse and its sinister heavy metal chorus.

Steven: Yeah, I'm not a massive fan of "Freedom Fighter." I do like the album, but there's only nine tracks on it, and two are written by people outside the band and two are instrumentals. One of those leans heavily to Beethoven's "Ninth" for inspiration. The fact that we've got original songs like "Freedom Fighter" that run out of steam a little bit, it really doesn't seem, in my opinion, that a ginormous amount of effort was put into the songwriting (laughs). You do have to wonder how much they had prepared and ready.

Because "Freedom Fighter," it's happy and it's poppy and it's all a bit throwaway. And then you get to the chorus and the guitar riff sounds like it's made an escape from *Rising*. It doesn't really belong on this album. It's all mean and moody and much deeper in feel. And it's not even what this song's verse and lyric are doing, never mind what the rest of the album's doing. And don't get me wrong, Ritchie turns in a great solo, but it actually feels like it's been tacked onto the song. Because they had it and they didn't want to waste it. So ironically it's actually a waste of a solo. The solo feels like it was lifted from somewhere and placed in here. And I suppose you could argue in parallel that the chorus doesn't seem like it was written for the same song as the verses.

Rich: As far as I'm concerned, "Freedom Fighter" is in a similar poppy vein to "Magic," although it's one of the band's own tracks. Joe's had a hand in writing this and I think it works well. It's got a triplet rhythm over a 4/4 beat, not a Maiden gallop but it's using the same trick of playing like a triplet rhythm. The lyrics are quite intelligent. They show how far we've come from the Ronnie era, with Ronnie's fantasy side of things, which I love. But now we're two albums later and Rainbow is singing about contemporary issues and political things on "Can't Happen Here" and "Freedom Fighter." Great melodies in the verse, really heavy chorus and the middle eight section is really good as well, with like a call-and-response between Joe and the backing vocals. So yeah, I like this one.

John: Blackmore, Glover and Turner here on the writing credits. The opening B minor riff really gives me Thin Lizzy vibes—I don't know, it just makes me think of Thin Lizzy. So we start off in a minor key and then the verse moves up to a major key, the relative major of B minor, which is D major here. So that's why the verse has this uplifting effect.

Martin: They lose the gravitas that's been conjured, but then the clouds sort of part.

John: Yes, exactly. We lose the heaviness. The whole thing about this album in general is that they don't want to go too heavy. Or they only want to give it to you in small doses and then it's over to these more melodic but still hard rock-sounding things. So that's what we get in the verse. Honestly, this one falls a bit flat for me. It's a little bit stock, but I do like the heaviness of that main riff. I also like the guitar solo, where we drop down to F sharp minor. It adds back some darkness to the song, for me, with Ritchie doing these crazy bends and whammy bar things which I think are pretty cool.

Jamie: "Freedom Fighter" sounds very Broadway-like to me. I picture Joe Lynn Turner singing this on stage with all sorts of dancers around him. I imagine them making a video where there are dancers that Joe is trying to recruit as freedom fighters. Joe is standing on a little, like, mini-hill and they're below him dancing. He's reaching his hand out and they're coming up on the hill as they get recruited and fireworks are going on behind them.

But I've also heard some people say this sounds like a Kansas song. I see that too and can understand connecting Joe with Steve Walsh. As for the lyrics, although there are some smart lines, they can get cringy too. "You can't take my freedom/You know it is my right/ If you try and stop me/I'm going to fight/With all my might." That rhyming there is pretty darn simple. Oh my goodness gracious; not good at all.

But yeah, it sounds like something off *The Elder* by Kiss. And I know a lot of people like *The Elder*, but I'm sorry; that's not a compliment coming from me. This sounds like it should be part of a rock opera, but an off-off-off-Broadway production. Like out in the East River. That's how off-Broadway. People would need binoculars to see what's happening on the little floating stage. "I see the freedom fighters out there, honey."

Martin: That sounds more like the story of the next song, "Midtown Tunnel Vision." But seriously folks, I never liked this song. Then again, I don't like "Mistreated" either.

Jamie: Yeah, "Midtown Tunnel Vision" is down and dirty, bluesy, almost a little doomy. But Joe Lynn Turner is singing his heart out and Ritchie is doing some damn fine guitar work. This might sound odd, but it's probably my favourite track, but at the same time, the album's least memorable. But given the fact that I remember some of these songs for the wrong reasons, that's probably a good thing. And when I say least memorable, It isn't striving too, too hard to have a hook. Nothing feels forced from a songwriting point of view. It's not trying to make itself dance, nor is it a singalong-type song. It's not trying to be cute and it's not trying to be a hit on the radio. It's just being nasty and ballsy. This album needed more of this. Because when they tried too hard to produce a hit on this album, they fall flat on their face.

Rich: When I interviewed Joe, he picked this one out as one of his favourite deep cuts from his time with Rainbow. He was quite keen to stress the lesser-known tracks on the albums he did. It's got what I would call the Hendrix chord on it, the chord on "Foxy Lady." I'm not sure what key this song is in, but I looked this up, because a lot of guitar players call it the Hendrix chord. It's that high bit, the bit Garth dances to on *Wayne's World*. It's odd-sounding and funky. Apparently, when Hendrix plays it, it's E seventh, sharp ninth. And it sounds like Ritchie is playing the same chord, like a seventh sharp ninth chord. I'm not sure if it's in the same key, but it's very much that Hendrix thing. And at the beginning, before the band comes in, Joe says "Comin' to get ya," which is obviously from "Foxy Lady." That's a little vocal lift from Jimi there.

John: "Midtown Tunnel Vision" is another Blackmore/Glover/Turner tune. As Rich explained, that's the Jimi Hendrix chord at the beginning, which is this E seven sharp nine chord that he used all the time, like in "Purple Haze." So you get these bluesy riffs here, with Blackmore playing off of this Jimi Hendrix chord. It's got a nice laid-back feel to it, the song in general, but it's pretty heavy too. What I find interesting is it's a very bluesy song, but right at the end of the guitar solo, he throws in a little bit of "Snake Charmer" on us, a couple of notes that dive into that modal thing he does. Pretty cool that he was able to sneak a little "Snake Charmer" into basically a bluesy thing. I do dig, at the end of the song, this sort of flanging chorus thing that takes the song out. I'd like to think that's deliberate, like they are painting the picture of driving through a tunnel.

Steven: Yes, with "Midtown Tunnel Vision," we slide off into deep, bluesy, English territory. But we've got a great singer here who unfortunately feels absolutely lost, I think. You asked what type of singer Joe is. Can he bring the Lou Gramm? Can he sing the higher parts and can he give you emotion and theatrical appeal? He cannot do gritty and dirty. As his voice evolves and gets older he can. But wow, the gritty and dirty parts on this song, that's not something he should get involved with. He sounds out of character and, pardon the pun, all bent out of shape on it. I imagine Roger or Ritchie are going, "Joe, try it this way. We need this on here. This song requires that. Imagine Ronnie, he could have done this here."

Joe Lynn Turner is not that singer. He's a fantastic singer. I love some of his vocals on this album, but he should play to his strengths. This type of delivery is not his strength. But the instrumental section on here, that's another example of Rainbow moving into that AOR territory. They hadn't gone all-in. The singles make me think they have, but the guitar work on here, you can imagine it on *Long Love Rock 'n' Roll* or *Rising*. And you could imagine Graham Bonnet singing this song. We still don't quite know where we are. The song is okay, but this album is beginning to peter out now. It really is losing a lot of steam.

Martin: Unfortunately that's the way I see it too, with the last selection, "Difficult to Cure." I'm just not an instrumental guy and I actually argued with Ritchie about it once, and he won the argument with, "Instrumental music—imagine that." That's why they pay him the big bucks (laughs).

Rich: Oh man, that's great (laughs). Yeah, when bands go classical like this, it can be cheesy or it can be great. Nobody's going to be surprised by Rainbow doing something like this at this point, but it's more elaborate than anything they've done before. But it does bear out what Ritchie has always said about having classical influence on his own riffs. If you listen to the riffs in the middle of this, when it goes into the darker minor key section, it's very much in a Rainbow style. And it's very well arranged with the band and the instrumentation.

Around the same time, Sky—I don't know if they were big in Canada and America—but they did a version of "Toccata" by Bach. And they were doing a very, very similar thing. Not quite as heavy. Sky were a band of classical session guys. I remember a guy called

Herbie Flowers. But yeah, they used to do these rocked-up versions of classical tracks and they had quite a big hit with this "Toccata" by Bach about a year before. So that would have been contemporary. I'm not saying that Ritchie was jumping on the bandwagon, but Sky had scored a big chart hit with that, with platinum albums in the UK. So around that time, something like this was a smart move because there was a precedent for it.

And it doesn't come across as a big, lumbering, awkward fusion of rock and classical that doesn't work. It's very light on its feet and it's a good match. I think Roger is very much the secret weapon on this album. His bass playing is so melodic and tasteful, and he never overplays. There's some great syncopation or synchronicity between him and Bobby Rondinelli on this. And Ritchie solos really good; he keeps within the theme of the track. Again, it's just a really great fit. So the album's bookended at either side. You've got the classical-influenced pop or pop rock of "I Surrender" and now we've got a full-blown classical rock track at the end.

John: Good stuff. "Difficult to Cure" is based off of Beethoven's "Ninth Symphony," Beethoven's final symphony, mostly based off of the final movement, the "Presto" movement. In fact, the opening lick that Blackmore plays, the opening melody, is straight-up lifted off of the opening of the fourth "Presto" movement from Beethoven's symphony. The little thing that Ritchie's playing is in A minor and then the drums build up and we drop to F major for the "Ode to Joy" melody. In the original Beethoven symphony, there's a choir and everything, and it's very triumphant-sounding and happy-sounding and that's what you get here.

It's interesting that they modulate this. They play the melody, the "Ode to Joy" medley and then it modulates up to A major, an unrelated key to F major. But it gives it an uplifting feel. Ritchie does this very well with his riffing, with these modulations, to give songs either a lifting or a dropping feel.

Eventually we find our way to D minor for the keyboard solo, which takes a bluesy approach, which is interesting because everything's been very classical up to this point. But we get a really bluesy Jon Lord-style keyboard solo here. I have to admit that there's some sound in there I can't identify. I don't know if it's a sequencer, but it's a "giga-giga-giga" sound that I find slightly annoying, that runs through parts of this song.

Eventually, we arrive back to F major for the "Ode to Joy" medley, finally landing in D major, the original key that Beethoven wrote "Ode to Joy" in. I don't know if that was intentional or not (laughs), but when they play the melody for the last time, it's in the original key that Beethoven did it in. Ritchie gets to go crazy here at his solo. I forgot to mention this earlier, but his solo drops down to F sharp minor, a very guitar solo key. Ritchie wants it to be in a minor key so he can go crazy and shred and everything. And very classical-sounding too. There's also all these little nods to various licks and melodies in the "Ninth Symphony" that Ritchie throws into his solo.

Then at the end, we get this big drum fill and everything sort of comes crashing down and there's this laughing sound, a repeating laughing thing. Which almost makes me think that, okay, hey, they realized that this whole thing was over-the-top and sort of crazy, and even they're having a laugh. They're not taking themselves too seriously here with this particular song.

Jamie: Some might like that they get to hear Ritchie plays something like this. And they might think it's well done. Okay, I get it. I just wish they didn't do it. Or I just wish it wasn't on this album. The main issue I have with this is that the signature melody reminds me of Christmas. And if I'm listening to an album at any time of the year other than December and a song reminds me a Christmas, it's an instant skip for me.

Also, we've all heard Beethoven's "Ninth" a thousand times, even though we don't know what it's called when we're hearing it. Who keeps track of all those numbers? Beethoven's fifth, ninth, sixth—I don't. But we've heard it in commercials and cartoons and movies. We've heard it our whole life. So it becomes very bland-sounding to our ears, even when it's being played by Ritchie Blackmore and Rainbow. It's like if they just remade "Happy Birthday." Plus it does feel a little tacked-on. It feels like the album originally had eight tracks and then was reissued recently with this bonus ninth track on it.

Steven: With 2024 hindsight, closing a chart-chasing album out with another ode to Beethoven is just bonkers (laughs). And yet, you get past the two-minute mark, and I can't help but marvel at just how much fun the band is having. And that's not always a theme of across this album. The performances are tight and everyone is excellent on this album but they don't always have an awful lot to do. I've barely spoken about the rhythm section because it doesn't really have much to do on *Difficult to Cure* other than hold it all together.

But Roger Glover and Bobby Rondinelli are absolutely bounding along here and Ritchie is just living out his fantasies. You get that mid-song break, and Don Airey, who has been making these mid-eighties noises up to this point, has suddenly found his Hammond organ. And before you know it, it's like a 30-year-earlier audition for Deep Purple (laughs). You listen to it and you go, wow, did a certain Mr. Lord walk into this session and go, "I'll have a shot. Can I have a go now?" The second half of this track plays like vintage Purple and it's really impressive. You can't but help whack the volume up—it's exciting. By the way, I can understand what Rich said about Sky. I can see that, because they were huge for a period of time. And I do have those albums here. I can't say I listen to them particularly.

Martin: But Ritchie owned that territory anyways, already. It doesn't sound out-of-place, or that he's copying another band's successful formula.

Steven: Absolutely. I don't necessarily think that Ritchie was looking elsewhere for those kinds of inspirations because he always had them. You just have to go right back to the start of Deep Purple. And much of it was Jon Lord as well, but they did *Concerto for Group and Orchestra*. That classical bedrock is in that band all the way through.

I know it's not this album, but more successful is "Snowman," from *Bent Out of Shape*. I don't know if *The Snowman*, the film from 1982 was a thing outside of the UK. It's a Raymond Briggs book, music by Howard Blake. I was ten-years-old when *Bent Out of Shape* came out. Your friends would come around and they weren't having hard rock. There'd never been a great massive hard rock scene in the UK. I always lament a little bit when you guys talk about being with your friends and talking about these albums. We had a very small group of people who were interested in any of this stuff.

So my friends would come over and I'd and go, "I've got a song to play you," and I'd put on "Snowman." And they'd recognize it as the song from the program. We'd listen to and after two minutes we'd all go, "Er, can we turn it off now?" Because Ritchie had started to play! It's not what people wanted. People didn't want him to reinterpret what was a respected piece of music known from a kids film. It was a strange move. And as a song or a piece of music on that *Bent Out of Shape* album, it actually makes me disconnect with it. It has a different connotation for me. We still get *The Snowman* on the telly here every Christmas. It's a staple. It's definitely not a rock 'n' roll mainstay (laughs).

It's funny; I don't know why, but *Bent Out of Shape* has always been the one that lacked for one or two killer songs. I seem to have more love for this one, *Difficult to Cure*, than most people, and less love for *Bent Out of Shape* than most people. It's an album that I put on and I never quite find my way in. I don't dislike any of it, but I'm never really overly excited by very much of it. I almost get the feeling that Ritchie is going, "I'm a bit bored with this now."

Martin: Interesting. Now you guys have got me wanting to take a second look at "Difficult to Cure." Okay, does anybody have any closing comments? I've always had it in for this album. It seems like they are ticking the boxes of Rainbow styles and then turning in a middling song to cover off each example or stylistic placeholder, sort of thing.

Rich: Totally, yeah, there's a lot of variety in there and I can see that that could be polarizing. I enjoyed *Difficult to Cure* at the time when I bought the album. I enjoyed the fact there were so many different moods on it. But I think that could work against it. I definitely see what you're saying. For someone who's been listening to the band for longer, it could definitely feel that way, especially after *Down to Earth*. It's not exactly formulaic, but definitely, we have this structure and it's following a pattern.

They're all very different from each other on this album and I wonder if that's somewhat by dint of the fact that Joe is such a versatile singer. He really can do anything. For example, remember those silly rumours that there was a Bon Scott version of *Back in Black*? That turned out to be complete BS, but it had sort of flared up again because of a tribute album version of "Back in Black" sung by Joe. I actually interviewed Joe about this for a *Record Collector* special on AC/DC, and he said he could always sing like that. He just made his name doing something different. And there's the video of it on YouTube, with people swearing that's Bon Scott. And it's from an AC/DC tribute album called *Thunderstruck*. It's his job. So with a singer like that, who can turn his voice into anything, I wonder if maybe Rainbow went a bit too far for some people.

Jamie: I doubt *Difficult to Cure* is an album I'll play that often in the future because it doesn't even have that one big hit like "Stone Cold" to draw me back to it. Now look, I know every album, no matter how crappy it is, has that group of people that think it's a misunderstood classic. But if you did a poll for worst Rainbow album, you're either going to get *Stranger in Us All* or this one. Okay, granted, maybe *Bent Out of Shape* as well. *Difficult to Cure* does give me a certain kind of emotion, but not the kind of emotion they were hoping for. Frustration is that an emotion. And the production is thin, which doesn't help the songs whatsoever. I hate to hate on it. Some people love this album and God bless them.

Steven: All I know, as I say, is that I'm looking at this material, and the instrumentals and covers… almost half that album is taken up with those four songs. And then I get to an original, and I'm thinking, were they really careful enough about this song when they were constructing it? That's my issue with the Joe Lynn Turner era. It's not whether it's popular or commercial. I come from an AOR/melodic rock mindset. I'm happy in that world. But you gotta mean it. You gotta go all-in. And *Difficult to Cure* does not go all-in on that. It goes all-in in places, but it's frightened of it. It's almost frightened of what it's become.

Martin: Like I say, it's a smorgasbord of expected styles.

Steven: Yeah, absolutely; very much so. It feels like an album made by committee. And that doesn't make it a bad album, but it definitely makes certain songs or parts on them very questionable. Yeah, and I think one of the main issues with *Difficult to Cure* is not necessarily that it's got X amount of good, bad or indifferent songs on it, but that it doesn't really hang together as a journey from start to end. This is a collection of songs, not an album.

And that last instrumental, "Difficult to Cure," sums up what a confused album it has become. You've got bonafide chart-chasing singles, a couple of instrumentals, nods to Beethoven all over the place, a few early Rainbow passages and a song that could have come off a Deep Purple album. I don't really dislike anything on here; this used to be my go-to Rainbow album. When I was young and really heavily into melodic rock and AOR, this was my go-to Rainbow album. But I must admit that with a lot of more years under the belt, as an album, it just doesn't hang together at all.

As individual songs, I like quite a lot of this. I'll go beyond that— there are individual songs that are really top-notch. As an album, nobody really seemed to know where we were going. And I think that speaks to the next two as well. We're still always answering questions that didn't even need to be asked, right up to the end of the Joe Lynn Turner era.

RAINBOW
STRAIGHT BETWEEN THE EYES
RAINBOW
Straight Between The Eyes
mercury
Manufactured and Marketed by
PolyGram Records™

RAIN BOW
RAINBOW
STRAIGHT BETWEEN THE EYES
DIRECT MASTER
60

STRAIGHT BETWEEN THE EYES

June 10, 1982
Mercury SRM-1-4041
Produced by Roger Glover
Engineered by Rick Blagona; assisted by Robbie Whelan
Personnel: Joe Lynn Turner – vocals, Ritchie Blackmore – guitars, Roger Glover – bass, David Rosenthal – keyboards, Bobby Rondinelli – drums

Side 1
1. Death Alley Driver (Blackmore, Turner) 4:36
2. Stone Cold (Blackmore, Turner, Glover) 5:15
3. Bring on the Night (Dream Chaser) (Blackmore, Turner, Glover) 4:02
4. Tite Squeeze (Blackmore, Turner, Glover) 3:15
5. Tearin' Out My Heart (Blackmore, Turner, Glover) 4:00

Side 2
1. Power (Blackmore, Turner, Glover) 4:23
2. Miss Mistreated (Blackmore, Turner, Rosenthal) 4:25
3. Rock Fever (Blackmore, Turner) 3:40
4. Eyes of Fire (Blackmore, Turner, Rondinelli) 6:41

RAINBOW
STRAIGHT BETWEEN THE EYES

A *Straight Between the Eyes* Timeline

December 1981. Rainbow, with David Rosenthal in place of Don Airey, set up at Le Studio in Morin Heights, Quebec, Canada to record what will become the band's sixth album.

December 17, 1981. *The Best of Rainbow* is certified gold in the UK.

March 26, 1982. "Stone Cold," backed with "Rock Fever," is issued as the advance single from Rainbow's forthcoming sixth album. It reaches No.34 on the UK charts and No.40 on the Billboard 200.

April 14, 1982. Rainbow issue *Straight Between the Eyes*, their second album featuring Joe Lynn Turner on vocals. The album reaches No.5 on the UK charts and No.30 in America.

April 28, 1982. *Straight Between the Eyes* is certified silver in the UK.

August 18, 1982. Rainbow play San Antonio, Texas, with the show being documented on the band's commercial video release, *Live Between the Eyes*, issued in February the following year. Saxon is support on the bill, with Riot joining them the following night in Dallas.

May 11 – August 1982. Rainbow tour the US and Canada promoting *Straight Between the Eyes*, support coming from Iron Maiden, later, UFO and Riot, and down the stretch, mostly Scorpions.

October 12 – October 22, 1982. Rainbow tour Japan, followed by an extensive European leg which runs from Oct. 29 through Dec. 1, with support coming from Girlschool.

Rainbow
STEREO CD 45
7DM 0044 ¥700
レインボー
SIDE 2 RAINBOW ROCK FEVER
STONE COLD

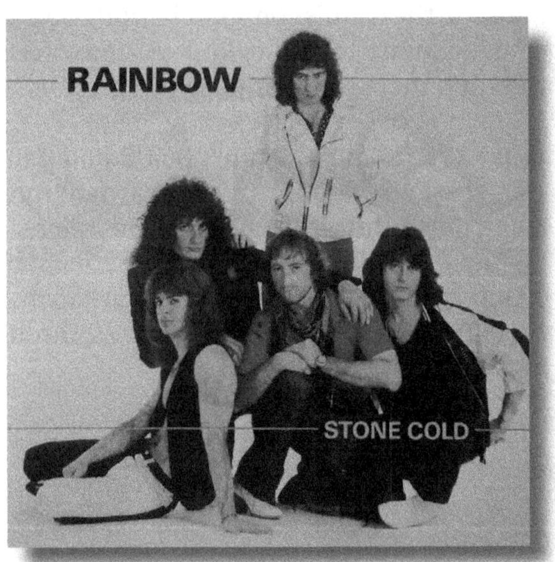

RAINBOW
STONE COLD

Martin talks to Tim Durling, Peter Jones, Peter Kerr and Luis Nasser about *Straight Between the Eyes.*

Martin Popoff: Back for the attack, Rainbow delivers a second album of the Joe Lynn Turner era. What are your general impressions, first of all?

Tim Durling: I think that *Straight Between the Eyes* is a vast improvement over *Difficult to Cure*. The songs, on the whole, are better, the recording's a little better and it just seems like they're starting to gel. I've just always preferred *Straight Between the Eyes*. I see *Difficult to Cure* as a test-run for that line-up.

Martin: Pretty cool that it was recorded at Le Studio.

Tim: Yeah. I've read Joe Lynn Turner talk about that, and seeing The Police. I don't know if he mentioned seeing the Rush guys there. But it's interesting because they're such a European band; you wonder how they ended up in Quebec making an album.

Martin: And what is Ritchie's role as a guitarist in rock history? And to what degree has that shifted now?

Tim: When he said he wanted to get on the radio, he meant it, because this album is dominated by melody more so than riffs, for the most part. You can tell that the directive was we want hooks, we want something to catch somebody's ear every so many bars. To some extent, he only comes out for solos.

Peter Jones: I will say categorically that I am a fan of the Joe Lynn Turner era. But with this disclaimer: it's got really good peaks but it's got some really low valleys too, and not much lives in the middle. It's either a strong track or not. Ritchie's direction here is where he always intended to go, even if his timing might have been a little out of whack. Going into '82, maybe the heavier material from the earlier records would have been better suited given the New Wave of British Heavy Metal and everything. It is what it is. We've got the established band of Blackmore, Turner, Glover and Rondinelli and David Rosenthal is now on keys. It's a good rock 'n' roll record.

Peter Kerr: *Straight Between the Eyes* is much more, what we call in Australia, American-orientated rock—that's what AOR means over here, oddly enough. But it's the same thing, your Styx and Foreigner and other corporate rock. But in the States, you call it album-oriented rock.

Martin: Or adult-oriented rock!

Peter Kerr: That's right (laughs). In any event, Ritchie is wanting to push the barriers of breaking through into the charts. *Difficult to Cure* had a commercial breakthrough in the UK with "I Surrender" going to No.3. And some of the other singles started to chart and they were getting moderate radio airplay in America. So it was a full-on assault. He really wanted to conquer America; that was the modus operandi of this album.

Roger Glover's production is meat-and-potatoes. I don't think there's anything fancy. Ritchie and the vocals of Joe Lynn Turner are the two elements in the production that are pushed to the fore. It's very tailored to being played on radio. The riffage is simpler and Ritchie's guitar playing is very much contained. He's not going as wild as he did in the past. He's almost straitjacketed, although it's by choice. Let's say he's tailoring it in service of the song, not the other way around.

Luis Nasser: This particular album had Roger Glover and Ritchie Blackmore writing some really good stuff, and *Difficult to Cure* and *Bent Out of Shape*, less so. They got the blend right for this one. I speak to you as somebody who was a kid when it came out, and when I bought it, I could not stop playing it. So it has a special place in my heart, because it is part of my musical DNA growing up. I didn't even mind that it wasn't like a Dio album, because it's just such a good hard rock album.

I really like David Rosenthal on keyboards. I think that that guy is a musical master that people often overlook. He worked with Happy the Man and The Muse Awakens. I believe he is now the music director for Billy Joel. The dude is a phenomenal musician and arranger and just great all-around. What he brought to this record was something difficult to pull off. He used some of the best-sounding keyboards of the era and managed to pass on the worst of the technology. There is no Velveeta—he has good taste. He was able to tweak them and make them sound right, even today. As I was studying up on this album, it struck me how good the keyboard sounds are, and how bad they could have been. Bobby Rondinelli does his best Cozy impression. He's attempting to play through the drum like Cozy; he's trying to propel the songs forward like Cozy did. He doesn't sound like a Cozy, but he provides the same kind of propulsion. I enjoy this album immensely.

Martin: That's quite a shock of an album cover, isn't it?

Tim: Yeah, it's pretty silly. One of my biggest complaints is that I'd like to see them use the actual Rainbow logo, instead of just this block Arial or Helvetica font. And the illustration makes the album look heavier than it actually is. But in terms of getting attention in the record rack, it does the trick. Maybe something a little classier would have been in order.

Peter Jones: It's one of the ugliest album covers I've ever seen. The logo stinks. It's like, what's the point? I get it, metaphorically, but it's pretty ugly. After *Rising*, the quality of the album covers dropped pretty substantially throughout the rest of their career.

Peter Kerr: It's up there with *Abominog* by Uriah Heep as a bit of a sheep in wolf's clothing. You think, wow, this is going to be something powerful, but the music is completely different to the image in the sense that it's melodic and considerably radio-friendly. It's the polar opposite.

And yet I like it! In a day and age when Rainbow were dead and not represented in record stores, at least here in Australia, if you're a rock fan and you see that image, you would gravitate to it. And it's basically about how Jeff Beck described Jimi Hendrix to Ritchie Blackmore. He said, "He gets you straight between the eyes." So Ritchie probably recalled that, maybe described it to the artist and you got that image. I think it's great. It hooks you in.

Luis: As a kid, that cover was the reason I bought the record. As an adult, I'm not a big fan. But as a kid, I thought it was the greatest thing ever. Rainbow never came to Mexico when they were touring in those years, but when I saw videos of those live shows, and they had the actual eyes on stage with the lights, I thought that was the greatest thing ever. And *Straight Between the Eyes*, as both a cover and a title, it also makes a promise that I think the record pretty much delivers, which is that it's supposed to blow your mind with guitar, right? That's basically what I get from it.

Martin: What are your thoughts about the delivery of these songs from a sonic standpoint, the production? I always saw it as more powerful and fuller of range than the last one, but not recorded particularly heavy metal, which is not a bad thing.

Tim: I agree that it's a lot better than *Difficult to Cure*, which is almost clanky-sounding, low-budget. This is a good, full-bodied recording, but like you say, not heavy in the least. There's a sort of a blanket thrown over everything. And then with *Bent Out of Shape*, they throw two blankets over everything. But it was perfect for radio at the time. The frequencies were such that nobody would be turned off by too many jagged edges. And yet it doesn't sound particularly pop either. It doesn't sound dated, it sounds like real drums, it's analog and yet competitive. When I think about this production compared to, say, Martin Birch's at the time for Whitesnake, if we're going to keep it in the Deep Purple family, this is easier on the ears. It would sound better on FM radio than the Whitesnake productions from the same time.

Martin: It reminds me of the way that Pat Travers complains about *Heat on the Street*, or the Max Webster guys—or at least the fans—complain about the last Max Webster album with Jack Richardson, *Universal Juveniles*. It's like hi-fidelity and lush with more than adequate bass and treble, and yet not aggressive.

Peter Jones: It's produced by Roger Glover. Mixing is a very, very specific art, and can really make or break a recording. And the reason I say that, a lot of times back in the day when people were making pre-mixed tapes, pre-mastering tapes, you're like, well, let's check the mix. Well, what would you do? You'd listen to it in your car, you'd listen to it in your stereo at home, you'd go to as many different environments as you could to hear how that mix translates in different environments.

Okay, this album, and the ones you mentioned, especially the Max Webster, is not an album that sounds good at low volumes. All of the low end of this disappears. There is no foundation to it. And I realized that when I was listening last night, before I put my headphones on, I'm like, okay, I'll put my headphones on and put a little more juice in. And it just absolutely exploded in sonic spectrum—it woke up. And I'm like okay, this needs some power. And once it's given power, it's a very rich and very comfortable sounding record. Nothing's harsh, nothing's out of balance, all the instruments are in their spots and even the panning is nice. But just do not listen to this at lower, everyday volume, because it'll just suck all the low end out and sound really thin and wimpy. So I agree with you completely.

Martin: Nicely put. And *Difficult to Cure* is quite midrangy and tight, right?

Peter Jones: Yeah, it's definitely got more aggressive upper mids and lower highs on it than this does. This has—and you used the word— it's more lush. It's rich and opulent, if you will, more foundationally secure. *Difficult to Cure* might sound better in a car where you're not really getting a lot of low end unless you've got a really good quality system. But on a home hi-fi, it's going to sound comparatively brittle, sharper.

Luis: Yes, agreed, *Straight Between the Eyes* doesn't have the same cut to it. More frequencies are there, but they're trying to go for that polish for AOR radio. It's still Ritchie Blackmore trying to get a hit. I don't know what happened to that guy. Maybe at some point he decided that the success he had with Deep Purple wasn't enough and that he wanted to make more money and have the charting songs. So he put aside that hard rock edge, precisely what you're saying there. It's a quintessential early to mid-eighties album to me. It's typical of the era but, lucky for us, before things got silly.

Martin: All right, the album opens with a barn-burner called "Death Alley Driver." Is it unanimous that this is one of the high watermarks of the JLT era?

Peter Kerr: Definitely. Rainbow, and Deep Purple have always had a knack for doing a cracker of an opening track. So this is a really banger. It's Rainbow's version of "Highway Star," Purple upgraded for the eighties. It's got all the classic elements, including a Baroque little keyboard flourish (laughs). And incidentally, I've got to point out, Ritchie was always looking for his next Jon Lord, and David Rosenthal fits that bill here. Although when I interviewed Bob

Daisley, he told me that Ritchie treated his keyboardists very badly. Still, I feel like David Rosenthal is the closest that he ever got to Jon Lord, and he definitely shines on this particular track. It's a rollicking track, sort of, "Here we are—this is Rainbow." It had an interesting film clip. It begins with Joe playing a video game, and then he's on a motorcycle being chased by an antique car. Ritchie is in the back of the car, sort of satirizing or living up to his image as the Man in Black. It had a little bit of impact at MTV. But, look, if you want a furious, rubber-burning album-opener, this is the track for you.

Tim: Yeah, it's a great rocker and a good way to start the album. Joe claims the song was written about this highway in New Jersey called Highway 99, which Bruce Springsteen also wrote about, where it was a known spot for drug deals to go down. And he claims that a buddy of his took him for a drive and didn't tell him what was going on and he's like, "Don't ever take me there again." It's probably the heaviest thing on the album and maybe a bit of a red herring, because it really doesn't represent what's to come. But maybe it was a way to ease the old-school fans in. It's telling the guys that had been hanging on from the Dio years or even the *Down to Earth* years, "Hey, we're still Rainbow; we're still a hard rock band. It's going to be all right." I really like it. It's got some good guitar/keyboard interplay. Joe's equally good singing a fast rocker like this as he is singing a ballad.

Peter Jones: As far as an opening track goes, Ritchie's learned his lesson from the previous album. Here we've got a roadrunner. "Death Valley Driver" is introduced with driving, chunky, up-tempo guitar with strong drum support from Bobby. It's even got a lot of the same syncopations and accentuations as "Highway Star." So again, Ritchie is copying from Ritchie. Joe Lynn Turner comes in and I feel like his voice suits this just fine. The lyrics are pretty decent; it's another song about cars and racing and driving fast. Ritchie's guitar is thick, the drums are heavy and the production sounds good, even if the keyboards during the verse are non-existent. It's really just bass, drums and guitar.

When they transition into the end of the first chorus, Rondinelli fires off one of the great drum fills of all drum fills, with some really great choked high-hats right into the chorus. That one's a keeper— good one, Bobby. I stole that one a million times. It's very Cozy-like, and that's an interesting paradox because there's a running joke. Cozy used to wonder where Bobby would go next. Because Bobby followed him in Rainbow and he also followed him in Black Sabbath. The keyboards finally take over and it's heavy synth, although at first it's more just interesting noises before it settles into some actual playing of licks. But it's an aggressive track. It's got a lot of energy, it's propulsive and I love the way it ends: super-tight, concise, bam, 4:42—perfect.

Luis: "Death Alley Driver" is a much better opening track than "All Night Long" or "I Surrender." It just takes off! Ian Gillan would have sounded great on this. Perhaps my only critique is that it makes the album a bit front-loaded. But that's a minor quibble. That's me as an adult and a musician overthinking things, right? You always wonder what it would sound like if you got to re-sequence it. But it is what it is, which is a product of its time.

Even though David Rosenthal is a phenomenal musician, the keyboard sounds firmly place it in the early eighties but yet tastefully. Rosenthal is only too eager to inject some of his own personality through his choice of organ and keyboard patches. It's actually commendable that it does not have a lot of the cheesy keyboard patches from that era. When we were making that transition into the eighties, everybody just went nuts with whatever toys were available, and they forgot that they had really good-sounding instruments that they shouldn't ditch, okay? Rosenthal seems to remember that and it sounds admirably or relatively timeless and yet fresh at the time the album came out.

And as far as I'm concerned, Roger Glover has always been underrated as a bass player. If you listen to the old Deep Purple records, songs like "Pictures of Home," he does some incredible things. He pulls magical notes out of the ether and he just drops them in there. I think that's why he's such a good producer. He has all the chops, but his superpower is his ear and the way he blends the instruments on this track is brilliant. It's just a great song from any perspective. It doesn't do anything wild with harmony, but then again, neither does "Highway Star." It's more about the delivery and the punch. The drums are driving, the bass line is relentless, but it's also melodic—the perfect album-opener.

Martin: Next is "Stone Cold," and for the first time, the JLT era of the band is in possession of its own sound, rather than offering up a new version of something they'd done before just for continuity's sake.

Tim: Yeah, that's a nice way of putting it. "Stone Cold" is just a great song and fully deserving of its hit status. It's one of those oddball ones that was a Top 40 hit, hitting exactly No.40 in the States (laughs). I think it did a little better in Canada. It's the first song I ever heard by them and I remember seeing the video on MuchMusic. Mick Jones and Lou Gramm wish they could write a song like this. Obviously they didn't do too bad (laughs) but to me this is supercharged Foreigner.

I like the understatedness of the drums. It's a very simple drum pattern but it's Bobby Rondinelli, so every few bars he'll do a quick little snare fill and then hit a crash. There's a lot of cymbal whacks, but they're not all fully committed. Sometimes it sounds like he's hitting the bell of the ride or something.

I like the way that the guitar and the keyboard mix together and I really like the solo in this song. I'm surprised that it didn't chart higher, but at the same time, they didn't have that look that I suppose you would have needed by then. They're actually like a lot of the Canadian bands, like April Wine and Aldo Nova and Loverboy. That's the milieu they're working in and that's the piece of the pie that Ritchie Blackmore is looking for. He's saying, "I want the people that buy those records to buy our records." One last thing, when I was a kid—and it still stays with me today—I chuckled at the, "You put me in the deep freeze" line. To me that was a little too literal. I still think it's a great song.

Peter Jones: "Stone Cold," was the biggest single of their career, in terms of chart success in America, anyway. It's medium tempo and not really a ballad, more of a slow, quiet rock tune. It's got simple, straightforward chording from Blackmore over an equally simple but effective drum pattern from Rondinelli. The keyboards are a nice touch, but it's singular of note. It's not big and chordal or anything like that.

The intensity picks up as it gets to the chorus.

It is interesting during the chorus, how many crashes Bobby chooses to play. You don't pay attention to it until all of a sudden you notice it. It's very AC/DC-like, having a lot of crashes in a simple straightforward chorus. Ritchie's solo is very calm, focused and centred around melodic elements. This isn't about showing off or anything else and I think it works perfectly.

Great job presenting the vocal and the melody here. Again, it does sound a bit rooted in the eighties. It's never been my favourite track. It's extremely well composed and well executed. I think it's a strong track and it's in a good spot in the running order, at number two behind that flame-thrower opener. And I agree; it's pretty much their first really good attempt at one of these Foreigner-type songs. I don't want to say it's overtly intentional. But whatever the inspiration is, it lives in that camp. And the proof is in the song's popularity and success outside of an album that as a whole really didn't do that great. Unlike Foreigner and Journey, a single for Rainbow really doesn't elevate the rest of the record along with it. It lives on as a standalone track.

Peter Kerr: Martin, you can tell which songs on this album they spent time on and that they crafted, and "Stone Cold" is the best example of that. The filler between the tracks, you feel that they didn't spend as much time. With "Stone Cold," you can tell that they've carefully mapped out how it's going to be. I think this is one of their best power ballads or best sort of slower songs. It's got drama, and the hero of this song is actually not just Ritchie Blackmore and Joe Lynn Turner, but it's David Rosenthal, with those keyboard textures and chords that just boost it up. I can imagine Jon Lord easily slotting into this song and doing his thing.

The background to the lyric is that Roger Glover came into a recording session one day and said, "My wife left me stone cold." So Joe Lynn Turner, out of drama and misery, that's where art is created. He came up with the lyric and it becomes one of the most-played Rainbow songs on radio in America. It's got crossover appeal, a lot of emotion, and it's got one of Joe's great vocals. But the hero for me is Rosenthal, who just adds that extra oomph in the keyboards.

Luis: A lot of people call "Stone Cold" a power ballad, right? And people think it's easy to write a ballad. It's like, whatever. No, it isn't. It's easy to write a ballad that sucks. It's not very easy to write a good one. I think "Stone Cold" is an example of a great ballad. There's nothing about it that I would say, oh, here we go, this chord progression again. No, it's actually sophisticated but it also just makes sense.

And the vocal melody is nicely composed. I'm sure that came from Joe and I don't know how much credit he gets for it. But through that process, singers often tweak the existing musical melody in powerful and interesting ways, and this record has a lot of really thoughtful vocal melodies. That's another thing; it's memorable. I could go through the chord progressions, but it's more a question of, does the song function? This certainly does, and in the running order it's is a little breather after "Death Alley Driver." It sets up the next one, which is another rocker.

Martin: And what do you feel, just in a general sense, that Joe Lynn Turner brings to the band?

Tim: Well, I'm a big fan of this era; I lean towards the more commercial-sounding stuff anyway and I'm all about the AOR-sounding Rainbow. I think he brings a supercharged Lou Gramm feel to things, perfect for the time.

Peter Kerr: I've changed my view over time. Back in the day, not so much of a fan. I was very much from the Ronnie James Dio school and thought Joe was not as strong a personality. But over time, as I've done a deeper dive into the discography and grown to appreciate this album in particular, I'm on board. Ritchie Blackmore is always looking for a Paul Rodgers. So when they were going for *Burn*, Mk. III, he got David Coverdale. Not to be controversial, but I think Joe Lynn Turner's much more interesting than Paul Rodgers. I find Paul Rodgers a little bit bland. I'm not a big Bad Company fan and just never got the Free/Bad Company thing. I find them a very low-wattage type of band.

But I find Joe Lynn Turner fascinating. He's always good for a soundbite, he's controversial, he's got a big ego, he's the sort of singer that you get when you want to get noticed and conquer America. So he's definitely not bland. There's a lot of soul and R&B in his vocal intonation. I hear it here and even more so on the live material on *Finyl Vinyl*.

I don't agree with a lot of what he says. He's outrageous, but he's always good for a soundbite. And if you want somebody that's got personality and charisma to push the band, he's the person for you. And also, Ritchie did sort of remark that he noticed that the audience was starting to get more females. Previous to that, with Dio and Graham Bonnet, it was all blokes. But now they're starting to get more girls because he's got sex appeal. Ritchie has also said that Joe was a little bit on the feminine side and I think Joe played to that.

Luis: Joe's a competent singer but I wouldn't go as far as Peter in terms of him standing out or having a strong personality. I've read interviews with him where it's framed that he's like Roger Daltrey, in The Who. Pete Townshend was always talking to people, but Daltrey rarely said anything. He rarely even introduced the songs. It's more like he was there to sing and he was happy to be there and that's what he did. The rest of it was handled by others.

Martin: All right, next is "Bring on the Night (Dream Chaser)," which supports that thing I mentioned earlier about Rainbow being practitioners of Teutonic metal-lite or goth metal-lite or goth-lite. In other words, they've placed themselves at the nexus between classical-based heavy metal and AOR.

Peter Kerr: Yep, Ritchie Blackmore and Rainbow love mining that slight "Kashmir"/"Stargazer"/"Gates of Babylon" thing, or as you famously called them, Egypto chords. This is a slight deviation into that wheelhouse from their new AOR reality, not as overt as "Eyes of Fire," which will be coming up right at the end of the album. Is it the strongest song? No, but it's got a bit of groove to it, and you're right, it fuses a couple sub-genres.

Tim: "Bring on the Night (Dream Chaser)" is where you start to see Ritchie and Joe as these night people, right? There's that candlelight séance-type thing. Apparently Joe was knee-deep if not hip-deep into that stuff and as for Ritchie, we've all heard the stories about recording *Long Live Rock 'n' Roll* in France and summoning Baal (laughs). So Joe would write lyrics like this anyway, without Ritchie having to coax him. But it's a catchy hard rocker, heavy, a good change of pace after "Stone Cold." So people are thinking, okay, we're not going to get a full-on pop album now.

Luis: "Bring on the Night" has that Arabic harmonic minor twist, but I find that the chorus melodies are a bit too mainstream. It's still a great song.

Peter Jones: Ritchie begins "Bring on the Night" with about ten seconds of cool, effects-laden guitar soloing. When the drums take over, it's got a nice, driving feel to it. I really appreciate the stronger, more aggressive vocal approach from Joe on this and the harmonies are great. They introduce a phase-shifter effect when we get to the chorus and I'm not a big fan of that. It's a studio trick that hasn't dated well. And then the song starts to become a bit predictable, because when Joe sings, "Let the dream chaser take you away," here comes the double bass. I'm listening ahead of time and thinking, "He's gonna put double bass right there." And sure as heck, there it is. And then it disappears back to his groove. You're like, okay, that's a little contrived.

Martin: The other thing that bothers us with that part is that it's a complete lift of a Ronnie James Dio vocal melody too, right?

Peter Jones: Well, you can't avoid it. Ronnie's stamp is so much a part of Rainbow, even if Joe is so adamant that he's his own guy and wasn't really a fan of that old-school Rainbow style. But you can't avoid comparing. If he sings the word higher or fire or anything, we're gonna think about Ronnie.

Martin: But that specific example, it's a bit like how Tony Martin relentlessly re-used Ronnie's vocal melodies in Black Sabbath.

Peter Jones: That's a great point, exactly, although it happens less often between Ronnie and Joe. But I love the added harmonies when they get to the last verse—that's a nice touch, and it's strong vocally overall. There's interesting bass playing here from Roger. He's usually a hard hat, lunch bucket guy, basically out of the way. He's gonna foundationally do what the song needs. You'd miss him if he wasn't there, but you don't really notice that he's there either. This one has never been performed live. But it's a good mid-side track and a nice contrast to the slower track that is ahead of it. Pretty good from a sequencing point of view.

As for your goth-lite idea, absolutely, yes. It happens on a secondary level as well, beyond the riffs and the chord changes. He's able to move forward with what is accessible to a general audience, but a lot of times, often during his solos, he'll put in a flavour or play a scale or a lick and your ears perk up because you recognize that as part of Ritchie's history and tradition. You're like, oh, that was a nice touch, a toe-hold back to the old camp. That's combined with the forward progress into the more commercial material that he's writing. It's a delicate blend that it could come off as cornball if he does it incorrectly.

Martin: Next is "Tite Squeeze," with that curiously undermining spelling, not that it's much of a song, basically "Maybe I'm a Leo" crossed with "Mistreated," but unfortunately closer to "Mistreated." It's also in that loping rhythmic space with songs like "Run with the Wolf" and "L.A. Connection."

Tim: Yeah, a half-time shuffle feel. I don't know how well this one holds up. This is their attempt to be sensual or something, sort of in a Whitesnake zone. It's Joe Lynn Turner trying to appeal to the ladies that might be listening, although the audience was still woefully male. One nice thing sonically, it's got that section in the middle where it sounds like Ritchie is playing with an Octavider effect on his guitar.

Peter Jones: Glad you brought up "L.A. Connection," because yeah, instantly at the beginning, you hear that they are really similar. There's a slight treatment to Ritchie's guitar that distorts the signal just a little bit. It's slow and driving. From your comment about the last track, where you said "Let the dream chaser take you way" was very Ronnie, here you've got "Ooh, give it to me/You got everything I need/Ooh, do it to me/Bring me to my knees." This is just juvenile eighties tropes, trivial nonsense. They're bad lyrics that don't age well. Because you know what? Lyrics are important and good lyrics are really hard to do. It's the art of prose, it's writing, no different than a poem or a short story. The words matter. You can have the greatest melody, you can have the greatest musical accompaniment. If I'm singing, "I went to the store to buy some shoes," you're gonna be like, "Screw this; I don't care." Because they have to work in tandem.

I do like that they change up the feel and do more of a halftime or double high-hat feel and then they go right back to the groove. I do like that. Ritchie plays a very strong solo here and I love that he uses the octave harmonizer on this. It's an element that he didn't use very often. He pulls it out again on Deep Purple's "Bad Attitude," which is one of my favourite Ritchie solos of all time, because I just think that's tasty as heck. But that effect is all over this strong track. Musically, the band's playing great, but Joe isn't working for me on this one. I'm glad this one was never performed live. I'm glad they didn't subject anybody to it.

Peter Kerr: There's a bit of an R&B groove to "Tite Squeeze," but I agree, the lyrics are a bit throwaway. If you look at the lyrics on this album in general, they're not super-strong. I think it was only on *Bent*

Out of Shape that Joe became better as a lyricist. But having Joe being able to create an R&B vibe and do a little bit of Paul Rodgers or Lou Gramm, that gives Ritchie something extra to work with. If you've got somebody that's just meat-and-potatoes hard rock, you're limiting yourself as well as limited in how big your audience might be. But this guy has sung back-up to Cher, he's done radio commercials jingles, he's versatile. As I've read more about Joe Lynn Turner and all the work he's done, I appreciate him more. But at the time it rankled me. He's not Ronnie James Dio. And that's why a lot of people dismissed it.

Martin: I guess you could call "Tearin' Out My Heart" a proto-power ballad.

Tim: Absolutely, although I'm not quite sure it works as a power ballad. It's Joe Lynn Turner being very dramatic, but I don't think it delivers the punch that they would want a power ballad to deliver. I'm thinking about similar songs from this period, maybe some of the Y&T ballads like "I Believe in You." This doesn't quite get there. It's funny; it's listed as 4:02 but it feels longer to me and that's not a good thing. It's one thing if a long song feels shorter, but this one feels like it goes on too long.

Martin: To me, it feels like a quieter version of "Love's No Friend" from the last album. It's an oppressive, dark and doomy situation, isn't it? And certainly as heavy as that song when it comes to the chorus.

Peter Kerr: Yeah, and it's also about the same volume as "Stone Cold," albeit with a different architecture. I guess they didn't want two power ballads in a row to be released. It's emotive, it's got that slow build and Ritchie does a smoking guitar solo on it. And anytime Ritchie plays his solos, Roger puts him high in the mix, he ramps him up. It's like if you were looking at it on an equalizer it would spike, because that's the dramatic apex of what is already an emotive song. Even if the lyrics are banal and a little bit clichéd, you believe Joe is sincere in the way he's delivering the song.

Luis: There's nothing innovative about "Tearin' Out My Heart," but it's a masterclass in how to use this genre to its fullest. I love it.

Peter Jones: "Tearin' Out My Heart" opens up with light picking from Blackmore and some soft keys underneath, while Joe carries the verse vocally with very minimal support from the band. He has the voice for this and I think it's nice and it works. A more aggressive metal singer would butcher this. It wouldn't have the delicacy or the light touch needed and Joe was good at that. He's maybe not as heavy on the power side as Ronnie or Tony Martin or even Ray Gillen. But he does have a very strong AOR voice that can pull this off.

Over to the chorus, the riff is effective and there's some strong percussive accompaniment. I have to comment on how clean the recording sounds, specifically on this track. The drums sound huge and impactful. I've often wondered in my brain what this would sound like with a little violin behind it and Steve Walsh singing. It's got those elements to me.

Martin: Wow, you're right, Joe quite often sounds like Steve. That's never crossed my mind.

Peter Jones: He does. When he says, "Oh, it's killing me"—that's Kansas. Steve Walsh has sung that line a million times (laughs). There's a strong solo section, which goes back to the light opening riff. It's just great playing from there on out. It's a solid track that deserves a little more focus, although I don't know if it's quite single material. Kansas could pull it off. They'd probably throw in a really cool prog element and then somehow convert it to something that somebody would listen to on the radio. I'm not sure how that magic always worked for them, but it did. But I don't see that working here for Rainbow.

Martin: Flip the side and we've got an uncommonly happy and straight-forward song for Rainbow. Even though it's an outlier, I've always liked it.

Tim: Yeah, "Power" is a fun one. It's a rocker, and as the title might suggest, it's anthemic. I do like the drums at the beginning of this one. Nothing's very complicated here, not the riff and not the drumming. But it's positive; I can almost hear this song as part of a soundtrack during a training montage, like a *Rocky* movie or something. It might be my second favourite on the album after "Stone Cold." But I could see this being one that they would always play in concert because it's upbeat and it rocks. But you're right; the only thing that sounds Ritchie Blackmore about this is that it's in the key of G and he likes writing in the key of G. But yeah, it's happy. I hear what you mean. I wonder if it would have had more depth if they had slowed it down a few BPMs.

Peter Jones: To me, Ritchie's and Bobby's opening of this track feels a bit like "Hot Blooded" from Foreigner, until the verse kicks in. But in the beginning, it's these odd double snare hits and pounding bass drum. Here's one of life's ironies: the pattern that he's using is the same that Cozy uses in the middle of "All or Nothing" on *Slide It In* from Whitesnake. So now we have the egg chasing the chicken, or the horse before the cart or whatever. Because this time Bobby did it first, while Cozy followed him and did it later. So good on you, Bobby, because you got the one-up on him this time.

It's then very straightforward until the pre-chorus, where we get a nice riff. But again, it's so predictable—here comes the double bass: "I got the power," It's so contrived. And there's another element in here that I was trying to isolate. Once you get to the chorus, the snare drum is affected in some way. It's either got a handclap in it or it's not a true snare. It definitely doesn't sound like it did on the earlier songs, especially that really clean snare on the intro to "Stone Cold," which is crisp and clean and cuts nicely. There's an elemental attachment to it during the chorus, which makes it sound dated, although it's quite slight, mind you. So "Power" is another good track, but it's not going to get anybody's attention, really.

Peter Kerr: I don't know, I've always thought this was filler, not the strongest opening to side two. But I like it a lot better live, and we'll talk about that when we get to *Finyl Vinyl*, where he's got the backup singers and there's more soul and more oomph. The studio version seems a bit muted and doesn't hang together as well as the other songs. I'm not sure if it's rushed. Talking to Bob Daisley and a lot of other folks and also reading about Rainbow and Ritchie Blackmore, he's not a multiple take sort of guy. He'll plan it, he'll rehearse it, but then it's one or two takes because he's got a short attention span. That's probably why he's got so many members coming and going— he likes new blood. But "Power" seems unfinished. It needs a bit more polish, and maybe a few more takes.

Luis: I just don't find that Ritchie Blackmore is a guy that can pull off a cheery song like this, or a simple power chord song like this.

But he tries, and kudos to him for that. But yeah, even when he takes solos, it's usually darker and more minor key stuff. It's a song that I remember loving as a kid. But it's a three-chord thing, and as an older guy, I'm just not that drawn to it anymore. I wonder if the band dynamic had anything to do with it. I feel like Blackmore is more so calling the shots now. Before, both Cozy and Ronnie had strong voices in the band. But that is getting diluted. People basically do what Ritchie tells them to do, and I don't think that's necessarily for the better.

Martin: "Miss Mistreated" is a cool track, sort of thumpy Foreigner with definite Lou Gramm vocal phrasing. But it's got that patented keyboard/guitar alloy with respect to the power chords, which you don't get from Foreigner.

Peter Jones: Yeah, it's got an aggressive, heavy feel. I like the sort of psychedelic keyboard intro with the echoed vocals from Joe. The verses are mostly keys with drums and a droning bass line from Glover. Blackmore really just adds these intermittent big power chords to it and then gets out of the way and lets those sustain underneath, which is a nice change of pace. He doesn't do that very often.

Ritchie fires off a nice solo here, but it doesn't have much support in the backing tracks, because they're just playing the same thing straight through the song that they did once it got started. So there's not much contrast or variety. The track builds to a section where there's more double bass. The track has more power and intensity when played live. I actually prefer the version of this on *Finyl Vinyl*. I think the elements are there. But it's nothing fancy; it doesn't throw us any curveballs and just sits and plateaus a bit from start to finish and doesn't give our ear something else to hold onto or hook onto. That "Miss Mistreated, who's mistreating who?" phrase really isn't a hook that you can wrap yourself around; it's more of a shouty lyrical riff.

Tim: "Miss Mistreated" is a good mid-tempo one. I've always been amused by how they capitalize "MISS" in the credits. The idea is that no one dare get it mixed up with "Mistreated." The two songs have nothing in common. This song's like a slightly heavier "Stone Cold." If you wanted to sum up the Joe Lynn Turner era in one song, maybe something like this would work because it's got melody but also more menacing chord changes than "Stone Cold."

Martin: But of course this is the rock 'n' roll business, so inevitably they can't keep their story straight. On the original vinyl, it's "MISS Mistreated" on the back. Then on the lyric sleeve, it's all capitals with the "MISS" bolded. Finally, it's just simple all capitals on the record label, no bolding. Three different ways. Which of course allows us in this book to say enough with the stupidity, we're calling it "Miss Mistreated."

Peter Kerr: Absolutely; I agree—so dumb. But is this a potshot at Mr. David Coverdale? Maybe. Are you aware of the famous bit of a punch-up between David Coverdale and Ritchie Blackmore? *Kerrang!* was the press outlet where a lot of people used to take potshots at each other, and Coverdale would take potshots at Rainbow. And Ritchie was getting quite riled-up. So Rainbow were playing in Germany and Coverdale rolled up backstage. There were some members of Queen and there were some fisticuffs to be had. And they still talk about it. They're all friends and it's all cordial now. But there was a really big brawl between Whitesnake and Rainbow because they were very competitive, and probably on an even par in the chart stakes around the world, or at least in Europe. So I think this is a bit of a shot at "Mistreated," doing it as "Miss Mistreated." It's an in-joke with respect to the lyrics and the name of the song.

Luis: Whatever the story, it's a little self-referential and tongue-in-cheek. The music, again, is just right and the lyrics are coming at it from a different perspective. The original Coverdale thing was the perspective of the guy, right? And now you could imagine it as the continuation, but from the perspective of the woman, what her life was like, or at least it's addressed to the woman's concerns. So I really enjoy that. Even as a kid I thought that was smart. And the music, what's surprising about it is not a particular chord choice or a section. What's surprising to me about this one is just how well assembled it is. It's an almost perfect Blackmore blues song, deceptively simple, and is even better than "Love's No Friend."

The first impression of it is, okay, we've all heard this before. But then when you deconstruct what the keyboards are playing, and you match it up to the guitar, it's quite thoughtful. And it has that really nice B flat, C thing, that little interlude, which is unexpected. He does that little lick and then he shifts it by a fourth.

Plus it's right in the wheelhouse for Joe Lynn Turner; it doesn't sound awkward for him. Sometimes you do catch lightning in a bottle and "Miss Mistreated" belongs to that ecosystem of songs. It doesn't sound weird to me. It's fun. I loved it as a kid when I first heard it, and as you get older and you think, well, now I know this much about music theory, blah, blah, blah, I need to revisit this. Turns out I'm still enthusiastic about it. People can be cynical about it if they want, but I'm not. It's just a very good, basic blues rock song, but with surprises if you actually pay attention.

Martin: With "Rock Fever," we get a carry-over from "No Time to Lose" and "Can't Happen Here" en route to "Drinking with the Devil" and "Make Your Move."

Tim: Yes, it's another of Ritchie's widdly riffs, as you call them, or twiddly riffs, as I call them (laughs). I'm a guitar player, and I don't know how else to describe it, but it's in "Spotlight Kid" too, where he's taking his hands off the fretboard and it's a circular riff. What he's doing is he's using a lot of open strings and just fretting certain notes, and it has a circular structure because it repeats.

Lyrically, it doesn't sound much like Rainbow, which is similar to what we said about "Power." It sounds like they're trying to be a hair metal band. It's something for the ladies in the audience, like David Lee Roth pointing at girls in the audience and getting the security guards to escort them backstage. I like it, but it's a bit out of character. It's like Joe is singing to an imaginary audience with girls that are screaming at him.

Peter Jones: One of the better riffs on the record from Ritchie; then the band crash in and drive it nicely, providing solid syncopation. Great drumming from Rondinelli. However, it sounds a bit muted sonically in comparison to the earlier tracks. It's not as clean on the high-end. Sounds to me like it was recorded in a different session or they treated the mix differently.

As for this family of riffs from Ritchie, all of us as musicians, whether we want to admit it or not, the more creative you are and the more stuff you put out there, you can break down elements and say, "Well, that's a Ritchie-ism, that's a Ritchie thing, Ritchie does that." But that's one of the ways to identify them as unique to him. He has transition pieces that he uses to connect parts. He says, "Okay, where am I? I'm going from here to here. What do I have in my toolbox? Oh, I've got this." The same thing happened with Jon Lord. When Ritchie was writing with Jon, it was like, "Okay, if we're getting from here to here, what if we do a unison keyboard/guitar thing that'll get us to here? And then we'll use that same transition to get us back out of it to here."

So you start to see those ideas repeat themselves throughout, the more material they release over their careers. So, yeah, it's elemental to him. He's going to do what's familiar, and we're all going to fall into trends. It's hard to break out of that; every band does it.

The lyrics, again, are not so great, a bit cringy: "I can feel your blood run hot/Burning with a fire." I'm like, no. But I do love the syncopations the band fire off during the pre-chorus, and then everybody hitting the brakes together on that "Fever takes me higher" line, before we cruise into the chorus proper. It's done well musically. It's one of those tracks where the music outperforms the lyric content and the melody of it. With a different vocal melody and a different subject matter, this might've risen to a higher standard. It's not a horrible track, but what positive measure is that? Calling a song not horrible (laughs).

Peter Kerr: No worries, because I also think "Rock Fever" is a bit of a filler track. Like Peter says, Ritchie is very good at recycling riffs. So you might hear a riff from Mk. I pop up in Mk. II and then it goes in Mk. III. If he's got a riff, he'll just do a slight alteration to it and then recycle it and bring it into a Rainbow album. So I think the main riff, and some of these tailing licks too, sound like they're recycled from Deep Purple.

Martin: Peter Jones politely calls out the vocal melody and now I can't unhear it as not exactly optimal (laughs).

Peter Kerr: Yes, there's the juxtaposition between the sweet and the hard. Ritchie will play these guitar lines that say, hey, I'm Ritchie Blackmore and we're still in this European metal or hard rock or classic rock theatre. But then Joe will put a pop spin on it with his vocal melodies. The verse here is a perfect example of that.

Luis: I listen to "Rock Fever" and the edge has been polished off or something; it's sounding a little different. And of course that intro is great, another example of David Rosenthal doing interesting things that have dated well. He's innovative, and his part here sounds carefully designed. But the whole record is just so well put-together. Because sometimes you get records where there's like three tracks that are just dynamite, and then the rest are not great. I'm not saying every song here is great, but what I'm saying is that there is no single song that sounds like it doesn't belong in the flow.

Martin: Okay, we close with Rainbow proposing a "Gates of Babylon"-style epic but with Joe Lynn Turner unfurling the parchment manuscript rather than Ronnie James Dio. Are they successful in selling it?

Tim: Sure. I certainly wasn't paying attention to Rainbow when this came out, but I would think "Eyes of Fire" would have satisfied anybody who enjoyed the early stuff. It's as gothic and mysterious and nighttime-feeling as any of the Dio stuff, and I don't think Joe's vocal sound out of place. It might be his best vocal on the album. He really goes through the paces. It's very dramatic. It's long, and I know a lot of that's a long trail at the end, but, sure, of course—this is the most traditional-sounding Rainbow song on the record. I think "Miss Mistreated" is the most emblematic song of the JLT era, but "Eyes of Fire," you hear that and you say that sounds like Rainbow. It's the only properly gothic, Middle Eastern-sounding metal song on here, really, because "Bring on the Night" is goth-lite.

Peter Kerr: Well, you can't get more Egypto chord than "Eyes of Fire." This is their "Stargazer," their "Gates of Babylon." Joe Lynn Turner shared an interest in the dark arts with Ritchie Blackmore, so I guess that was probably a bonding process. He likes all the seances and the spiritual side of things. So this song really goes into the laneway of both Ritchie and Joe.

Not many songs can be as great as "Stargazer," but "Eyes of Fire" has that sort of drama. It's got the strings, because I think if Ritchie was born in a different century, he would imagine himself as a Mozart or a Beethoven. He loves two periods of music; he loves classical music, which is Mozart and Beethoven, and he loves the Baroque music, which is Johann Sebastian Bach etc. So he regularly has to mine those two periods, and maybe through use of a string arrangement. But yeah, "Eyes of Fire" has that magnificent, elaborate introductory passage at the beginning, with Roger doing that octave-jumping on the bass. It's got your Egypto chords and it's traditional Rainbow through and through, although we've got a different singer.

Luis: Which begs the question: might this have had more impact with Ronnie James Dio and Cozy Powell on it? Interesting, but placing it at the end sends us off thinking about that, thinking about old Rainbow. It's a reminder of the seventies albums, as if to say, "Don't forget that we are those guys." It's not that it's the best Rainbow song or anything, because it's like they're making it nice. They've cleaned up for the photo (laughs). Still, the idea is, sure, we've changed the music that goes with the brand, but deep inside, there's this other thing that's still part of what we do.

Peter Jones: "Eyes of Fire" opens with a gong, which, you'll get no complaint from me. Anytime a drummer whacks a gong, I'm okay with it. There's a lot of multi-tracking, slide parts and things from Ritchie here. And the drums are presented interestingly, because they come in as a fader sliding up; they're already existing, which is different than anything they've done on the record. You don't hear that too often from anybody, actually. Plus you think the song is one thing—as it's starting; you're getting a sense that it may go a certain direction—but then all of a sudden, there's a big right turn and in come these sweeping Middle Eastern flavours.

And Ritchie is not subtle on this one at all. This is Ritchie in his full neo-classical element and I love it. It's so recognizably Rainbow, and it creates such a strong sense of familiarity and comfort for me. Of course, this is something that was utilized heavily during the Dio era and one of the signature musical staples of that period. Through the use of orchestrated strings and heavy keyboards, you get that Middle Eastern thing. It's also caused by the use of specific minor scales. Minor keys are used in rock all the time, but Ritchie specifically liked to use the harmonic minor scale as well as occasionally using the Hungarian minor scale.

Without getting too specific, a harmonic minor scale is a regular minor scale with the seventh tone raised a half step. What this does is create a "leading tone" or half step that pulls very heavily to the root of the scale. It's full of tension and our ears are really clamouring for it to resolve. Once it does, it's very satisfying. A natural or regular A minor scale is A-B-C-D-E-F-G-A., i.e. no sharps or flats. The A harmonic minor is A-B-C-D-E-F-G sharp-A. Like I say, occasionally, Blackmore will also use a Hungarian minor scale. That takes the same elements of the harmonic minor, but it also raises the fourth note and thus creates two sets of leading tones within the scale that also creates a "tri-tone" or "the devil's interval," that whole celebrated sound you hear in "Black Sabbath."

Anyway, it pulls on us to resolve. We can feel our bodies almost moving forward, going, "Can you resolve this now, please?" That one wants to just go down. "Powerslave," from Iron Maiden, is dripping with this, between the verses and the chorus. Oh, it's just like heaven to me. It's just home. It's something I really, really love from rock music. And I love that Ritchie pulled this out. It's a good vocal from Joe Lynn Turner. I think he's up to the challenge here. And I also really prefer these kinds of lyrics.

Ritchie's solo is totally vintage in its flavour and its tone. And they even pull out some of the old tricks. There's heavy left and right panning, like he does in "Tarot Woman" and "Stargazer," where his guitar is bouncing back and forth. So they brought that back into the mix. It might be my favourite riff on the record. It's exotic, it's different. It really makes the track stand out from a compositional standpoint. The drumming and rhythmic backing is rather simple but it needs to be. It's a refreshing way to end the record.

Martin: Still, I feel it's a little forced, a little clunky. I much prefer the way these influences are massaged into a few different tracks across *Down to Earth*. Here, it's like he loaded them all up into one song, and it's the last song, like it's him remembering, "Oh yeah, we should stick on one of these."

Peter Jones: Sure, if you could talk to Ritchie, you might say, "You seem a little conflicted. You say publicly, 'I want this, I want this and I want that.' And you may do that, although I feel it's begrudgingly. Where really, if you just had your druthers, this 'Eyes of Fire' stuff is where you live. This is your thing."

Now, he's also an individual with a personality who just doesn't give a hoot what anybody else thinks. Clearly, his track record with hiring and firing people tells you that in spades. But he does want success. He does want recognition. He wants to be able to say, "See? I can do this." And maybe the best way on this record is to try one of everything and see what sticks.

Martin: And you don't get one of these on *Bent Out of Shape*, although there are licks here and there. Instead, you get a cohesive, integrated presentation. I don't quite know how to explain it, but there's a sense of mission finally accomplished on that record for me.

Peter Jones: He brings it back much more consistently on *Stranger in Us All*. "Hunting Humans" and a lot of the other stuff that's on there, that's more his style, but even that album is confusing. Because then you'll have some other more AOR tracks that don't fit, and you're like what?! And then they even reprise "Still I'm Sad," and "Hall of the Mountain King" is a substitute for "Sixteenth Century Greensleeves," because they come from the same traditional classical background.

So again, if you could talk to him, you might tell him, "You may say that, Ritchie, but you take all your time off and then you come back and what do you do? You go back to what you were known for originally. And put your feet back in the sand or on the ground and go, 'Okay, here.'" And maybe it's just destined to not be commercially accepted. Doesn't mean it's less art. It certainly doesn't mean it's not well done or that it doesn't have a ton of merit. It does. "Street of Dreams" tried, but it couldn't match "Stone Cold" success-wise. And to me, that one sounds more dated than "Stone Cold" because it sounds forced.

That reminds me. I want to tell you a quick story. I know I'm not part of the *Rising* chapter, but this is *Rising*-related. Freshman year in college, the university overbooked so I was in temporary housing in bunks down on the lower floor of our dorm. So we had to walk upstairs to use the restrooms and come back down. First half of the year ends, and as this happens in most colleges, people flat fail out. Or they lose their financial aid and rooms become available. I'm going to move upstairs.

Okay, in years past, all the walls between all the dorm rooms had been painted over the decades by various students, with flower motifs or whatever. I get ushered upstairs to the first floor to see my room. I walk around the corner to see my room and what is on the wall right next to my door but a full-sized hand-painted mural of Rainbow *Rising*, right next to my door. It's the full wall between our doors. Enormous, gorgeous—wow! And I thought, I'm home, and what irony is that? Yeah, I'm like, holy shit. So there's the fist. Every day I'd come in and out of my room and slap that hand on my way in. It was frickin' fate.

And I thought, wow, 99% of the people who have walked by this don't even have a freakin' clue what it is. But I met my new roommate and he was a hard rock and metal fan as well. We loved the room so much; we stayed there 'til our senior year. There was no text on it; it was just the artwork from the album cover with the little guy down on the rocks with the waves.

Martin: Sweet—love it. All right, shall we wrap this up? Tim, any closing thoughts?

Tim: Well, it's interesting, because I've been listening to a lot of Kansas lately. And that same year, they put out *Vinyl Confessions*, which doesn't hang together as an album, because you've got some very traditional Kansas-sounding songs, but then you've got John Elefante coming in and writing more commercial-minded songs. And it almost seems like they wanted something that would appeal to everyone. So they're just throwing everything at you.

Straight Between the Eyes is the bells and whistles album. You did that *History in Five Songs with Martin Popoff* podcast episode about the hair metal bands called "Go to Vancouver and Try Harder." I guess if there was such a thing as "Go to Quebec and Try Harder," that's what they did here. Because they really did. Blackmore really wanted to be up there with the Journeys and the Foreigners of the world. I know they did well as a touring act, but I'm surprised by the fact that none of these albums certified. That is really strange to me. Surely at least the first couple would be very close to gold by now.

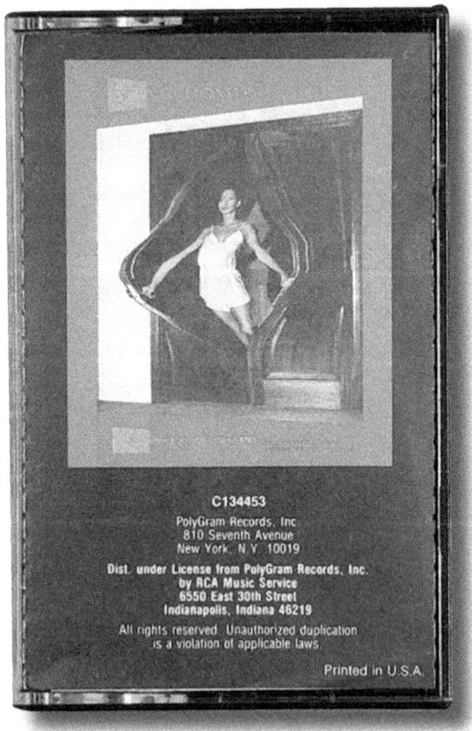

C134453
PolyGram Records, Inc.
810 Seventh Avenue
New York, N.Y. 10019
Dist. under License from PolyGram Records, Inc.
by RCA Music Service
6550 East 30th Street
Indianapolis, Indiana 46219
All rights reserved. Unauthorized duplication
is a violation of applicable laws.
Printed in U.S.A.

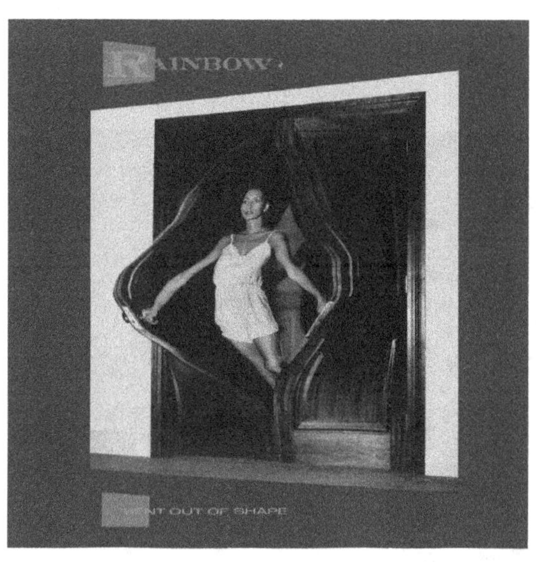

BENT OUT OF SHAPE

August 24, 1983
Mercury 422-815 305-1 M-1
Produced by Roger Glover
Engineered by Flemming Rasmussen; assisted by Thomas Breckling
Personnel: Joe Lynn Turner – vocals, Ritchie Blackmore – guitars, Roger Glover – bass, David Rosenthal – keyboards, Chuck Bürgi – drums

Side 1
1. Stranded (Blackmore, Turner) 4:30
2. Can't Let You Go (Blackmore, Turner; intro by Rosenthal) 4:22
3. Fool for the Night (Blackmore, Turner) 4:05
4. Fire Dance (Blackmore, Turner, Glover, Rosenthal) 4:31
5. Anybody There (Blackmore) 2:41

Side 2
1. Desperate Heart (Blackmore, Turner) 4:37
2. Street of Dreams (Blackmore, Turner) 4:27
3. Drinking with the Devil (Blackmore, Turner) 3:45
4. Snowman (Blake; arr. By Blackmore) 4:33
5. Make Your Move (Blackmore, Turner) 5:25

A *Bent Out of Shape* Timeline

May 1983. Rainbow works at Sweet Silence Studios in Denmark on what will become their final album (until a semi-Rainbow affair in the nineties), namely *Bent Out of Shape*, wrapping up the following month.

August 19, 1983. Rainbow issue "Street of Dreams"/"Anybody There" as a 7" single in the UK, adding "Power" (live) for the 12" version. "Power" is lifted from the *Live Between the Eyes* VHS video. The video for "Street of Dreams" is directed by Storm Thorgerson, continuing in this field after the dissolution of design house Hipgnosis. The song reaches No.52 on the UK charts and No.60 in the US.

August 24, 1983. Rainbow issue *Bent Out of Shape*, the third album of the Joe Lynn Turner era and last studio album of the band's catalogue until quasi-Rainbow comeback album *Stranger in Us All*. The album reaches No.11 on the UK charts and No.34 in the US.

September 6 – October 7, 1983. Rainbow embarks on a European tour in support of *Bent Out of Shape*. A handful of US dates follow in November.

October 1983. Rainbow issue "Can't Let You Go"/"All Night Long" (live) as a 7" single in the UK, with the 12" version adding "Stranded" (live). The song reaches No.43 on the UK charts.

February 28, 1984. Rainbow is nominated for a Grammy, with the instrumental "Anybody There." Meanwhile, Ritchie Blackmore separates from his third wife, Amy Rothman, with their divorce taking place in 1987.

March 11 – 14, 1984. Rainbow plays its last dates before the brief nineties era of the band. These are all in Japan, with the band recording "Difficult to Cure" at Budokan with a full orchestra.

RAINBOW
Street of dreams

mercury
Time: 4:20
Thames Talent
Publishing, Ltd.-
Lyon Farms
Music, Ltd.
(ASCAP-BMI)
19
STEREO
45 RPM
815 660-7
2-57687
Produced by
Roger Glover
STREET OF DREAMS
(Blackmore-Turner)
From the Mercury album 422-815 305-1 M-1
BENT OUT OF SHAPE
RAINBOW
℗ 1983 PolyGram Records, Inc.
MANUFACTURED AND MARKETED BY POLYGRAM RECORDS, INC., 810 SEVENTH AVENUE, NEW YORK, N.Y. 10019

Martin talks to Phil Aston, John Gaffney, Peter Kerr, Jamie Laszlo and Matt Thompson about *Bent Out of Shape.*

Martin Popoff: All right, we arrive at the last Rainbow album before the reunion, although reunion isn't exactly the right word for *Stranger in Us All.* Nor is it the right word for what Ritchie put together with Ronnie Romero years and years later.

Phil Aston: No, it isn't (laughs). But yes, with *Bent Out of Shape,* I know the call from Deep Purple was coming soon after this emerged. And in some ways, I understand that. That reunion turned out to be great to the extent that *Perfect Strangers* is, for many people, the best thing that Deep Purple ever did. But these Joe Lynn Turner Rainbow albums, first, *Difficult to Cure* was faulty, a bit broken around the edges. I do like it but they were finding their feet. I think Ritchie had decided that this epic swords and sorcery stuff wasn't going to buy him big cars and big houses. He wanted to be like Purple again. He was listening to Foreigner and Abba and all sorts of things. He wanted hits. But *Difficult to Cure,* although it had a massive hit with "I Surrender," was a bit mismatched; there are things on there that don't work. *Straight Between the Eyes* was a step in the right direction. "Miss Mistreated" and "Eyes of Fire" are great tracks, as is the ballad "Stone Cold." *Bent Out of Shape,* I felt, brought in some of the aggression from *Rising* and the first album and melded it with the AOR melodic aspect that he was trying to go for.

Martin: Nice; yeah, it's my favourite of the three. I don't think I'd agree that it's got any *Rising*-style aggression, although, sure, I think people tend to forget that there are fully four significantly up-tempo and hard-rockin' tracks on it. But whatever the reason, I do think it's far and away the triumph of the trio.

John Gaffney: I'm happy to hear you say that, because it seems like everybody dumps on the Joe Lynn Turner era, and I absolutely love this record. To me this record has a sophisticated cool about it. Everything from the production to the songwriting, there's a maturity to this album. It's all about the songs. There's no shredding, there's no unnecessarily long keyboard or guitar solos. It's all like, hey, we're all grown-ups here. Let's just write really good, solid songs.

But yet there's this mysterious vibe to it at times. And maybe it's the album cover, with the girl coming out the wall all bent out of shape. You can make what you want of that image, what it might be implying. But also Roger Glover's production, it's very clean and it's muted in a good way, in the sense that there's no frequencies to jump out and hurt your ears or anything. It's got this cool, misty vibe to it. Whatever it is, there's this mysterious feeling to this record that I just really, really like.

I love Joe's singing as well. I mentioned it earlier, but Joe has this cool, crooner vibe to him, almost like Frank Sinatra. He's never straining, never shouting, and he really comes into his own on here. He and Ritchie both put in some fantastic performances, although Ritchie picks his spots. In the end, it's all about melody. You don't get a lot of Ritchie just throwing his fingers around the fingerboard. He doesn't do a lot of that in general, but on this record in particular he steps up his game as far as melodic playing and serving the song when it comes to his solos. Chuck Bürgi joins us here on drums and puts in a solid performance and once again it's David Rosenthal on keyboards, who adds some really nice textures throughout the whole album.

Peter Kerr: My theory on *Bent Out of Shape* is that we really get the fruition of Ritchie's appreciation for Abba and Euro pop music. Ritchie has always had a fascination with pop music, and he loves those sweetly melancholy melodies of Björn and Benny and I think that he was starting to implement that more in this album. It's also more polished, better production, the songs are more thought-out, and maybe some of the rock crunch is muted, although like you and Phil said, there's some heavy material here.

But in general he was going for more of a Euro pop sound. And that's an interesting direction, because that Euro pop sound is not what America was listening to. 1983 is an interesting year because AOR was starting to morph into hair metal. It was the end of the lifespan for a lot of those AOR acts and hair metal was starting to take off. It was an interesting decision to record in Copenhagen, Denmark, but it makes sense on one level, given that the musicology and the melody lines were classical and Euro pop-orientated, albeit still within the Ritchie Blackmore universe of rock.

Jamie Laszlo: Man oh, man, this album gets dogged on and I really don't understand why. But when you start dissecting these albums, you start thinking in a different way and you come to grips with certain things. In the end, I absolutely love this album. I think it's the best post-Dio-era album by a landslide. I want to state that I'm only one guy with one opinion. I'm not sitting here thinking I'm giving facts. When I say this is a great album, my job is to give an opinion. It's the reader's job to agree or disagree. Either way it's great, because we're all thinking about and discussing music. The funny thing is, there's not much I can say about the songs. They are just great songs played well, but it's actually the uniformity at a high level that is this album's advantage, isn't it? I will also say this might not be a guitar player's album. Ritchie Blackmore fans that want to hear him do the things that they love, maybe this isn't for you. It's more of a songwriter's album.

Matt Thompson: We have a different line-up for *Bent Out of Shape*, as we've switched out Bobby Rondinelli for Chuck Bürgi, who comes in late in the game and is probably under-utilized. But it's a lame duck album in that the band is going to break up so that Deep Purple can reform. There's been some conversations prior to the album, where maybe the reunion might not happen. And for whatever reason, it doesn't seem like it's going to happen. So Rainbow is still a thing. But already, there's conversations going on. But unbeknownst probably to most of the band members, the writing is on the wall. This turns out to be the last Rainbow record for a period of time.

As for the record, it's very professional, well performed, and it's professionally and conservatively recorded. That helps its stand up over time quite well. This is a 1983 album, and in '83 there's some weird stuff going on production-wise with a lot of their contemporaries, right? One of the bands we've talked about before, this sounds more like *Fire of Unknown Origin* than *The Revolution by Night*, for a peer who is always playing around with sound. So it's conservatively recorded and just very well done and it holds up quite well.

And Joe Lynn Turner has more involvement in this record. He's got much more lyrical contribution to this record, rather than it just being the Glover and Blackmore writing show. Personal opinion, he's not a great lyricist. But I think he's passionate about what he's writing on this record. He can get behind what he's doing, I think, both on the record and then what he does with these songs live for the most part. I think he's in it; he stands behind the songs. It's a very good performance from him and maybe he took his involvement in the songs a bit more personally. I think the catalogue overall is of this time period, but the Joe Lynn Turner era in general is pretty consistent. It's not like one's a total flop and one's a masterpiece.

Martin: Except I feel like the first two check off boxes of the different styles and this one holds together almost like a concept album.

Matt: Yeah, that's an interesting take. It has a more consistent feel to it. I don't think they have the intellect to pull it off as a full concept lyrically, but yeah, it's more cohesive. In some ways it's more cohesive than almost anything from Rainbow, right? Like we talked about the debut not being cohesive. This is the opposite.

Martin: Yeah, when I say concept, I mean arrangement-and production-wise, but sure, semi-thematically with the lyrics and even with the album cover. The whole thing is absolutely that British racing green colour throughout. Speaking of that, where do you guys stand on that cover art?

Phil: Well, for starters, I don't like the *Straight Between the Eyes* cover; it's possibly a good idea, but it falls down on the execution. And *Difficult to Cure*, of course, wasn't even meant for them. But it's pretty cool; I like the way they're all looking down on the patient on the back cover. It makes sense. But this one, *Bent Out of Shape*, just having a random girl on the front—no. I imagine at this point in their career, maybe they just looked at covers and went, "Yeah, that'll do," like they weren't involved in it. Or perhaps the people at the label were thinking we don't want it to be too rock, so that we can cross over into different markets. But that's a tricky thing to do in late 1983, into 1984, when we're starting to see Bon Jovi, Europe, Ratt and Dokken. These other bands are starting to queue up to go after this same niche, really.

Peter: The cover plays into Ritchie's interest in the spiritual in regards to how he loved magic and the dark arts, astral traveling and things like that, time travel, spirits, portals. It's Ritchie's affection for mysticism. He's the dark prince or whatever it is. I don't think it's a funny album cover just to grab attention. I think it shows his personality. Is that lady bending time? Is she emerging from a portal? Is that a mirror or a wall? What it has to do with the album, Martin, I don't know (laughs). Ultimately it's like clickbait, an attention-grabber, but it doesn't really have much to do with the music.

Martin: To me it also looks very uptown eighties, like a New Romantics album cover, say Duran Duran or Spandau Ballet. Or post-punk like Echo and the Bunnymen or The Teardrop Explodes.

Peter: Yeah, with the lady and that forest green and the text treatment; absolutely. But there are two versions, the widely known green one, and a white one, in the UK. I don't think the green one dates well.

Jamie: Well, on that cover, she is indeed bent out of shape, I guess. I don't mind the greens and the whites. I just don't know how I feel about that goofy image of that woman bent out of shape. It doesn't bother me as much anymore because it's just the album cover to me now. It's what it's been for my whole life. Album covers stop bothering me at a certain point.

Martin: I think it's them trying to look upscale. It's like, if we're gonna be rock, we want to be part of the rock elite. It's almost like they're overcompensating or even apologizing for the contents. They are saying take us seriously. It's expensive-looking, ostentatious.

Jamie: Okay, sure, for 1983 it definitely is. It looks like a Hipgnosis cover, but it's not. And sure, it's not terrible like *Straight Between the Eyes*. We're not alienating anyone here. *Straight Between the Eyes*, someone might hear "Stone Cold" and go to the record store and see that cover and go, "You know what? Never mind. Never mind, I'll just grab the 45" (laughs). But with the *Bent Out of Shape* cover, you hear "Street of Dreams" and you're in the record store and you go, "What album's that on? Oh, this one? I'll take it. Take my $8.98."

Martin: I like that (laughs). Matt, what are your thoughts on this?

Matt: Well, I guess they're making a literal picture of the American phrase "bent out of shape." They're purposely trying to continue to crack America. This is not a British phrase. It's an American phrase that struck them as interesting and now you're trying to do a fit, right? There's a woman coming through and things are being bent, literally, in that picture. The very important song on the album is "Street of Dreams," and this album cover has that matching dreamlike look to it.

I like your point about them trying to look classy. You've got the British racing green and the little geometric shapes right behind the fonts, which is not a heavy metal thing, and more like Duran Duran, like you say. Yeah, that's interesting; I never picked up on that before.

Martin: All right, the album opens with "Stranded," which again, as far as I'm concerned, represents this band's unique way of marrying classical with AOR.

Phil: Yeah, I'd class this as melodic rock. It's 1983 and Ritchie has seen this music around him in the charts. He's seen what's going on in the US, but it's also quite aggressive, with these hard elements, with respect to the riff and even the soloing, although his guitar style has now moved on again. He's always had that little bit of echo on the end of his licks and stuff. That's still there, as are the Middle Eastern scales that he likes. But the songwriting is more accessible, to two audiences, actually, the audience that *don't* know about him and the audience that *do* know him. I think the songs are stronger and they serve both camps equally.

John: "Stranded" is one of the heavier songs on the album, maybe, or at least one of the darker and more urgent-sounding ones. When the chorus comes in, when they're saying the "Stranded!" line, repeating that line over and over, it sounds really heavy because everything sort of drops down and Blackmore is emphasizing his lower strings there, while Joe's singing lower and more intense. It really makes that pop out. The other chorus here, with the "Don't leave me stranded out here" part, Joe soars over the top of that. Roger Glover's bass too; he starts playing these sort of octave lines that propel that particular section of the song along.

"Magic and madness, it's so very strange/Sometimes I think it's all prearranged;" that's a great line (laughs). Joe's mentioned that he and Ritchie used to like to mess around with seance boards and stuff like that. Maybe this reference to magic and madness is about things that he and Blackmore were dabbling in at the time. Joe's even talked about them unleashing spirits that sort of haunted them throughout the making of various records.

Martin: They're creatures of the night too, right? They're kings of dreams, chasing dreams, on the street of dreams. They're fools for the night.

Peter: Exactly, yeah (laughs). Okay, "Stranded" is probably one of the rockier songs, so it follows the path of Rainbow that they have to have a starchy rock song to kick things off, so it doesn't tick off the core audience or the people that are predisposed to buy a Rainbow album. Track one is always vitally important because if the first track is something that is at polar odds with what the audience expects, they will just lift the needle, put it back in the sleeve and go back to the record store. So it's important. Every album by Deep Purple and Rainbow has a cracking rock opener. Is "Stranded" one of their best songs? No, I wouldn't even put it in the greatest hits. But it's a rock song. It's one of the more starchy songs on the album, and therefore, it does its job as the first track.

Jamie: Is it me, or does the song have gang vocals, Martin, with the "Stranded!" line? So it looks like Rainbow is dipping their toe right into 1983 and beyond with that. And even though it rocks, there's a certain smoothness to it; it goes down easy. In fact, this whole album goes down easy. There's just this low bottom end tone to the album that coats the music. It makes it easy to swallow. And the song does have an interesting little almost proggy part in the middle, just to satisfy the music snobs who might be listening.

Matt: Right off the bat, it's a good example of this production palette we're all trying to articulate. You can hear everything really well. So as opposed to the first record, it's not cluttered at all. The bass sounds great and is consistently that way throughout the album. Roger Glover's not a complex player but he plays to the song throughout and it cuts through the mix really nice. You get a little bit of keyboard ear candy on this song, but otherwise it's a straightforward, lean, efficient, professional rocker, which is a good way to open any record. Very well done. As for the guitar solo, Ritchie's got a bit more of a heavy metal tone and attack here. It's a little less melodic than some of his other solos. It starts more as sort of sound effects before going into those fast, choppy licks that he does. You've got a shouty chorus to it, which not sophisticated, but for a rocker, I think it works.

Martin: Let's see if we can find some additional ways to describe this plush production job Roger presents to the band.

Phil: I think it's of its time. I do like the guitar sound. I do think the guitar solos sound vital, and as I said, the echo and reverb he used is really good. The keyboard sound is of its time because they're using the synthesizers you'd expect in the eighties. But it sounds good. I played it at fair volume before we started talking this morning and your ears adjust to it quite quickly. It's aged better than *Difficult to Cure*, and I would say it's clearer than *Straight Between the Eyes*.

Peter: I think the production job on *Straight Between the Eyes* is very much meat-and-potatoes, a bit middling. This is glossier, and more pop and less rock. So the edges are smoothed down. I wouldn't use the word muted because that's got a negative connotation, but I don't think it's as rock-orientated. So yeah, it's interesting. They've gone from a rock/AOR production sound to something that is more tailored for big pop. I don't know what the modus operandi was. Maybe they thought that it would be even more radio-friendly and that radio will embrace those sorts of sounds. I'm just wondering if management at Polygram were sitting around tables and throwing things at Ritchie and saying, "This is what we need you to do to get into this market." Because records in the early eighties were becoming more directed by corporates, more accountants, and they were looking at target markets. So you get out the daisy wheel printer and print out all the charts with demographics and stuff. I don't know.

Jamie: You may have noticed, I haven't brought up Roger Glover much at all. Because when it comes to Roger Glover, I just don't notice him much in these songs ever. But I will say he did a damn good job producing this record. It might sound dated to a younger person hearing it for the first time, but I'm grandfathered in. This was my first Rainbow album. It sounded great to me as a kid and I've carried that feeling into my 50s. But it's so funny. I had a K-Tel album called *Masters of Metal*, with Triumph and Dio and Twisted Sister on it, and it also had "Street of Dreams." on it. And that's not even close to being a metal song.

Martin: I feel like the narrative of this record as a concept album builds with "Can't Let You Go." It's pop and yet it's still regal, so in other words, yeah, goth-lite, just like "Stranded."

Phil: Yes, plus "Can't Let You Go" sort of underscores that idea through its very gothic, church organ-type opening. Lovely lyric, lovely chorus, lovely melody and the guitar solos again are structured, well thought-out. Plus there's the second narrative carried over from previous albums, where Ritchie is letting others strut their stuff.

John: Yes, I love the *Phantom of the Opera* church organ intro here from David Rosenthal. It gives it a really spooky haunted house at your local amusement park atmosphere (laughs). There's also a video that goes along with this song that plays into this whole haunted house/vampire/Hammer Horror type of B-movie thing. So that church organ sets the song up for me. It's interesting; the church organ part is in G minor, which sets up this nice resolution, again, this circle of fifths thing. You hear me reference this a lot; it's a classical move. So they start off in G minor and then we drop into five lower here for C sharp minor when the guitar and the whole band kicks in. That gives us the idea of moving to a different place in the song.

To me, this is Joe Lynn Turner's money zone; it's melodic and so he can show off his range and sense of drama, his thespian tendencies. When the chorus kicks in, the way Joe just opens up and goes for it, he sounds great. He's powerful and never sounds like he's straining. And I just love the pre-chorus in this song. The "I don't want to say goodbye, but I don't want to live a lie" piece is a great section in the song that sets up the chorus. I love that line and I love the way it leads into the chorus.

The verses also have the classic Blackmore root fifth octave thing, like he does in the verses of "Smoke on the Water." That's a classic Ritchie thing that works really well here. Ritchie has the maturity, if you will, to know what to do. This is another thing that I love about him. He knows when to step back or drop down. And right here, the mandate is to let the vocal melody shine. He has no ego or no problem to just drop down and play subtle little things underneath the vocal so that the vocal melody line can speak and can jump out at you.

It's the same thing as when a lot of times when the keyboard players are soloing, going all the way back to Deep Purple. Ritchie will sometimes completely drop out or just drop down and play real quietly behind the keyboard player because he knows like, okay, now it's their time; let them do their thing. A lot of guitar players don't do that. They need to be the centre of the spotlight at all time. But Ritchie has the musicality and musical sense to know when to step aside and just blend in.

Peter: "Can't Let You Go" represents the more saccharine end of

Rainbow and it was readymade for FM radio. It's a nicely crafted song. This is Joe Lynn Turner as crooner, purveyor of rich, beautiful tone. You can understand why Ritchie rescued him from Fandango because Fandango were going nowhere. There's less of David Rosenthal and his keyboards on this album, so he just chimes in where it's necessary, providing atmosphere and colour. But he's less of a Jon Lord character than he was on *Straight Between the Eyes*. So all through this album, he does these quirky synth lines and little sort of ear candy hooks and riffs and that's perfect for the pop market. But no, he's not a Jon Lord character where he's like a fully-fledged pseudo-rhythm guitarist; that's one thing I've noticed.

Jamie: "Can't Let You Go" was the second and last single off the album, after "Street of Dreams," which is definitely the one you want to lead with. It's totally AOR, and I for one think AOR is a type of music that's of its time. The best prog came out in the seventies and the best AOR came out in the late seventies to mid eighties. And you have to be careful with AOR. I don't even know if you call this a genre, but it's definitely a sound. It's like djent—is that a genre or a technique? Whatever. You have to be careful with AOR. It's like a souffle. You have to be delicate. It can turn out great, but one wrong move and it falls flat.

Maybe some people would say in this case that AOR stands for "I'm admiring older Rainbow" and their seventies albums. They might think that their later period albums suck. Normally I'd be right there with you. Except for this AOR masterpiece. And I'm calling it a masterpiece within the world of AOR. This is as good as the genre gets. It's on the top of the mountain. That mountain might be made out of cheese, but it's still a mountain and it's right on top of it.

I think "Can't Let You Go" should have been a huge hit in 1983. We should be talking about this song today the same way we discuss any famous Journey or Foreigner song. But it's weird how it starts with a church organ. Because I can only imagine… I don't remember hearing it on the radio. It probably came and went pretty quickly. But if it's being played after a rockin' song—I don't know, Aldo Nova or something—and that church organ comes on, it doesn't exactly make you turn up the volume while driving your car. But there's a limit for me anyway, because I'm not a big AOR guy. Like when it comes to Survivor—too far. You've gone too far for me. But there are things on this song that are keeping my attention and making me like it.
Matt: Yeah, that intro is quite the statement. You've got this

improvised pipe organ sound from David Rosenthal. It's not a real pipe organ; he's playing it on an emulator. But Ritchie had liked that sound, and asked for something similar to Bach's "Toccata in D Minor," right? So it's got this very classical church organ-type sound to it. And then it goes into the verse. This song sounds like it could be on *Perfect Strangers*, the first part, at least. So you maybe get a foreshadowing of what Ritchie's going to do next with the very successful *Perfect Strangers* record.

But the transition to the chorus, I would say, is more of an AOR pop-type passage. Which is what Rainbow is trying to do, right? They're trying to be more like Foreigner than Deep Purple. Then you get the chorus, and it's a very strong vocal by Joe Lynn Turner, really professional. Then it's a terrific guitar solo, in this case, rhythmically very interesting. Ritchie does some sweep-picking-type stuff, but then goes into the slow bends. I really like when Ritchie combines the slow and fast stuff, that type of phrasing or dynamic; it's a fairly unique approach. Plus they do the proper production video, and it's like *The Cabinet of Dr. Caligari*, the silent German film. So the band must have liked this song. It seems hit-worthy to me as well.

Martin: It's so ridiculously in the Joe Lynn Turner zone, isn't it? How did the acquisition of Joe go over in the UK?

Phil: Well, I think he was a bit too flamboyant, as many people have said, for the UK, seeing him jumping up and down and flicking his hair back and stuff. He was not quite what the British audience could cope with. To be honest, I don't think that British audiences could have coped with someone like David Lee Roth in Rainbow either (laughs). Ritchie is the main focal point. The singer is someone who's supposed to be just slightly in his shadow. So someone who was trying to be out in front of Ritchie and trying to take the limelight off him was never going to win. But I still think that his voice was perfect for this part of Rainbow's evolution. I took to that straightaway.

Jamie: He's got a lot of soul in his voice, especially on this album. That was really lacking on *Difficult to Cure* and it started coming in on *Straight Between the Eyes*. But on this album, I feel like he's really found his groove, vocally. And having soul goes a long way in my book. Someone just asked me recently, last Saturday, how can you like Counting Crows but not Dave Matthews Band? You know what my answer was? Soul. Counting Crows have a certain soul that Dave

Matthews Band will never have. That's what this album has.

Martin: Even though "Fool for the Night" is a little faster and more of a wall of sound, darn it if it continues in this goth-lite vein that this band owns, for better or worse, as the AOR and the New Wave of British Heavy Metal begin their fade and hair metal is in ascendance, right?

John: Yes and no, and I'll get to the yes in a minute. Because after the darker tones of "Can't Let You Go," this one opens with a triumphant major key-sounding intro. I could picture that played by a horn section, actually. But to agree with you, here's another point I want to make about the Joe Lynn Turner era versus the Ronnie James Dio era. People always saying the Joe Lynn Turner era is about Foreigner and AOR rock. I truly believe that if you changed some of the lyrics to these songs, it would change the feel and people would perceive these songs as being heavier.

For instance, if this song wasn't called "Fool for the Night" and it was called "Demon of the Night"… Listen to this; here's a quote from the song: "Running through the shadows like a phantom in the night/And as the curtain raises, you get ready for the fight." That's something that Ronnie could have written anyway, right? So sometimes there are still some slightly heavier-sounding lyrics that you get out of the Joe Lynn Turner era. It's just that in general, Joe stays away from the demons and wizards and stuff like that. But you do occasionally get those here, like in this line that I just quoted. But something even more evil and with Ronnie singing it would go just fine on this music. The verses have this nice, chromatic, descending bass line, which is the exact same bass line that you get in the verses of "Stairway to Heaven." It's a classic minor chord progression.

Peter: "Fool for the Night," has a bit of groove to it, but I think it's filler. It's one of those songs that I don't think they spent a lot of time crafting, compared to like "Street of Dreams" or "Desperate Heart."

Matt: This one doesn't work quite as well for me either. It doesn't really have a riff to it and the lyrics are a bit pedestrian. For the guitar solo, it sounds like Ritchie's playing it through an octave pedal. It's melodic but it has a weird sound to it. The *Kerrang!* review at the time said that this is one of only two songs that were uninspired on what is otherwise a generally well-crafted album. And I would agree;

I would say this one's probably the least inspired of the songs. But it's still professionally done; it's well performed. But the songwriting and the quality and quantity of riffing isn't quite on par with the rest of it.

Martin: And here we are again, with Joe and Ritchie bonding over their love for all things nocturnal.

Matt: Absolutely; that's right. And they also bond on dream life and reincarnation and the séance-y Ouija board type stuff. Ask him and Joe will give a pretty lengthy description of the lyrics of "Fool for the Night." That's very much his nature. I don't think the execution of the lyrics quite deliver all the meaning that he's imbued into them. It ends up being a bit more pedestrian and less mystical than, say, "Street of Dreams" does, which works great, right? If he'd leaned a bit more into the supernatural vibe you get with the nocturnal, rather than just this party feel to the allure of the night, we might have felt more of a sense of mystery.

Jamie: I see no flaws with this song, which carries over to pretty much the whole album. It's a great hard rock ditty. It might be hard rock that you can listen to with your mom, but who cares? It opens up the opportunity for you to bond with your parents. And maybe that should have been this album's sales pitch to teenagers in 1983. "Going on a long trip with mom and dad? Throw on some *Bent Out of Shape*. They'll like it more than Iron Maiden."

Martin: I imagine your parents would like "Firedance" a little less, because Ritchie turns up the heat when it comes to the riff. It's a substantially heavy song on here, and I guess the fastest in terms of BPMs.

Jamie: Correct. This is one of the true hard rockers on the album. Mom and dad might want you to fast-forward through this song on that long trip you're taking with them. But I do like David Rosenthal's keyboards. That intro lick sure sounds like fire dancing, so mission accomplished. And I love Joe's vocals on this, and how he almost strains himself at times. It adds a little edge to the music that maybe some people think is lacking on this album. I'm gonna make a deep cut reference. And I wouldn't do this if you weren't Canadian and the band wasn't Canadian. On this album Joe sounds a lot like the lead singer of a little-known Canadian band called White Wolf, and the dude's name was Don Wilk. And if you compare the first two White Wolf albums and the vocals to this song, holy cow, it's almost like the same guy.

Phil: Nice one. Yeah, "Fire Dance" is one of the rockers, and it has the riff from "The Battle Rages On" hidden in it, doesn't it? It's a little motif that he's obviously thought, that'll be useful one day.

John: It's the most metal song on the record, softened up maybe because of the production. It's not a very metal-sounding production. The finger-twisting main riff is pretty cool, the way it bounces off of the open strings. There are some pretty dark Dio-style metal lyrics in this one, right? "Visions of Artemis, goddess of the moonlight." Artemis is the goddess of wild animals.

Peter: Totally agree: "Fire Dance" is heavier, but it's muted. The edges are softened through the pop production, so it doesn't have that crunch. If this was recorded on *Difficult to Cure*, the guitar would have been ramped-up in the mix. But the template here is for a pop metal album, so the impact is deliberately lessened. It winds up a bit nondescript and, dare I say, a bit anonymous.

Matt: With "Fire Dance" it's mystical Joe again, but he's piling on a bit more detail, because you get the visions of Artemis stuff. It's fantastical with an actual mythological reference. That's a level of reference and sophistication that's unusual for Joe Lynn Turner. You've got a wicked cool guitar riff, and with the swirling keyboards it's like Deep Purple, where you get that great combination of heavy guitar and keyboards, and then you get that keyboard and guitar solo before it goes back into the great riff. It's like "Burn" or something. Maybe not much of a chorus in there, but that would be my only knock on it. It's a very successful song given that for a Joe Lynn Turner song, it has a lot of Deep Purple in it and even some Dio.

Martin: We close side one of the original vinyl with "Anybody There," an instrumental ballad very much like "Weiss Heim," as it were.

Phil: Yes, and actually both "Weiss Heim" from *Down to Earth* and "Maybe Next Time" from *Difficult to Cure*. It points to a direction Ritchie might have pursued more seriously, doesn't it? You take this song along with "Snowman," and lots of his fans I feel would have thought one day Ritchie might do an album of those kinds of instrumentals and it would sell like hotcakes. But he never did. But I think both of those instrumentals, they feel to me that Ritchie Blackmore was comfortable and happy with what he was doing, playing this more laid-back guitar instrumental-type stuff. Just overall, his solos were becoming less… frantic is the wrong word, because I love Ritchie Blackmore when he plays like a demon. But equally I think he was thinking more about melodic structure. He was about serving the song rather than serving himself. He wasn't thinking about whether he'd be in the Top 20 guitarists in the *Sounds* poll that year.

John: I love when Ritchie does instrumentals. This evokes for me post-Roger Waters-era Pink Floyd. It's got that vibe to me, with the keyboards and everything. David Gilmour, Ritchie Blackmore… both guys play Stratocasters and both guys emphasize melody over flash. And so we get this beautiful, atmospheric song.

Peter: I think Ritchie puts a lot of soul and emotion into both of the instrumentals on this album. People look at Page, they look at Eric Clapton, they look at all the greater guitarists and they say they play with emotion, but Ritchie doesn't get spoken about. On the instrumentals both here and on *Difficult to Cure*, besides the divine tone, Ritchie is really putting his heart and soul into it. You could close your eyes and listen to this and think Ritchie Blackmore's got the most defined tone in all of rock 'n' roll.

Jamie: Did you know "Anybody There" was nominated for a Best Rock Instrumental Performance Grammy? It lost to Sting's "Brimstone and Treacle" from the movie of the same name. And I'll tell ya, I listened to that Sting song yesterday and it stinks. This is ten times better. And it should have won (laughs). It has what the guitar players came for, badass guitar playing along with really nice melodies packed into two-and-a-half minutes.

Matt: Structurally, it's really just slow keyboard chords for Ritchie to solo over. His playing is very expressive and quite beautiful and it works. This is a very well sequenced album. I like where they put the two instrumentals. It breaks things up and gives you a little bit of a moody ending to side one. Like Jamie says, it does get nominated at the 26th Grammys for '83. I think it's interesting who it's competing against. You have Stevie Ray Vaughan, Allan Holdsworth and then Pete Townsend for unused piano in *Quadrophenia* and of course Sting. So what a collection of rock instrumentals for 1983. As for the title, "Is there anybody there?" is what you say when you're doing a séance-type thing, right? You're reaching out and asking, "Is there a ghost here?"

Martin: All right, over to side two, we start with "Desperate Heart," which to me is of a mysterious verdant set of songs with "Stranded," "Can't Let You Go" and "Street of Dreams." Those tunes all form the conceptual foundation of *Bent Out of Shape* for me, of, yeah, a bunch of heavy Foreigner songs, or "Stone Cold" times four, basically. And then there's the symmetry of four fast ones and two instrumentals. It's like a re-drawing of *Rising*, in a way.

John: That's actually pretty cool, yeah. And "Desperate Heart" has this short but slightly medieval-sounding intro, pairing it up with what they do at the beginning of "Can't Let You Go." The keyboards there sound like a harpsichord. Throughout the song we get some very eighties-sounding keyboard-type fills that maybe date the record slightly. It's interesting how the verse is in D minor and the chorus drops down to A minor instead of rising up, which is a typical move, for the chorus to sound like it's lifting up and going higher. Here it drops down on you. Pretty safe song for me that doesn't have much to say in the lyric department; they're standard radio rock-type lyrics.

Jamie: We're still on that car trip with mom, and she might be on board with our album again. She might be liking "Desperate Heart." And yes, it sounds like early Michael Bolton, but Michael Bolton rocked in the beginning there on the first album or two. So it sounds like a good Michael Bolton song.

Peter: I love this song. It's got a lot of urgency. It's got a guitar line that's very similar to Stevie Nicks' "Edge of Seventeen," with that muted plucking. I love that it's dry and drives it along almost percussively. I'd say this is Joe's most urgent and crunchy rock vocal on the whole album. It cuts through the pop metal production. I would have put this as track one, side one. It's got those wonderful keyboard lines that act almost like ear candy. It's memorable overall and should have been a hit, to be quite frank. But yeah, it's that

"Edge of Seventeen" guitar line that propels it. Ritchie is a thief. He's thieves song snippets and guitar lines, but who doesn't? But he makes it his own. Because only he can play in that certain, special way, given his unique tonality. It's a totally underrated Rainbow song, but because it was put into the marketplace in 1983, there was a lot going on and it just got lost in the weeds.

Matt: Maybe comparing this to "Fool for the Night," to me, this is a much more effective and interesting AOR corporate rock song. The chorus vocal has a lot more variation, right? I like the way it melodically goes up at the end of lines like, "Don't start feeling you were sold out" and stuff. It makes it an interesting and catchy chorus. We get a Lou Gramm-style vocal on this song but it's very well done. You get some nice keyboard flourishes and excellent Blackmore solo that typifies his style at the time; there's rhythmic variation and some expressive whammy bar. It's another hit-worthy song, had they given it attention.

Martin: I know I lean hard on this and have tried to explain it a few times, but there's a parallel between Rainbow and something like MSG, and maybe more McAuley Schenker Group actually, this forging of a European hair metal aesthetic.

Matt: That's right; I completely agree. And that sets it apart from a Foreigner, right? Foreigner has none of those Teutonic medieval, classical elements at all.

Martin: Except for the verse chords in "I Want to Know What Love Is," although I'm sure there are a few others.

Matt: Yeah, that's dark enough. That's right. I wonder where that came from?

Martin: All right, onward to "Street of Dreams," and like I say, we barely have to make any sort of left turn.

Matt: Yes, it's of a similar arrangement and volume, isn't it? To the extent there's a hit, this is the hit on the record. It's a very well-done but unusual and poppy hard rock song. It's not even that hard, right? It's a moody rocker, I guess you would call it. And it's very well constructed. Joe Lynn Turner has called it his favourite song that he ever did with Rainbow. I think he's described it as like his golden child, or the diamond that they created.

We talked about the dream stuff before. Joe said that he woke up from a recurring dream where he's been haunted by a woman's face for years. So it's a lyric that touches on reincarnation, with that "Do you remember me?" idea. And so Ritchie is really keen on this; it's a common area of interest for them, around reincarnation and dreams and the importance of them. And Joe goes on and talks about how he later meets the woman and marries the woman. He very much is a believer in these dreams sending him messages, right?

Chuck Bürgi's talked about how they ultimately recorded it to a click track and that the feel wasn't right. Ritchie didn't want to record to a click and then, allegedly, they do it unbeknownst to him when he's out of the studio against his wishes. But Chuck has said that he had a thing in mind about how the feel of the drum track should go. I like how the chorus is very controlled. It builds up a bit, but there's restraint, which serves the song very well. It's sort of dreamlike, the way it never goes over-the-top with the chorus. The keyboard parts and guitar parts go really well together and the guitar solo is also restrained, just a solo that fits the song. Which for a guy who noodles a lot in concert, Ritchie could do that at times on the record with a lot of taste.

Martin: Matt, something funny about this. The verse riff is like arpeggiated octaves. Even Roger, throws in a few octaves and on "Stranded," Roger does more of that octave-jumping bass stuff. And then on "Desperate Heart," that keyboard lick from Rosenthal jumps octaves.

Matt: Yeah, very cool. Plus we just talked about how on one of Ritchie's guitar solos, he used an octave pedal. And there's times when he's playing slide he does some things with octaves. And what Ritchie is doing on "Street of Dreams," it's a muted arpeggiated chord, right? He's palm-muting, so the notes of the chord don't ring out. It's a three-note chord and then the palm-muting creates that effect where it doesn't ring out. And I just love the way it blends with the keyboards. For the eighties stuff that Ritchie does, when it matches with the keyboard, this is true on the later Deep Purple ones too, when it works, boy, it really works, doesn't it?

Martin: And we're back to night-time mystery, right? What's the eighties movie about that the crazy stuff that happens all through the night?

Matt: Is it *After Hours*?

Martin: Yeah, that's it. I look at these titles and play the lyrics in my head and it's just a big, surreal night of misadventure for Joe, with drinking and supernatural happenings and dangers of all kinds He's just wandering around the city and getting yanked from one adventure to another. It's a concept album, I tell ya!

Phil: Sure, sounds good (laughs). Whatever the case, "Street of Dreams" is the best ballad that they ever did. It didn't sell as well as Ritchie probably had expected. And he revisited it with Blackmore's Night, didn't he? Because Candy's had a go at singing it.

John: I absolutely love this song. It's so well written. There's not a note out of place, not too many notes, not too few notes. It's just a very well-crafted, well-written rock song. For me this feels like—and I don't have any quotes from Ritchie—but in my mind I think I've heard him say this is the song that I've been trying to write forever, a really well-crafted and accessible song, but it still has a slightly dark and mysterious tone to it, with the idea of a "street of dreams" and all that. The eighties-sounding keyboards really work here, and in the intro especially. They give it this really dreamy, ethereal quality.

But you've got these goth overtones from the Man in Black, and Joe's melodies are haunting and memorable. This might be my favourite vocal performance from Joe. I love the melody at the part in the song where it goes, "I've seen this place before, but you were standing by my side." That is a great melody and it's a great lyric overall; it conjures so many images. The chorus is very restrained and sublime, but also catchy. It's not big and bombastic but it fits the mood of the song so well. Those little keyboard flourishes inside the chorus are perfect. There's a beautiful guitar solo from Ritchie. I remember reading where when it came time to do this solo, he was so impressed by Joe's melodies in this song that he felt pressure, like I've got to come up with something that can hang with the melodies that Joe is singing here.

It's a shining example of Rainbow being able to write a dark, moody song but in a melodic AOR format. You can still do this. You can have a radio-friendly song but it can have a dark mood too. For me, "Stone Cold" is like the predecessor to "Street of Dreams." It's that melodic, slightly moody, like you said, gothic Foreigner or gothic AOR thing. "Stone Cold" establishes the formula, but they perfect it with "Street of Dreams."

Peter: They're definitely looking for another "Stone Cold" because "Stone Cold" got to No.40 In the US singles charts and was getting lots of radio airplay. And just talking to folks that I do my shows with, it still gets played to this day on classic rock radio. It's probably their second most well-known song in the Americas because it was getting a lot of traction.

But I love "Street of Dreams." It's mining Ritchie's love for Abba. It's got melancholy, it's got that chordal progression and I was just thinking, I could imagine Agnetha singing this in Abba. I could imagine a lot of pop acts doing it. But we're talking about Rainbow here, so it's got the European, the classical.

I believe it stalled because there was a video clip that had hypnotism, and it got banned by MTV, inexplicably. MTV was very much a deal-breaker in America. If you didn't get your clip played, then you were dead in the water. I've seen the video; it's pretty tame. I don't get the rationale behind MTV banning it, but I understand it got played and then there were some complaints. It's got some occult themes and violence, but when you compare it to a lot of the videos of the day, like in heavy metal, where a lot of them are borderline sexist now, it's a real head-scratcher, why they got banned. So coming back to the root, because it simply needed to be played on MTV and it wasn't, what could have been their breakthrough hit ultimately failed. It might have been a whole different trajectory for Rainbow.

But look, this song is just so well crafted, I can really imagine that the band sat down, maybe got out a big piece of paper and worked it out. Like some Rainbow songs, as I said to you earlier, they sound like they came from a jam and just come out as filler tracks. It's where they're working it out in the studio and it evolves into a song that the better songs are realized. Where they've actually sat down and planned it out and really thought about the arrangement. "Street of Dreams" sounds like one of those; it's the perfect Rainbow pop song.

Martin: Next is "Drinking with the Devil," and I'm seeing yet another unifying theme, and it's how most of the fast songs lapse into melodic, chordal verses. It's that Sammy Hagar "hanging chord" thing I complain about, although here there are more chords. But the heaviness definitely evaporates or at least wanders off (laughs).

Jamie: Right, right. This was the first Rainbow album I ever got, and I remember thinking that the rocking songs on here, to my 13-year-old ears, oh, that's pretty rockin'. And now a song like this is barely even metal to me. Still though, "Drinking with the Devil," man oh man, this is a great one. And if we're in that car trip, mom's giving us that look again. Yes, this rocks a lot like "Fire Dance." But do you know what I see this song as? The predecessor to Deep Purple's "Fire in the Basement," especially when you compare the two choruses. And let's face it, *Slaves and Masters* is pretty much a Rainbow album, and a really good one too. And then of course you might call "King of Dreams" the follow-up to "Street of Dreams," although musically it's quite a bit heavier.

Even though Joe is using more of his metallic voice or metal guy voice, he's retaining his soulfulness. So it's a hard rockin' party song, but with just enough soul in his voice to make it sound genuine. It doesn't sound like they're doing a hard rocker just for the sake of doing a hard rocker on the album. It sounds like it belongs on the album.

Martin: Funny, now you got me thinking about *Slaves and Masters*, and "Fortune Teller" on there reminds me of "Desperate Heart."

John: Yeah, you could compare those two albums all day. As for "Drinking with the Devil," it's a hard-driving rocker that fills the space, I guess, on the record. The guitars are pretty aggressive here. Coming after "Street of Dreams," it sits well on the record, providing maximum contrast. Ritchie's solo here is almost chaotic, a little noisy-sounding. The lyrics are a bit stock and boring; they're clichéd rock 'n' roll lyrics, I suppose. "Drinking with the devil/Gonna raise some hell/I'm just a rock 'n' roll rebel/Got my soul to sell." Eww (laughs). But there's a pretty cool chromatic walk-up from the five chord of D back to the root in G minor they do in the song that I think is pretty cool, and I do like the fast, bluesy guitar flourishes at the end of the song.

Peter: No one has mentioned that odd howl or scream from Joe at the beginning—when it starts out, it actually sounds like guitar. It's a fast-paced rocker and the lyrics are about having a good time and just raising hell. Like John says, it's bit clichéd, but this is where Rainbow have to periodically check in and punch the clock. Rainbow song? Check! (laughs). I guess they deliberately sequenced it after "Street of Dreams" because a lot of the older, classic power metal fans of Rainbow *Rising* might be in shock after hearing "Street of Dreams" and thinking, oh no, what's happened to Rainbow? So they've got to put a rocker in just to yank them back. So I think it's deliberate with respect to sequencing, that they've done a rocker straight after the saccharine Euro pop song.

Matt: "Drinking with the Devil" is a straightforward rocker and, again, well produced. This whole record sounds good on crummy speakers. So it was ready for radio in a lot of ways because everything is just so clearly and cleanly recorded. Each instrument has its space.

Martin: Although Matt, I disagree with you in that respect because I believe it was Peter Jones that brought up that because it's such a beautiful analog recording with such low bass, if you were driving on the freeway in your car, because it's not a very midrangy record, you'd have difficulty hearing it.

Matt: Yeah, you'd lose the bottom end, but I don't think you'd lose the bass, because Roger Glover keeps adding these little parts to each of the riffs, that end the riffs, so that they cut through the mix. So I agree; you're definitely losing the low end to it, but I think the bass guitar continues to add interesting parts that would come through on your car stereo.

Martin: Nice. And would you say this one has one foot in that collection of widdly, circular Ritchie Blackmore riffs that we've talked about?

Matt: I'm not sure, or let's say, yeah, partially. It's a little bit swingy, right? Like he repeats a motif. He plays it across one chord and then plays it across another one, so it's got the same rhythm but then in a different place. So I don't know; he's such a weird guy. He actually complains about some of the funk and R&B parts in the later stages of Deep Purple, but he has such a blues background that he keeps using. He'll play these swinging, R&B-ish type things and then go off and do his classical stuff. He really has those two sides, that non-bluesy, very European and then this funky side that comes out in these note-dense riffs that are, on the face of it, quite significantly heavy metal.

Martin: And what do you make of this lyric?

Matt: Like you were saying, Martin, it's all part of Joe's night out, right? It's about the dangers of drinking and having the devil as a bar companion. That's subject matter that lots of bands have addressed and again, it might have been more dramatic or impactful if it was more about the devil and less about the drinking. Because other bands have done a better job with this. You've got AC/DC with "Have a Drink on Me;" "Forget about the check/ We'll get Hell to pay." I think that's a little better executed version of this. Or like even later with The Mighty Mighty Bosstones and "Devils Night Out," where the devil is this better-dressed interesting character and is dancing up a storm.

Martin: It also reminds me of Ozzy Osbourne's "Demon Alcohol," or Yesterday and Today's "Alcohol."

Matt: Yeah, and The Kinks have an "Alcohol" too. So it's a common subject matter, but probably done a bit better by some of these other bands.

Martin: It's back to the instrumentals for the second to last track on side two of the original vinyl. This is pretty much my favourite of all the instrumentals.

Peter: Yeah, "Snowman" is wonderful and extremely emotive. This guy, through the strings, he just sings. I'd actually never heard Ritchie Blackmore talk until the last ten, twenty years, this is before YouTube. You'd read the occasional interview but I never heard Ritchie Blackmore speak, which added to the mystery, like the olden days when we didn't have this multimedia madness where if anyone farts on TV, you hear about it. But not hearing Ritchie speak and not knowing much about him, this man of mystery, you listen to a song like this through the headphones and you just get lost in the tonality of his guitar playing and what he wants to create. I would have loved to have heard a Ritchie Blackmore instrumental album. I think it would have been quite wonderful. And yeah, this is not filler in any shape or form. I think it's one of the strongest songs on the album.
John: "Snowman" is a song written by Howard Blake for a children's

animated movie called *The Snowman*, which was adapted from a Raymond Briggs children's book. The song in the movie is actually titled "Walking in the Air." The story of the movie and the book is basically like a British version of *Frosty the Snowman*, where a snowman comes to life and he befriends a young boy.

This can almost bring me to tears when I listen to it, especially if you're at all familiar with the storyline in the movie, with the original song, "Walking in the Air," where the boy and the snowman are sort of flying through the air. So I just love this song. It's so emotional. The keyboards carry the main melody, the "Walking in the Air" melody at the beginning here. But they sound so atmospheric, it sounds like you're up there floating in the air.

When the guitar arrives, it enters with so much force and it's so powerful and majestic and yet so melodic. I'm getting a shiver up my spine talking about it. The chord progression is super-interesting. It just moves to all these really nice places. Again, Ritchie loves to solo over interesting chord progressions. Most rock guitar players love to solo over one chord so they can just play one scale and just jump up and down and move their fingers around without really having to think about it. Ritchie is the opposite. He loves playing over moving chords, because it forces him to be even more melodic than he already naturally is. There's a part in Ritchie's solo where the way he builds a solo, it's just so well done, so well crafted. I mentioned this earlier, but it's interesting to me how Ritchie opts for instrumentals that are showcases for melody rather than flash.

There's a fading bell sound at the end of the song, as it's sort of going out, that's just great. This should have ended side two. It would have been a perfect bookend. Side one ends with an instrumental. This should have ended side two.

Jamie: I said that this album is pretty much flawless, and I did say "pretty much." If I could change one thing, I would narrow it down to one instrumental on this album and not two. You could either pick "Snowman" or "Anybody There." I don't care which one you pick. But that being said, "Snowman" is a cool and moody piece of music that gives the album some added depth and creativity that maybe a relatively simple AOR album like this needs.

Matt: As John explained, Howard Blake gets a writing credit on "Snowman" because he's an English composer who wrote this "Walking in the Air" song from the animated movie called *The*

Snowman. The song itself has a lyric, but this is an instrumental, where he's taken that core melody to that song. One thing that's interesting about Howard Blake, he also wrote the orchestral score to *Flash Gordon.* Of course, Queen does the soundtrack to it and he was, I guess, disappointed with how little of his orchestral score was used. So I think Queen muscled him out of his music being used.

The percussion on this is sequenced, so Chuck Bürgi is not on this one. You get a long intro that's mostly keyboards. So even though this is a Ritchie showcase, it does start with an interesting keyboard passage. Again, it's another slow and melodic instrumental and more about the atmosphere of the song. Sequence-wise it works really well because it's coming in between more rockin'-type songs. I think it does break things up nicely.

Martin: *Bent Out of Shape* closes with a fourth up-tempo, action-packed, wall-of-sound-type song in "Make Your Move," after which Ritchie and Roger will make their move over to Deep Purple.

Jamie: Yes, "Make Your Move" is just pure Rainbow, if you ask me. It has that driving beat, the guitar is in sync with the keyboards just like Ritchie likes, until he does that fiery little solo. Chuck Bürgi is killing it on drums.

Peter: They reinforce and leave the listener with the message that Rainbow is a rock band, a hard rock band, but still very polished, very professional, plus we write good songs. It's in that sort of template. Is it a top-tier Rainbow song? Probably not. But it's there for a purpose, to finish the record on a rock high, so to speak.

John: For me, "Make Your Move" is a bit unremarkable, a bit forgettable. It's up-tempo but it's too similar to "Drinking with the Devil." It occupies that same fast, slightly chaotic, rock 'n' roll space. Joe tries coming across as tough with lyrics like, "Better not mess around with me/You know you better think twice." But man, it just doesn't work for me. Those type of lyrics work with Phil Lynott and Bon Scott but not with Joe. I like Joe when he's in that sort of austere, sophisticated romantic zone but with a bit of darkness or even despair. This type of thing just doesn't do it for me with Joe. I do like the guitar melody that Joe doubles with his vocals, right before Ritchie's crazy, shredding guitar solo. Again, I just wish that the album had ended with the instrumental and they had maybe either dropped this song or replaced it.

Matt: "Make Your Move" is another song that *Kerrang!* cited as maybe being less inspired than the rest. I think that's true to the extent that, again, it doesn't have much of a riff. So it's a bit underwritten. Plus you have the clichéd lyrics and not as many interesting chord changes. But it's really well performed and it's got a quick and fiery Blackmore guitar solo. The bridge is a little underwhelming, but then you get that great guitar solo, as well as some cool outro guitar soloing. Joe is rocking out. He's not going through the motions. So even though the song's a little underwritten, he's definitely putting out the energy and the effort in terms of execution. So I disagree with *Kerrang!*. I don't think it's uninspired. I think they're feeling it. The effort is there. It's just maybe not as well crafted as some of the others.

Martin: All right, any closing thoughts? I want to reiterate, for me anyway, this is where Rainbow finally settle on a sound and it's an intriguing one, or sort of a nuanced hybrid that puts them in a class of their own. But trends are pointing elsewhere, away from any version of AOR, which is something this pretty much is.

Phil: Yes, I agree. The first time I really felt this defined persona for Rainbow come together was "Stone Cold," but I think on this album it's quite developed. That's what I was saying at the start of this segment. You almost wanted another one after this. Because this one got to No.11 in the charts in the UK. It felt like Ritchie had found the way forward, combining his aggressive guitar playing with the more commercial, melodic road that he wanted to go down. Because he could rock out with things like "Drinking with the Devil"—fantastic song, great guitar playing on it, great lyric, well delivered by Joe Lynn Turner. "Make Your Move" is another great song, great guitar outros and stuff. But that's equally balanced with "Desperate Heart," with its great keyboard motifs. I agree that out of all the albums from this period, *Bent Out of Shape* sits at the top.

Martin: It's like the birth year of hair metal, yet *Bent Out of Shape* is of a previous generation. It's more like Sammy Hagar and Loverboy and Night Ranger, more of a 1981 or 1982 album. But they want to be the upscale, almost regal or elite version of that, the band with pedigree operating in this space. Or maybe the best *British* band operating in this space.

Phil: Yeah, and I think that was how it was received. It might actually have gotten five stars in *Sounds*, saying he's back on form. I remember buying it and absolutely loving it as soon as I heard it. It sounded polished, it had enough Ritchie on it for me, I love the instrumentals, I love the hard rock songs, I love the ballads. So I was quite surprised when we heard that Purple were coming back together. But Ritchie said, "I'm putting Rainbow on hold." He didn't actually say he was stopping. He just said I'm going to pause it for a moment. Although he paused it for quite a long time.

Martin: Well, again, I like it for its cohesion, and to put it bluntly, for me that's represented by the album having four "Stone Colds" on it, namely "Stranded," "Can't Let You Go," "Desperate Heart" and "Street of Dreams."

Jamie: Yeah, and those are all great. It's not like you listen to one and you go, oh, that's just a copy of that one. They're all great somehow. Maybe if they made 12 songs that sounded like that, we'd be going, okay, all right, you went to the well too many times. But four or five? Perfect number. Great. Talking about "Street of Dreams," I'm just gonna say it—it's one of the best songs to come out of the eighties for me. Here's the thing. I started this off saying how I'm just one man with one opinion and I'm not saying facts. Well, I'm taking that back for this one song. If you think this song sucks, you're just plain wrong. This is perfect songwriting and then perfect execution. Is it metal? No. Is it hard rock? Barely, right? The kids today would call it dad rock. But who cares when a song is this good? It doesn't matter what label you put on it. When I hear those opening notes, I instantly smile and I wouldn't change one damn thing about the song. I will never get tired of it. Ever.

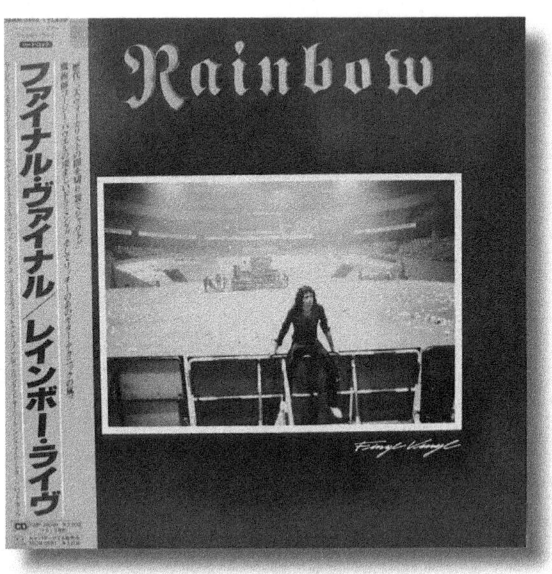

FINYL VINYL

March 1986
Mercury 422-827 987-1 M-2
Produced by Roger Glover; Executive Producer Ritchie Blackmore
Personnel: various line-ups (live and studio compilation)

Side 1
1. Spotlight Kid (Blackmore, Glover) 5:00
2. I Surrender (Ballard) 5:45
3. Miss Mistreated (Blackmore, Turner, Rosenthal) 3:21

Side 2
1. Jealous Lover (Blackmore, Turner) 3:10
2. Can't Happen Here (Blackmore, Glover) 4:15
3. Tearin' Out My Heart (Blackmore, Turner, Glover) 8:04
4. Since You Been Gone (Ballard) 3:40
5. Bad Girl (Blackmore, Glover) 4:48

Side 3
1. Difficult to Cure (Beethoven; arr. by Blackmore, Glover, Airey; orchestral arrangement by David Rosenthal) 11:15
2. Stone Cold (Blackmore, Turner, Glover) 4:30
3. Power (Blackmore, Turner, Glover) 4:22

Side 4
1. Man on the Silver Mountain (Blackmore, Dio) 8:20
2. Long Live Rock 'n' Roll (Blackmore, Dio) 7:12
3. Weiss Heim (Blackmore) 5:10

A *Finyl Vinyl* Timeline

November 2, 1984. Ritchie Blackmore, having knocked Rainbow on its head, sees the release of Deep Purple Mk. II reunion album, *Perfect Strangers*. The album reaches No.5 in the UK and No.17 in the US. The band's US tour for the album would be the year's biggest, after Bruce Springsteen.

March 1986. Rainbow issue a posthumous live and studio double album compilation called *Finyl Vinyl*.

January 12, 1987. Deep Purple issue *The House of Blue Light*, the second album in the eighties for the reformed Mk. II line-up.

June 1987. Former Elf and Rainbow drummer Gary Driscoll is found murdered at a friend's house in Ithaca, NY. The case is never solved. Driscoll was 41 years old.

1989. Ritchie Blackmore meets future collaborator and wife Candice Night. Meanwhile, also in '89, Glenn Hughes and Joe Lynn Turner get together to write a few tunes and record some demos, but the collaboration stalls. Same year, Turner is featured on an Yngwie Malmsteen live album called *Trial by Fire*.

Martin talks to Tim Durling, Peter Kerr and Matt Thompson about *Finyl Vinyl.*

Martin Popoff: All right, I feel like with *Finyl Vinyl* we're dealing with a tangle of things all over again, just like *On Stage.* It's a double vinyl release, featuring live material plus studio rarities, and when it comes out, Rainbow is no more. What's your general view of this album, first of all?

Peter Kerr: It seems like a contractual obligation album. It's wildly uneven in regards to the sequencing, which is all out of order. It was heavily criticized at the time and you can understand why. There's very limited Ronnie James Dio, which to the Dio-era Rainbow fan is disappointing. And to rub it in, it was the short-lived *Long Live Rock 'n' Roll* era of the band we hear from, which had immense potential and they only get a couple of tracks. This is like a lost opportunity where they could have put out something epic. Instead, it seems to be cobbled together in a ramshackle way.

What's on vinyl, the recordings are fine and there are some fantastic performances. But it leaves you wanting more. I take umbrage with the presentation, I take umbrage of how it's been put together, and to me it just smacks of the dreaded contractual obligation album. It was put out in 1986. So that was one year before *The House of Blue Light.* Polydor were probably thinking that there was an appetite for this among Purple fans. *Perfect Strangers* was a smash album and smash tour. We've got to put something out. Oh, Rainbow. Let's go into the vaults and cobble something together. I imagine that Ritchie wasn't too involved with it.

Tim Durling: *Finyl Vinyl* is a weird release. It's a posthumous release. Blackmore's back in Purple, at least for now. It's this weird grab-bag of songs. And I've got a lot of criticisms of it. Obviously it's not like they didn't know, but if you're going to mix studio tracks and live tracks, and you're doing it as some sort of career retrospective, which this certainly looks like by the title alone, you should never put live versions of your hits on one of these. Put the single versions on or put the studio album versions on. If you're gonna have live tracks, you put live versions on there of "Death Alley Driver" or "Stranded" or "Freedom Fighter." Don't put on live versions of "Stone Cold" or "I

Surrender." The cassette edition extra, "Street of Dreams," is also live and that was a hit song too. That was on the CDs too, by the way, just not the original vinyl.

And like a lot of bands did in the eighties, these live versions are all way too fast. They're so far past the original versions. And they're not the only ones. Whitesnake would take "Walking in the Shadow of the Blues" and like double the speed. Judas Priest on the 1987 live album did this too. I think a song lives within its own tempo and when you alter it too much, it's not the same song anymore. Plus it sounds like they're just racing to get through it like they are bored. I'm sure there's lots of good, white powdery reasons for that, but that's one of my criticisms. Plus don't put live versions of your hits on there. Save the live space for the B-sides and the deep album tracks if you want to show off your band's live sound. But yeah, the track listing looks better than listening to the actual album. Because you look at this and you go, oh, it's got "I Surrender," "Street of Dreams," "Can't Happen Here" and "Since You Been Gone," but they're all live versions.

Matt Thomspon: As Peter explained, *Finyl Vinyl* comes out after the band is broken up and it's between the two reformed Deep Purple albums, *Perfect Strangers* in '84 and *The House of Blue Light* in '87. So this one's smack dab in the middle of it, and they're emptying out the vaults, with studio songs that didn't get released on the records and then a bunch of live songs from different versions of the band. They're capitalizing on the pretty exciting reunion. That makes business sense. *Perfect Strangers* was very successful and they were a big touring entity supporting that and they got good FM radio play out of that album. So it's moving some units and the touring's doing well; they were a hot band.

Martin: How do you feel about the album cover?

Peter: Is that an inviting album cover? Ritchie looks like he's saying, "I'm exhausted." Is that the message you want to convey? Live performance is supposed to be about excitement. You want to see electricity and you've got Ritchie at the end of a concert looking half spent. Yeah, from a marketing point of view it's not very inviting. So I saw this in the record stores and I stayed away from it. And I'm a Deep Purple tragic (laughs). I love all the various roots and tree lines. But I stayed away from this album for a considerable period of time because the album cover didn't look inviting. I looked at the track listing and it was in all the shops, but I just resisted until I eventually succumbed. I don't mind it, but the way it's put together is just codswallop.

Martin: Okay, well, it starts sort of cohesive enough. Side one is three songs from Japan, March 1984. But like *On Stage*, they are calling fifteen minutes a side of music.

Peter: Yeah, this has been wildly bootlegged, the very final concert at Budokan. And doesn't Japan love Rainbow? They're up there I think like No.2 behind the Beatles. Maybe it's all the mysticism and mythology that they're interested in, or just the fact that they also love Deep Purple so much. But this was the final tour and I like the three tracks. "Spotlight Kid" is always a great opener. Ritchie shows his dexterity on the guitar, especially with that lead break and that sort of... how would I describe it? It sounds like a Greek or an Italian melody line in the middle—that's always amusing.

Tim: "Spotlight Kid" is okay, even though, again, it's ridiculously fast. It's one of the better songs on *Difficult to Cure* and it was a long-time set-opener for them.

Matt: It's the late-stage Joe Lynn Turner version of the band, at the Budokan in '84, so you've got Chuck Bürgi drumming on these ones. And it's interesting because first off, they present "Spotlight Kid" and "I Surrender" in flipped order versus the studio album. *Finyl Vinyl* opens with "Spotlight Kid" and it works great. Actually, it starts with "Somewhere Over the Rainbow" from *The Wizard of Oz*, that little opening piece. "Spotlight Kid" has got a lot of what you like about Ritchie Blackmore and his band. In some ways it's almost like an overture to the concert. Because you get the guitar solo, the keyboard solo and the doubled parts with the little classical solo. I think the keyboard solo's better on this one than on the studio version.

Martin: Next is "I Surrender," with Joe ducking notes and again, a little hectic-sounding at this increased tempo.

Tim: Yeah, I was never a big fan of this song anyway. The live version is adequate, again, like the first song. But at 5:43, with all those extra bars of soloing, it's too long. It doesn't need to be that long.

Peter: Joe does a good job on this live version, but it's got the backup singers. Initially I didn't like it, but I must admit it adds some R&B soul and colour and atmosphere, a little bit of oomph. It takes it into an extra dimension. As a bit of conjecture, did Ritchie add the backup singers because he wasn't confident in Joe Lynn Turner's vocals? Did he want them there to sort of reinforce and fill out the sonics? I'm not sure that's the case. But all-around, I think it's a good suite of songs. Again, this is one concert that should get an official release. I've got it on DVD—bootleg, mind you—but I think the show in itself should be released. In fact, across all the shows sampled here, there's six or seven albums that might be able to be expanded into full live albums. It's very frustrating, this album, just getting these snippets.

Matt: They stretch "I Surrender" out at the end, right? So they're solving the classic band problem of how do you do a live song when you faded it out on the record? And so what do they do? They extend it a bit. You get more soloing and then they come back to the opening riff. It's a classic way of solving that. It's Lin Robinson and Dee Beale doing the backup singing, Lynyrd Skynyrd type formation, where it's two backup singers. I think it works best when they are doubling Joe, like in the choruses. That gives him support and they sound like they're rockin' out a bit more.

Martin: "Miss Mistreated" is also bundled up and sent off for delivery with haste. It's quite punchy, and we've got the backing vocals doubling Joe as well as just doing oohing and aahing.

Tim: Yeah, "Miss Mistreated" is okay at 4:20. That's reasonable, and you're right, it's got a sort of face-forward energy to it. The cassette and the CD slot in "Street of Dreams" here, which is also played too fast.

Martin: Side two opens with non-LP B-side "Jealous Lover," and again, there's Rainbow playing with octaves.

Tim: Yeah, I like that one, but I can only enjoy it when I get past the fact that it reminds me of "Staying Alive" by the Bee Gees. That brings a disco feel to it. But it's a good song. It's weird that they didn't put it on *Difficult to Cure*.

Peter: "Jealous Lover" was on *The Best of Rainbow* which came out in 1981, in the UK. I'd say it's the greatest non-LP Rainbow song of all time. It should have been on an album and it could have been a huge hit. America got in on an EP at the time. It was getting a bit of radio airplay but it should have been bigger. It's punchy, it's got a compelling vocal line by Joe Lynn Turner and I like the lyrics to it.

Matt: I agree; "Jealous Lover" is a great song. It was the B-side of "Can't Happen Here" and then they put out a *Jealous Lover* EP, a little four-song thing, so ultimately they must have known that they had a good song. It's conspicuous in its absence that it wasn't on the album. It's got such a groovy riff to it and I love the way that riff comes back into the end of the chorus. That's the same move Purple do on "Smoke on the Water."

You covered this probably better than anybody in *Sensitive to Light*, but they recorded it in Minnesota using the Rolling Stones mobile unit. Joe Lynn Turner had written lyrics and melody for some other song and then Ritchie pulls a fast one out of that. He said no, we're doing this song, and Joe basically has five minutes to come up with a lyric for it and does a really good job. And he's talked about how maybe that helped the creative process, not spending too much time on it and just letting fly.

Martin: And then, wow, next we've got three live tracks in a row, each from a different show.

Peter: "Can't Happen Here" was a minor hit for them. It hit No.20 in the UK, which was a bit of a positive for Rainbow because their first big hit in the UK was "I Surrender" and that was a cover. For them to have a hit with this song proved that they could write their own songs and get some airplay. Anyway, with respect to the live version, man, again, like Tim says, it's almost comically fast. Bobby can barely get his fills in.

Matt: This is the only one where I really don't like the live version. It's one that supports my theory that this was probably more of a Glover lyric, because I feel like Joe Lynn Turner is blowing off the lyrics with his delivery, "All that you fear, they're telling you, can't happen here." The way he says "telling you" bothers me and he's ducking notes and rushing them, although that's partially the fault of the faster tempo. But I don't like that little affectation he puts on,

"They're telling you." I don't feel like he's taking it seriously. Maybe he's not particularly behind that song, just by virtue of it not being his own, which is understandable.

"Tearin' Out My Heart" is worth talking about just because that's a great version and it's double the length, right? So they take a four-minute song and do an eight-minute version of it. And Joe does a really powerful, emotional vocal. They speed up in the middle and we get this descending bass part. It's like how Blue Öyster Cult does "Veteran of the Psychic Wars" or "Last Days of May" in concert. You get that big jam section where things speed up but then it stops and then you've just got Ritchie noodling for a little bit on his own and then you go back to the fast part. Some things on live albums don't always warrant repeated listening, but if you're seeing them live, it would work so great. I'm sure the visual parts of this, with Ritchie doing his little guitar solo, would have been even better. But this was really good; they do a great job of that.

Tim: I disagree. "Tearin' Out My Heart" is too long and overwrought for a song that was never a single. It's almost like they wanted that to become the new "Mistreated," which is another song that they would always play too long. It's self-indulgent. But Deep Purple were always self-indulgent live too, so I guess this makes sense.

Martin: Last of this live trio is Rainbow with Graham Bonnet at Monsters of Rock, August 16, 1980.

Peter: Yeah, and that's another set that should have been released back in the day as a full album. It's Graham Bonnet's farewell, his final show, at Donington, no less. I like Graham. He's what you call, here in Australia, a belter. He just belts it out. There's not a lot of… you compare him and Joe Lynn Turner and Joe's got more colour and shade. But Graham, quality-wise, he's just one volume, one colour. He opens his mouth and lets it go. I've seen him live a few times and he's standing there, mic clenched in fist, mouth open all the way through; there's no variation. "Since You Been Gone" is a perfect match between the material and the singer. Ritchie's been really canny with his association with Russ Ballard, matching Graham smartly with this song and Joe with "I Surrender." This turned out to be one of Graham Bonnet's finest moments.

Matt: I guess the thing sticking out there is that it really sounds like he's having fun. He even cracks up when he's singing one of the lines. He's talked about what a monumental experience it was to do that show. It's a singer having a very good time and you can hear that attitude in the performance.

Tim: "Since You Been Gone" is only a bit sped-up, not like some of the other ones. Graham sounds good on it. I would have liked to have heard a couple more songs from him, but I guess it was such a short era and we're trying to cover a lot of bases here.

Martin: Illogically, side two ends with another B-side, "Bad Girl," from the Graham Bonnet era. Pretty weird, but for me, this reaches the exact same temperature—room temperature—as "Jealous Lover." I can't picture this song on *Down to Earth* at all.

Tim: I totally understand that. "Bad Girl" is okay. It's not a song where I go, man, if this had been on *Down to Earth*, it would have been even better. No, it's perfectly good B-side/extra song material. But if they're cleaning house, so to speak, they might as well put it out. It was useful at the time because "Bad Girl" had never been widely available before. Same with "Weiss Heim," and not everybody got the *Jealous Lover* EP. So I guess *Finyl Vinyl* has got something going for it.

Matt: "Bad Girl" was the B-side to "Since You Been Gone." So it's an outtake from *Down to Earth*. It's a groovy song with good guitar but lyrics that are throwaway. But that happens sometimes. I don't know that it should have displaced anything on the album.

Peter: I agree; it's a bit middling. But "Bad Girl" has a bit of groove and swing to it. I wouldn't mind if it was on *Down to Earth*, to be quite frank.

Martin: Next is the fancy-pants, frilly sleeves version of "Difficult to Cure," almost a different song in this guise. Wanna take a crack at explaining this, Matt?

Matt: Sure, so we're back to the Budokan show. This one is played with a Japanese orchestra. David Rosenthal did all the orchestration, and they had rehearsed with the orchestra. But because they played two shows, and they were already sold-out, they didn't announce that this is what they were going to be doing. So they're rehearsing in secret.

And so at that part where they're holding out the big chord, then the curtain opens up or comes down, and then you've got the rainbow-coloured lit orchestra in behind and you can hear the audience reaction to this, right? So that's a big moment. They're playing together with the band and then the band stops and you got the orchestra playing excerpts from Beethoven's "Ninth" which is what "Difficult to Cure" is based on.

And then on this one, this is maybe where we could talk about Ritchie's slide guitar. He plays a lot of slide on it. There's a video from this, from the Budokan show, and you can see him playing, and he basically hides the slide, right? I don't have one here to show you, but it's like it's under his hand. And it almost looks like he's holding a chord but the slide's actually under there. That's very unusual; I haven't seen anyone hold a slide that way before. And he's very accurate; he's playing very specific melody lines there. This is not bluesy-type slide, where sloppiness is almost part of it. It's precise, melodic playing, and he's very accurate with it. Ritchie's got a very good ear. When you're not using the frets, there's nowhere to go. You get the microtones in between when you're playing slide, so you have to be musical. It's like playing violin, right? You have to be precise with where you do it and he nails it. So that showcases part of his playing that you don't really get to see a lot.

Peter: It's Ritchie's fantasy to be Ludwig van Beethoven. So he gets to play it out at the final concert in Budokan. They do "Song of Joy" and it's a wonderful dramatic moment in the video. The band's in the front, and they've got this curtain. Forgive me, but this is from memory. A pink curtain lifts up, and then you see the Japanese orchestra. I'm not a big fan of band and orchestra. It's got to be done well to be successful and they plan this out really well. The band is complementing the orchestra and vice versa and they're both really going for it.

It's a nice arrangement where there's push and pull. There's counterparts where there's light and shade between the band and the orchestra. It's not like they're both going for it and soaring and it's like a competition; it's complementing each other. They've obviously worked out the arrangements, and it's been nicely planned and ends very successfully. But how it fits on the album is very frustrating.

Side three. So they have side one, which is the Tokyo show, and then you've got to jump to side three. Why? Why can't they put it in some sort of sequence? That's my big complaint about this album. It's all over the shop. They're just throwing songs around.

Martin: Case in point, it's back to San Antonio, Texas, two years earlier for a couple songs to close out the side.

Peter: Yes, well, at least I like "Stone Cold," the way they do it live. It starts off calm and muted and it builds. There's this restrained power to it. And Joe's live vocals on this particular track are really outstanding. This configuration of the band had immense potential. But it wasn't to be because Ritchie thought if there was somebody in the band that wasn't keeping up with him, they'd be gone. This was said about Bobby Rondinelli. So Ritchie gets studio musician Chuck Bürgi, who's Mr. Reliable. It's a shame because I think this band had good chemistry and they were starting to make inroads. But if something was irritating Ritchie in regards to the musicology side— and it always comes down to the musicology side—he would say, we need to get some fresh blood and move on to the next adventure. But "Stone Cold" and "Power" both come off great live.

Matt: Yeah, Bobby Rondinelli is in the band for this one. It's the earlier version of the Joe Lynn Turner-era Rainbow. He plays great on this; he's actually a really good live drummer. His fills are very snare-heavy, so everything cuts through. Instead of doing this overly complicated stuff, what he does adds power, pun intended, to these songs. He's a hard hitter anyways and those snare fills are really effective. And of course here's where Rainbow become the minor league of bassists and drummers for Blue Öyster Cult, right? Because you get Rondinelli and Bürgi, and then later you get Greg Smith on bass. Anyways, I think the songs are done very well and Bobby's drumming adds a lot to it.

Plus on "Stone Cold," what I like about that is the combination of the keyboard and the guitar. You get the little opening keyboard part, the extended keyboard solo, and then you go into the hit song. You get this little keyboard solo, and then when he plays the motif that everyone recognizes, you get that little pop from the crowd. But on the video, he plays a little excerpt of "Child in Time" on it. That's funny; it's not something they're gonna put on the actual Rainbow album, but it was recorded for it. But "Stone Cold" is great. When they talk about what the vision of the band was, which was to create an AOR/hard rock version of the earlier version of Rainbow, "Stone Cold" is one of the examples that works—it's really good AOR.

And I think the backup vocals elevate "Power" on this one compared to the studio version. On the studio version of "Power," the chorus is shouty, which is appropriate for the song, but I like how adding the female vocals to the shout makes it more musical. It's a little Rossington-Collins band (laughs).

Tim: They had shorter, catchy songs from the Joe Lynn Turner era, but they still did "Difficult to Cure" for 11 damn minutes. It's like, Ritchie just can't get out of his own way to say I'm sure the crowd would rather hear two more songs. They'd even rather hear Joe singing "Man or the Silver Mountain" or "Stargazer." He could do it. I've heard him sing "Long Live Rock 'n' Roll." He could deliver that stuff or a couple more songs from *Down to Earth* for crying out loud, to try and boost some sales of that album.

Martin: Moving onto the final side of the album, we've got a punk rock version of "Man on the Silver Mountain" from The Omni in Atlanta, June 24, 1978. I guess less punk rock in it is the guitar solo, the dreaded blues piece and the vocal vamping from Ronnie. But it's punk rock at the end again so all is right with the world. Then it's "Long Live Rock 'n' Roll" from the same show.

Tim: Yeah, this one is interesting because Ronnie's really playing to the crowd (laughs). He hadn't quite gotten into his persona of your wizard host for the evening. He's still wanting people to sing along and rock 'n' roll and all that. He sounds great, obviously. Again, "Man on the Silver Mountain" is way too long and way too fast. It doesn't need to be 8:18; it just doesn't. "Long Live Rock 'n' Roll" is a cool sing-along thing. I guess that's all right because it's a sing-along type of song. I'm really surprised that there's not more Dio on here and that it leaned so hard on the Joe Lynn Turner era. I guess that's proof that they were most commercially successful with Joe. But yeah, they could have taken off "Difficult to Cure" and put on "Stargazer" and "Starstruck" or something.

Peter: What a line-up; again a band of great potential. You can see this on the live DVD from Munich in 1977. But this one in Atlanta just shows that they are on fire. The bottom end of Bob Daisley and Cozy is arguably a better bottom-end combination than Jimmy Bain and Cozy. And I like the sped-up version, which is probably a contrarian view. It plays into more of my sensibilities because I like punk (laughs) and I like the fast, crunchy stuff. I find "Man on the Silver Mountain" on the *Ritchie Blackmore's Rainbow* album a little bit muted or even soft. I don't know if it's Martin Birch, but to me, the songwriting is great on that album but the end product is a bit polite.

Matt: To reiterate, the album overall is disjointed. You're jumping between eras as well as live and studio and stuff. But at least you're flipping the album over, with the original vinyl anyway, and are getting some Dio stuff. "Man on the Silver Mountain" is eight minutes, like it was pretty much always done in concert. But it's very fast and they actually complete the song in like 3:20. They basically have played the whole song at that point, because they do it very fast. But then they keep things going.

So you get the solo guitar noodling. Ritchie does his tremolo picking thing, that really fast picking like on "Highway Star," then adding various pick slides and other noises. He would do that in Deep Purple. Often he would have multiple solo pieces where he'd have one that was his noisy solo and one that was more like his technical solo. Here, he does both because he's doing the scrapes and slides and stuff. But then he goes into a slow blues part. And then you get Ronnie doing the vocal improvisations, which again, becomes part of how he does "Man on the Silver Mountain" forever at that point. He's talking about, "We're all going to climb the mountain" and "I'm the man" and "We're all the man" and all that stuff, which on the surface I guess is silly, but it's great in concert, right? It's Ronnie connecting with the fans and bringing us all together.

Martin: The version of "Long Live Rock 'n' Roll" here follows pretty much the same format, namely aggressive, sped-up performance of the song, extended guitar pyrotechnics, crowd participation and then back to the song, granted, with modulation.

Peter: It's their trademark anthem, their answer to "Rock and Roll All Nite" by Kiss. There were a lot of songs in the charts that had rock 'n' roll in them. I imagine Ritchie tapping Ronnie on the shoulder one day and saying, we've got to have a little bit of an anthem, we've got to have a song that the crowd can sing back to us, like a football chant. Because they can't sing "Stargazer" or some of the songs off the *Rising* album. Again, you listen to this and it's a missed opportunity, for more studio albums as well as some classic live album that is better than *On Stage*. Just one more album and they might have been enormous. But it was not to be.

Matt: As you say, similarly you get seven minutes with a bit of a jam in the middle and the audience patter from Dio. He's getting them to clap and then he's getting them to sing along—the, "Rock, rock, rock 'n' roll—yeah!" thing. And then *you* say it, cajoling the crowd to be louder. "It's not go home and drink a beer," he says. It's, "We're here to rock 'n' roll," right? If you didn't get to see that band in concert, I guess the reason we have these live albums is to recreate what that experience was. So you're getting, through those two songs, a glimpse at what it was like to see Rainbow in the Ronnie James Dio era, which included noodling and Ronnie James Dio audience interaction, for better or worse.

Martin: We close with "Weiss Heim," a ballad-form instrumental, which I guess makes some kind of sense because it sounds like the calming exit music you get at the end of a concert so the hall doesn't get wrecked.

Matt: Exactly (laughs). This was the B-side to "All Night Long," so you get the *Down to Earth* line-up with Cozy Powell on drums. It's an instrumental they recorded at Sweet Silence Studios. So they're in Denmark and you've got Flemming Rasmussen doing the engineering. They later go back there for subsequent recording, so this must have been a good experience for them. In an interview, Flemming said that he was excited to record Cozy Powell, but then when they set up the drums, the drums didn't sound good. So it took them a while to get a sound going. Then it was recorded over a single weekend. So this is a fast thing that they put together.

I like the way it's got piano in the beginning. It's one of these moody, melodic instrumentals of which we've now talked about at least three of them across these albums. The loose structure gives him a backing track to do his melodic soloing over. To me, "Weiss Heim" is as effective as these other ones that made the albums. They're great palate-cleansers when they're sequenced right on the studio albums. "Weiss Heim" means white home, although I don't think it's grammatically correct. But that's where the name came from and I believe it was Ritchie's idea.

Tim: I don't know; "Weiss Heim" is boring to me. I'm not a big fan of Blackmore's instrumentals across the board except the two on *Bent Out of Shape.* I really like those, "Snowman" and "Anybody There." But "'A' 200" on *Burn* and that non-LP one from Purple, "Son of Alerik," I usually skip.

Peter: I disagree. I love it; I think it's wonderful. So much emotion. I just love the interplay between Don Airey on piano and Blackmore. It builds up and it's Ritchie putting on his classical hat and banging out an instrumental tune. I would imagine he only did this in one or two takes, but yeah, this is the music that Ritchie loves. And it's probably a precursor or a sign of what he was going to do with Blackmore's Night for 30 years. In that sense it's a fitting way to finish the *Finyl Vinyl* album. Perhaps by putting it last and calling the record *Finyl Vinyl*, he was making the statement that this is what I really love. This is the sort of music that sums up who I am.

Martin: Tim, as a radio legend—and now an author of books on Y&T and Kansas too—you know your music stuff. Any closing thoughts on why we saw this record at all?

Tim: I just think it's that Blackmore was back in the forefront. And being with Deep Purple, he was now on the same label, Polydor/Polygram. And most bands eventually get compiled, so I guess this was just the inevitable best of Rainbow that would happen after the band was over. Why it came out in 1986, I don't know. But one could imagine thinking that it's two years since *Perfect Strangers.* Let's feed the hopper with something related while we all wait for the next Deep Purple album.

RISES AGAIN !!
RITCHIE IS BACK
WITH NEW RAINBOW !!
THE LEGEND LIVES ON....
Ritchie Blackmore's Rainbow
N E W STRANGER IN US ALL
ALBUM 孤高のストレンジャー
リッチー・ブラックモアズ・レインボー
(CD:BVCP 862 ¥2,500tax incl.)
■日本盤のみのボーナス・トラック1曲を含む全11曲収録!!
■日本のファンへのリッチー直筆メッセージ付
■日本盤のみの初回特典：最新ポスター
■抽選でレインボー・スペシャル・グッズが当たる応募券付き
NOW ON SALE
KING VICTOR
HARD'N'HEAVY
DYNAMITES
RCA
BMG

STRANGER IN US ALL

August 21, 1995
RCA/BMG 74321303372
Produced by Pat Regan and Ritchie Blackmore
Engineered by Pat Regan; assisted by Fran Flannery, Jesse Henderson, Ed Miller, Steve Moseley, John Reigart, David Shackney, Steve Sisco and Dug
Personnel: Doogie White – vocals, Ritchie Blackmore – guitars, Greg Smith – bass, Paul Morris – keyboards, John O. Reilly – drums, Candice Night – backing vocals, Mitch Weiss - harmonica

1. Wolf to the Moon (Blackmore, White, Night) 4:17
2. Cold Hearted Woman (Blackmore, White) 4:30
3. Hunting Humans (Insatiable) (Blackmore, White) 5:45
4. Stand and Fight (Blackmore, White) 5:21
5. Ariel (Blackmore, White) 5:40
6. Too Late for Tears (Blackmore, White, Regan) 4:54
7. Black Masquerade (Blackmore, Morris, White, Night) 5:36
8. Silence (Blackmore, White) 4:04
9. Hall of the Mountain King (Grieg; lyrics by Night; arr. by Blackmore) 5:32
10. Still I'm Sad (Samwell-Smith, McCarty) 5:24

BSCD2
STEREO
リッチー・ブラックモアズ・レインボー
孤高のストレンジャー
1995年作品
SICP 30388 / STEREO
Sony Music Japan International Inc.
定価¥1,890
(税抜価格¥1,800)
Ritchie Blackmore's Rainbow
STRANGER IN US ALL

LIVE IN CONCERT '95
Ritchie Blackmore's Rainbow
08.10.'95 · HANNOVER · MUSIC HALL
09.10.'95 · DÜSSELDORF · PHILLIPSHALLE
10.10.'95 · BERLIN · NEUE WELT
12.10.'95 · APPENWEIHER · SCHWARZWALDHALLE
13.10.'95 · LUDWIGSHAFEN · EBERTHALLE
14.10.'95 · STUTTGART · KONGRESSZENTRUM B
16.10.'95 · OSNABRÜCK · STADTHALLE
18.10.'95 · HAMBURG · SPORTHALLE
20.10.'95 · ERLANGEN · STADTHALLE
21.10.'95 · MÜNCHEN · TERMINAL 1
22.10.'95 · LEIPZIG · HAUS AUENSEE
24.10.'95 · OFFENBACH · STADTHALLE
25.10.'95 · HOF · FREIHEITSHALLE

A *Stranger in Us All* Timeline

November 5, 1990. Polydor issue Rainbow's *Live in Germany*, which sees re-release in 1994 and 1996 with assorted alterations.

1991. Ritchie Blackmore and Candice Night move in together, becoming engaged in 1994.

Mid-November – Mid-December 1992. Deep Purple, including Ritchie Blackmore, toil away at Red Rooster Studios near Munich on what will become *The Battle Rages On...*, with Ian Gillan finishing up his vocals at the stateside Greg Rike Studios, early into 1993.

August 3, 1993. The Deep Purple Mk. II line-up, having reunited (begrudgingly) for a second time, issues *The Battle Rages On...* in the US. The album only achieves a No.193 placement on Billboard, worse by far than its predecessor, even with Ian Gillan returning to the vocal slot.

September 24, 1993. Deep Purple play the first show of their second Mk. II reunion, in Rome. The European tour runs through November 17, a Helsinki gig that finds Ritchie quitting the band.

October 30, 1993. On this date, it is said that Ritchie had tendered his resignation from Deep Purple, although final concerts were still faithfully played, up until the aforementioned November 17.

November 18, 1993. The last scheduled Deep Purple gig, with Ritchie Blackmore as part of the fold, is cancelled. It was to have taken place at the Olympic Stadium in Moscow.

September 1994 – April 1995. Ritchie Blackmore and collaborators work on an album that will eventually be released as *Stranger in Us All*, by "Ritchie Blackmore's Rainbow," although Ritchie originally wanted to call the band Rainbow Moon, with Rainbow Flow also being discussed. The line-up consists of Doogie White (snatched at the last minute from Pink Cream 69), Greg Smith, Paul Morris and Ritchie, with no official drummer. The primary studio is Long View Farm Studios, North Brookfield, MA, with various locales around New York enlisted for overdubs.

August 21, 1995. "Ritchie Blackmore's Rainbow" issue *Stranger in Us All*, on BMG, but to limited release. As part of the deal to put the Mk. II-era Deep Purple back together for *The Battle Rages On...*, it had been stipulated that Ritchie got a solo deal as well. This quasi-Rainbow record was the result.

September 26 – November 7, 1995. Rainbow tour extensively in Europe, with Chuck Bürgi replacing John O. Reilly, who is the drummer on the album. Nine Japanese dates are also notched before the end of November.

June 27 – July 9, 1996. Rainbow tour South America and then are right back into Europe for 14 dates, winding up August 11.

February 20 – March 19, 1997. Rainbow embarks on a US tour, with John Micelli replacing drummer Chuck Bürgi, who quits abruptly to join Enrique Iglesias.

April 22, 1997. Blackmore's Night, featuring principles Ritchie and Candice, issue their debut album, *Shadow of the Moon*, but only in Japan. Playing keyboards on the album is Pat Regan, who had been co-producer with Ritchie on *Stranger in Us All*.

May 31, 1997. Rainbow play their final gig (until the modern, non-LP era), in Denmark. It is a one-off as two attendant Polish gigs (and some Spanish shows) had been cancelled, with Ritchie transitioning toward Blackmore's Night.

June 2, 1997. Blackmore's Night issue their debut, *Shadow of the Moon*, now in mainland Europe, following up in the UK a couple weeks later. It is released on February 17, 1998 in the US. In late '97, the band plays a series of dates in Japan, Spain and Germany.

July 1997. Polydor issues *The Very Best of Rainbow*. The liner notes are written by Jerry Bloom, head of Wymer Publishing.

April 5, 1998. Rainbow drummer Cozy Powell is killed in a car accident while driving his Saab 9000 at 104 mph in bad weather, no seatbelt and over the legal alcohol limit while talking to his girlfriend on his cell phone.

Martin talks to Tim Durling, Luis Nasser, Pontus Norshammar and Steven Reid about *Stranger in Us All.*

Martin Popoff: Not sure there's a messier end to a band's career than Rainbow, first with this late album and then much later a smattering of live gigs. But this book is all about the album. What's the narrative around *Stranger in Us All*?

Tim Durling: It seemed to come out of nowhere. Because when Ritchie Blackmore is not in the spotlight, he's completely out of it. There's no press. There's nothing to indicate that he was working on anything. But he was obviously toiling behind the scenes, as it were. He left Deep Purple in '93. He just played a little bit of the *The Battle Rages On...* tour, right? And then they had to get Joe Satriani. And so I would assume the fact that this came out in 1995, that he immediately set about assembling a new version of Rainbow. The end result is better than its reputation. Does it sound like Rainbow? Sometimes. But it's a good traditional hard rock album at a time when not a lot of them were coming out.

Pontus Norshammar: *Stranger in Us All* happens because Ritchie gets tired of the Mk. II reunion. I don't think he really wanted go back to having Ian Gillan in the band. He wanted so bad to have *Slaves and Masters* succeed and it didn't. And BMG told them, it's 25 years since the group formed, we want the old band back. Gillan agreed, they wrote an album and Ian's heart and soul is not in it, nor is Ritchie's. It's a very lacklustre affair. And during the tour, Ritchie behaves very badly towards the others. It's almost like a kid who wants to be thrown out of the house, right? So he leaves, but he was going to be thrown out anyway, because the others were tired of him.

And the others just said, all right, we'll continue without you. So Ritchie is going to do a solo album and BMG tell him, it's got to be a Rainbow album, right? Because then it's going to sell better. So he assembles a band. Doogie White, I know about. And there's Paul Morris on keyboards, Greg Smith on bass and John O. Reilly on drums. I hadn't heard of these people and haven't ever again. Doogie White, yes, but the others no.

But, this is the thing. *Stranger in Us All* is one of those albums that sits on the shelf. You play it two times, and something else happens and you put it back on the shelf. And preparing for this, I took it out, played it and I was pleasantly surprised. This is a very good record. It's the best Blackmore album, I think most people would say, since *Perfect Strangers*. I'd say *House of Blue Light*, since I like that album a lot. But he's got it more together than he'd been for many, many projects and he's turned in a solid record. The band is supportive of what he's doing. No one can argue that they are a backing band to him. Pat Regan produces, and I don't know very much about Regan, but I do think he gets a very good sound out of them. It emphasizes guitar and bass. It's a very sort of classic Blackmore album, and very well written.

And the sad thing, of course, is that no one cared about it when it was released. Had it been released in 1990, had this music been written and available for *Slaves and Masters*, they might have had a major comeback. Had it been released five years later, it would have come under the classic rock banner and been seen as a creditable comeback for Ritchie in that context. But it appears right when metal is splitting at the seams. So it disappears, which is sad because it's actually a good album.

Luis Nasser: *Stranger in Us All* is a conundrum. When it came out, I bought it immediately. Because I'm a Rainbow fan, of course I had to buy it. Here's the thing about that record: Ritchie Blackmore got a bunch of guys who were basically unknowns. Doogie White is a very good singer, who could evoke Ronnie and his style, which is something that Joe Lynn Turner never really tried to do. Joe Lynn Turner was himself, but Doogie could really do Dio. For instance there's "Ariel," which, to me, is a continuation of what Ritchie likes. I hear that and it reminds me of "Anya," from Ritchie's last album with Deep Purple.

Anyway, there are a lot of really good musical ideas, and I agree with Tim; it's better than a lot of people give it credit for. Still, it almost sounds like a cover band, and people picked up on that, which is a shame, because it's quite worthy. "Oh, Doogie's trying to be Dio." Well, yeah, but what else can they do? It's fucking Rainbow. If anybody has a right to do that, it's them.

It also has Candice Night contributing both backing vocals and lyrics, on three songs. It is surprising to me that this is what led to Blackmore's Night and Ritchie Blackmore dressing like a minstrel and playing a lute and other weird stuff. Because this band had potential.

I find the idea of this record fascinating, because on the one hand, it would seem to signal that Ritchie has an interest in the hard rock style that he pioneered. But at the same time, it's also sort of "yeah, but not quite." We'll take it this far, but the end result comes off a bit Spinal Tap, a parody of Rainbow.

Steven Reid: At this stage, I don't think anyone believed that we were about to have a record from not just Rainbow but Ritchie Blackmore's Rainbow. Some context for me, I was ten when *Bent Out of Shape* was released. So I had gone back and discovered all these classic and maybe not so classic Rainbow albums long after the event. So I personally was hugely excited when this album was announced. Because at this stage in my life, I was more of a Rainbow fan than a Deep Purple fan. Rainbow was the band of Ritchie's that I was into. So I maybe have a fondness for this album that some people don't, although I will admit that it's just a run through past glories. Still, it's a little bit better than it's given credit for. Maybe we'll emphasize the "little" because I've grown up a little bit too (laughs).

It was a band of complete unknowns that was being brought together here, and that in itself, I think, says an awful lot. Ritchie, in general, was quite good at plucking people out of relative obscurity. You could argue that none of the vocalists that he brought into Rainbow were unknowns. We all think they're mega-famous and he chooses mega-stars, but none of them were until they joined Rainbow. He did it again afterwards with Ronnie Romero. Let's not get into that, because it's not good.

Perhaps if he'd brought names in, they'd expect to be part of the spotlight. Given the line-up, that's obviously not what *Stranger in Us All* was all about. But I would also suggest that I'm not convinced that his patience could have dealt with the egos. I think it was important for him at this stage to have a group of musicians who would probably go, "How would you like me to do this, Ritchie?" And he would tell them and they would go, "That's great; that's what I'll do." And I think that, to an extent, sums up an awful lot of this album, because that's what you get. You get an awful lot of—for want of a better phrase—playing to order. And I'm doing a lot of talented guys a disservice there, because there's not untalented people on *Stranger in Us All*. But Ritchie could have used one or two people within the circle to say, "Are you sure?" every now and again. This doesn't feel like an "Are you sure?" album.

Martin: What is your assessment of Doogie at the all-important front man position?

Steven: It's interesting because you've got a singer here that can do the Ronnie James Dio-era stuff as well as the Joe Lynn Turner stuff. He doesn't necessarily go down the Graham Bonnet road, which is odd considering that Doogie is a fellow countryman of mine and he be spent most of his career following Graham Bonnet, in Rainbow, Michael Schenker Group and Alcatrazz. It's all very much, "Where Graham has been, I shall follow." But then you listen to this album, and to me, he's much closer to the other two singers in the band than he is to Graham Bonnet.

What I will say is his performance on this album is the best of his career. For the couple albums he did before, Midnight Blue and various things, he's really good. You can see why he ended up with this gig, Then he does this album and it becomes his best ever. I must admit, I struggle with him after that, on all these different projects and bands and career moves. I think he's decent, certainly better than I could be (laughs), but I don't think he ever re-finds this kind of power and gravitas. Honestly, I think in his latter years he's been a better live singer than he has been a studio singer. I don't really enjoy what he's done with Alcatrazz at all. I struggle with that as a concept anyway, how you can have Alcatrazz without Graham Bonnet. It makes zero sense to me. But I don't even particularly like what he's doing vocally. Live, when I've seen him over the years, I always walk away thinking, I've got him wrong. He's really good. And then he'll do a new album and I'll think, no, he's not great.

Martin: What are your thoughts on the album cover?

Steven: It's one of the worst covers that I can remember. Why? Worzel Gummidge was a children's character on TV and in books over here. And he's a scarecrow; he's an empty-headed scarecrow who could remove his head. And that is exactly what this image looks like. And I know that Ritchie's obviously meant to be a scarecrow on the front—I get all that. But to someone like me from the UK, the hat, the hair, everything—it's a Worzel Gummidge cover. It's the most bizarre thing to be stuck on the front. And I don't get the relevance to the title, *Stranger in Us All*. But there you go.

Tim: I don't know why he felt the need to call it Ritchie Blackmore's Rainbow again, even though they manage to make it look powerful and gothic with that type treatment. This album was never going to be a huge hit, but I would have called it Rainbow and used the classic logo. That's your branding. As it is, people would be like, is this a Rainbow album or a solo album? It's not much of a cover. It's Ritchie Blackmore made to look like a scarecrow. I guess he is a pretty intimidating individual. I'd be scared to meet him.

Martin: What do you think about the look of the band on the back? Look at those guys—it's a pretty cool shot.

Tim: Yeah, it's definitely competitive, right? It doesn't look out of place in 1995. It looks like a combination of some rock veterans and maybe some slightly fresher faces. Out of all of them, Greg Smith has had a bit of a career. I actually saw Greg Smith playing with Alice Cooper in 2000.

Luis: I quite like that cover. It's lo-fi, right? What I get from that is, Ritchie, by this point, has developed a reputation as sort of cranky and anti-social. And on that cover, he's the scary Man in Black. I suspect he's taking the piss out of himself by throwing himself up there as a scarecrow. It's like, I'm the big bad guy—see me standing in this cornfield. Calling the band Ritchie Blackmore's Rainbow, to me, is odd. I wouldn't think you would require his name in there at this point. Any potential fans were gonna find out about it either way. I don't know if it was the label that figured 12 years had passed and nobody would remember. But I don't think it was necessary.

Martin: It's interesting that it's the second Ritchie Blackmore's Rainbow album, and the first one was the debut.

Luis: That's right. Maybe he fully intended to have these two as bookends. You raise a good point; I hadn't noticed that. But yeah, I like this cover. Even though there's a sort of lo-fi indie vibe too it, I think it's cool.

Martin: All right, into the album—and it's the band's one and only from the CD age, so we won't be talking about side one and side two—we get a rollicking gothic rocker called "Wolf to the Moon." Is it a success?

Tim: Good opener, and immediately I'm thinking Doogie White might be the star of this album. His vocals strike a good balance between Joe Lynn Turner and Ronnie James Dio. He sounds like he could evoke the memories of both and therefore provides that extra connection to the band's legacy. I hear a little Coverdale in there too. And "Wolf to the Moon" is just a very Blackmore-sounding title, too. Cool sort of wandering vagabond lyric too, with, "One for the road/ Slave to the highway" and all that.

Luis: I like the neo-classical heavy metal intro riff to this one, before it settles in for the verses where we hear, as these guys have noted, vocals or vocal melodies that recall both Ronnie and Joe. Those harmonic minor scales are classic Rainbow and they got me instantly excited when I first heard this album as a new release. The solo is classic Blackmore and there are essentially no keyboard solos anywhere. The other guys play it safe on this song and throughout the album. You feel Candice Night's influence as a lyricist, and the overall mood, like I say, is that of a Rainbow cover band, only also not particularly commercial.

Pontus: It's a nice idea to open the album with an up-tempo shuffle like this, which is how *Long Live Rock 'n' Roll* started too. It's Ritchie providing these layers of gothic melodies that we used to hear and it has an energy that just glows through the speakers.

Martin: What do you make of this dynamic where both Candice and Doogie write lyrics on this record?

Pontus: I think that she won the battle, right? She won out. They became Blackmore's Night after this. So it becomes a transition to something else. But Doogie does a great job of it, and she helps out in the way that, let's say, Polly Samson helped out with the David Gilmour songs on *The Division Bell*.

Martin: It's almost like we have the man and the woman of the manor, and the rest of the band is the plumber and the gardener and stuff, right?

Pontus: Yeah, it is (laughs). One funny thing that I remember, there was a Swedish teen magazine called *Okej*, which I read a lot. And there was a journalist there called Anders Tengner, who's written a book about Yngwie Malmsteen. He did an interview with Ritchie in 1987 when they were here. And Ritchie is talking about wanting to do a medieval festival. He says, I want to stop playing rock and go back and have these feasts where people played acoustic music and ate a lot of food and had those gatherings. And that is actually what happens when they launch *Nobody's Perfect*. They launch it with that party. But that is also what happens with Candice Night and Blackmore's Night. They make this folk music/medieval music band, a bit like Clannad. So that must have been on his mind. But with *Stranger in Us All*, he decides to rock out, even if this is the last time he's going to do it.

Steven: You listen to "Wolf to the Moon," and you think it's answered all the questions right off the bat. What kind of Rainbow were we going to get? Because that's what everyone was interested in. Were we going back to the Dio days? Were we going to get that middle ground of the Graham Bonnet era? Or were we going to go down the Joe Lynn Turner route of melodic rock?

And really, "Wolf to the Moon" could have been lifted off any Joe Lynn Turner album. It's got that smooth guitar glide and slide to it, as well as Joe-style vocal hooks. It's maybe a little heavier. The guitars are a little louder, a little prouder, a little grittier. And the drums are similarly more powerful and higher in the mix. So it's a pretty strong start. It's not "blow your socks off" stuff, but it introduces you to the album in a way that gives you some hope that we're not just doing a retread of vintage Rainbow. We're not going to be one of those bands that has just turned up for the pay cheque, kinda thing. And Doogie's really good, to be fair. I've given him a hard time, but he sings with authority. He seems to be able to hit those high notes without any issues.

Martin: What are your views on the overall sound palette, the production?

Steven: It's unexciting, confused, middle ground. Neither one thing or the other. And that is a theme across the album. Even with all the hindsight we have now, it's difficult not to play the game of which era are we playing to now? The production doesn't know whether to be of its time or try and be vintage. As I say, it's a halfway house and we end up a little bit nowhere. At the same time, I think it's still trying to be a nod to the seventies. It's strange, and that's why I just find it ends up being really quite indistinguishable. It's trying to be everything at once and really not be very much at all.

We almost end up in that European power metal morass that was just so prevalent at that time. And I have to put that down to Pat Regan, because I'm not convinced that Ritchie Blackmore would have had the vaguest interest in what was going on outside his circle for all of those years. You could not tell me he listened to any of those bands and that power metal sound. And yet we end up there, with this song. I don't dislike it, but it's easy to pick holes in it.

Tim: It's just okay. It sounds like a veteran band putting an album out in the mid-nineties. Frankly, it sounds like a do-it-yourself type of production. I don't think it's bad. It makes me think of like Kansas *Freaks of Nature* or Y&T *Musically Incorrect*, where it's adequate, but it's not a big Bob Rock production or anything.

Luis: It's mid-nineties, right? So now you're getting into areas where people think that reverb is dirty and something you should avoid. This is after the grunge era. So I think that the production attempts to marry sort of the Joe Lynn Turner history of Rainbow with a mid-nineties aesthetic. Is it a greatly produced album? I wouldn't say so. The dynamic range is not particularly wide.

Martin: "Cold Hearted Woman" also plays to known Ritchie tropes. I'm hearing a "Jealous Lover" vibe with this one.

Tim: Yes, and also "Hungry Daze" from *Perfect Strangers*. But two tracks in, I'm definitely hearing more Joe's era than Ronnie's. But you're right; this riff comes from Ritchie's known bag of tricks, used for both Rainbow and Purple. I suspect part of the reason that he even wanted to do this album in the first place was to compete with the next line-up of Deep Purple.

Luis: "Cold Hearted Woman," I don't know how to describe it exactly, and this is gonna sound vulgar, but it's like a Rainbow lap dance. Like, it's only gonna get you so far. Although the album demonstrates potential, I don't think it fully succeeds. I have the nagging feeling as I listen to the songs that Ritchie didn't really believe in it. The investment emotionally by him is not there and you can hear it.

Pontus: "Cold Hearted Woman" is another one of those funky and yet goth-lite songs, right? Doogie sings great, and it's got solid backing with that thumping bass line.

Steven: This is a pretty strong song, although it sounds like the band is playing to order. John O. Reilly, who's playing drums on this, is he Cozy Rondinelli or is he Bobby Powell? Because he's neither. Similarly, Paul Morris on keyboards, he's laying down stuff that Carey or Airey would have done before him. It's not just, "We need you to play in this style." You can actually hear a lot of the same licks, a lot of those same signature moves that these guys were using on early Rainbow albums.

And that's already by "Cold Hearted Woman." You do start to think, okay, hold on, this is just a little too obvious for my taste. I didn't feel that way back then, I have to say, but I do certainly now as I revisit this album. But it's a good groove and Ritchie sounds invested at this stage. The riff is tight, it means business, and even if his playing is a little more contained than you might expect, he's not doing that dancing thing that you were speaking about earlier; it's not really that. And it's more the keys than the guitars that are pulling things along here. It goes into that slightly more commercial sound.

But I would say that—and this is unkind because they have been away and they've come back and it's a different line-up—in between *Bent Out of Shape* and now, how many acts did we have that thought that they could be the next Rainbow? More than I could even consider counting. This sounds a bit like those acts. It doesn't really sound like Rainbow. It sounds like all those bands who did quite a good job of sounding like Rainbow. And it's interesting to hear that come through.

Martin: Doogie writes these lyrics, but like Pontus says, it's almost like you've got two competing lyricists here and Candice wins out. Ritchie's enthusiasm went that way and not into a third Ritchie Blackmore's Rainbow album or ninth studio album overall or however you want to frame it.

Steven: Yeah, definitely. Who am I to say that this album—or the more recent tours—have been done just to make sure they can fund Blackmore's Night? I've come to the conclusion in recent years that it's not really a massive problem if enough people like what they do.

There are plenty of film directors like Guillermo del Toro, who will go out and make a ginormous blockbuster, get a payday and everyone thinks that's a great film, so that they can then go make a *Pan's Labyrinth*. Nobody says oh, it's terrible, he's sold out. No, they go, "Isn't he clever?" He can do a movie that's made pots of money and then he makes his own little bit project. If a musician does that, "Oh, he's a sell-out—total sell-out."

Martin: Next is "Hunting Humans (Insatiable)," an odd title, recalling "The Shed (Subtle)." An odd song as well, sort of thespian, like *The Phantom of the Opera*.

Tim: Yes, here we go with the goth-sounding title, and then the song is not nearly as dangerous as it sounds. It's not a bad song, but yeah, the title is a bit of a red herring. It's got some interesting parts, but it's not my favourite on here.

Luis: It's plodding and forgettable, a song not even Blackmore's solo can save.

Pontus: There' something about the melody of "Hunting Humans (Insatiable)" that reminds me of *90125* by Yes. It's proggy, it's slow and mysterious. It's also a modern sort of "Eyes of the World" with one of these atmospheric solos. In the early eighties, Ritchie changed the way he solos. It's very apparent on *Bent Out of Shape* and *Perfect Strangers*. This is Ritchie working that way as well, sort of careening and atmospheric.

Steven: This one is actually quite popular among Rainbow fans, but for me, things really come unstuck here. Changing the pace makes sense, but I just don't think this song plays to anyone's strengths other than Ritchie's. Doogie just sounds kinda weedy. He seems tired to me. He's not doing anything wrong, but I'm not wanting to stay the course with this slow, atmospheric feel. Comparing him to Ronnie James Dio is just unfair, but I think Ronnie could see his way through to making a simple, bare, spare vocal like this work where I don't think it does with Doogie.

Martin: He's forced into trying to play some psychopath, right?

Steven: Yeah, he's definitely in a role, and I can't say I'm buying it, to be honest with you. However, he's not helped by the rhythm section. John O. Reilly and Greg Smith, how they stayed awake during this, I have absolutely no idea. They are given nothing at all to do. It's a sin, in actual fact, that guys that are really good are given this little to do. "Here's a bass note. Go and play that. Here's the drum beat. We don't need a fill. Don't do anything crazy like that. Don't come off the snare drum. Don't do that" (laughs).

And yet the guitars are still pretty cool. It's measured and it's relaxed and it's atmospheric. The problem is that you can imagine other people from different line-ups of this band doing much more with it. And that's never a good place to be. And yeah, Doogie's trying to do the Dio thing but never quite does that. He's closer to the Joe Lynn Turner thing, but this is the wrong song for that. So where do we end up? Confused. I find this totally forgettable. But it does seem to be a favourite of certain people. Lyrically, it's about an affair and the guilt that it causes alongside what appears to be an inability to control the desire at its heart. The lyrics on this album are not great. We are covering just the "same old same old" with an awful lot of this. It's not very exciting, it has to be said.

Martin: Fortunately, there's a big change of pace for "Stand and Fight," which is rock 'n' rollsy, like "Can't Happen Here." It definitely succeeds in making me forget about Ronnie James Dio. I get more of a Charlie Huhn vibe from Doogie's performance, or Brian Howe also in Ted Nugent's band or in Bad Company.

Tim: Yeah, I like this one, and I get your point. While it's not Ronnie at all, it still really reminds me of the Joe Lynn Turner era. It could have come off of any of those albums, particularly with this vocal phrasing. As well as "Can't Happen Here," I'm hearing "Freedom Fighter" and "Power," and perhaps more so in the lyrics. It's one of those fist-in-the-air-type of songs that he would do.

Luis: "Stand and Fight," okay, I tried, man—I tried with this song. But it's just a blues rock number with lyrics that are clichéd. To me, the only musical surprise is that it features the harmonica, and quite a lot of it, which is unusual for Rainbow, right? Black Sabbath's "The Wizard" features harmonica too, but in an unexpected and interesting way. Otherwise, this is pedestrian blues rock. I like your reference to Brian Howe and I guess that's true, but I'm not listening to Bad Company. I'm listening to Rainbow. So that's the other thing. If you listen to this song without context, you might get a different impression. But it's not for me. I think it's a weak track on that record.

Pontus: "Stand and Fight" is the "Not Time to Lose" of this record. It's a good verse, it's a good chorus, there's no keys, but there is harmonica where there's supposed to be keys, right? And I'm not really sure about that. It's a funny thing. It's just suddenly there for the first time since '72 or whatever. I think the last time Ritchie used harmonica was on "Painted Horse" or something like that.

Steven: "Stand and Fight" is one of the more memorable songs, as far as I'm concerned. Phrasing-wise, I actually hear Graham Bonnet on this. I quite like the harmonica, from Mitch Weiss. It's not what you expect from a Rainbow album and it's a good addition that is actually quite prominent in the track. It adds colour and it doesn't feel out of place. There's a liveliness here, that certainly after the last song, I need. And even though it's a little more accessible and rock 'n' roll, it sounds natural. People are actually allowed to play and that doesn't happen quite so much on all the songs. I like the looseness. It's got a bit more of a kinda good-time feel about it.

Martin: Candice writes the lyrics to "Ariel," and it's very much in the Blackmore's Night wheelhouse, although at the music end, it's more "Kashmir" and full band. It's slow and thumping. Candice puts in a completely ethereal guest vocal as well, at the end. It's like an adjunct or coda, where we finally meet "Ariel."

Tim: Yes, and not exactly down a Dio pathway, more like a goth-lite Joe Lynn Turner-era song like "Eyes of Fire." "She's an angel dressed in the blackest lace/A sip of wine and the game can begin." That's very much both a Candice lyric as well as something Joe would write.

Pontus: "Ariel" is the epic of the album, with a trademark Middle Eastern riff bookending the verses, which are more chordal. Ritchie puts in an old-school "snake charmer"-type guitar solo. I think it's important for Ritchie to have Candice do lyrics and it's a successful collaboration. It's one of the songs that really stands out.

Steven: I don't know how much I love those big, echoing drums that usher in this song. But it's one of Doogie's best vocals on this album and maybe anywhere. The overall feel takes me to "Perfect Strangers," with its big, front-loading, menacing guitars. There's a real heft and a presence and there's a crawl to the tempo that's determined this time rather than ponderous.

And that's the difference—it seems to have somewhere to go; it's got purpose. The rhythm section is hardly pressed into action on this record, but there's a swing to this one, which I'm grateful for. There's not much flash, but they don't drag things down. And I do actually feel that, with all due respect, they do drag some of this album down.

Interestingly, the reissue that I've got from 2017 has an edited version as a bonus track, from its original 5:40 down to four minutes. I'm always fascinated by that. We've spoken about editing down singles for different albums. But why you would take one of the best songs off this album and then make it worse? I don't really know. It's smoothed-out and Candice Night's vocals are pushed way up in the mix. It's another example for me of a band who were never gonna have a hit making one of those songs worse, and then re-releasing it to the general public in the hope of having a hit. It's an odd concept. Everyone wants success. There's a lot of money that goes into making albums, especially back then. Everyone wants to at least make their money back. But play to your audience. Rainbow fans don't need to hear a song like this shortened.

Martin: "Too Late for Tears" is almost comically similar to "Stand and Fight" just two songs ago. Still, given that I quite dig "Stand and Fight," more of the same is A-okay by me (laughs).

Tim: Yeah, and "Too Late for Tears" reminds me of "Cold Hearted Woman" lyrically too. But I totally agree, it's really close to "Stand and Fight" at the music end—wow. For what it's worth, it's the only track that includes a credit to the producer, Pat Regan.

Pontus: "Too Late for Tears" could have been a Purple track. I can hear Ian Gillan singing that. It's the second mid-paced rocker on the album and I think it's good; it has its place.

Steven: This one doesn't work for me at all. It's repetitive, it's one-dimensional, but Ritchie pulls out a good solo towards the end. Doogie's left to do too much of the heavy lifting here, and that's a big ask for a complete unknown. He's released music with Glasgow bands at this point. But he's really left out there, to ad-lib and whatnot. It's gracious of the Man in Black to give him all that room, but for me it exposes him. As I say, it's unkind, but when you're walking in the footsteps of guys like Ronnie James Dio, Graham Bonnet and Joe Lynn Turner, like them or loathe them, they can all sing. Doogie can sing too, but I don't even think he's a Joe Lynn Turner, to be honest with you at this point.

And this song, again, it's a halfway house. Is this a Dio-era-sounding track? Not quite. Could it have been on *Down to Earth*? Maybe. Is it a Turner song? Almost. There's a less than subtle nod to "Can't Happen Here" in part of the riff. We are retreading old ground. And in that sense, it's a compromise. It's neither one thing or the other. You're left not really satisfied in any sense. It's not heavy with gravitas and it's not light and poppy and melodic.

And I know that for a lot of people, half the reason they listen to a Ritchie Blackmore-led album is to hear him ripping out riffs and hammering out solos. But this song only comes to life when the solo starts. He's playing a nice guitar line under the vocals at the song's end as well. It's almost like the whole song has been waiting for that point to come alive, and for Ritchie to come along and save it. It's a bit pointless, really. Why not do that upfront and let's get us all on board and excited? The last minute or so of the song is much more exciting than any of the rest of it. But I'm already checked-out.

Martin: We've talked about power metal bands raised on Rainbow. "Black Masquerade" really strikes me as something Stratovarius or Nightwish or Freedom Call might do. Or Labyrinth or Rhapsody of Fire over in Italy with their "soundtrack metal" thing.

Tim: Yeah, "Black Masquerade" is a good one, and it almost feels like Ritchie intended that to be the centrepiece of the album. "We'll go to that forbidden land" and "Let the darkness surround you"—this one's fully gothic and classical-based, underscored by having "black" in the title.

Martin: Yeah, it's funny. I never thought about this before, but this album gives me a little bit of a Tony Martin-era Black Sabbath vibe. Luis, thoughts on this song?

Luis: Well, it's exactly what we would hope for in a Rainbow song, right? It's the classic Rainbow song that nobody knows (laughs). Once again, it has the traditional A harmonic minor scale, which is just A, B, C, D, E, F, G sharp, A. It has that enigmatic feel, which is Arabic or flamenco, since Spain was basically occupied by Arabs for centuries.

It is also the song that gives the album its title—"stranger in us all" is in the lyric. The music is great, but I love the lyrics. They hold their end of the bargain. They have the same degree of sophistication as the music, which is something that's often overlooked. Why spend all this work on the music and then write the lyrics on a napkin in a diner and just be done with it? To me, it's a love song. But it also has like a veil of hidden danger and threat and I like that.

I love that neoclassical break that leads to the guitar solo. I like that it's one of the few instances in this record where the keyboard is allowed to play some melodies as well. One of the things that was great about classic Rainbow, which you get here, is that you're getting that mixture in the sonic palette between the guitars and the keyboards over a very beefy rhythm section.

Back to the lyric, "Now you'll see the dark side of me/In our black masquerade/Let the moonlight surround you/The game that we play is the black masquerade/The full moon unmasks the stranger in us all." It's like it's saying, we're all just pretending. But if you'll just take this chance with me, I can see right through you, I know who you are and I will let you see who I am. This is gonna be our secret. So I like that; I think it works. Ronnie James Dio never really wrote love songs, but I think this is a song that he may have gotten behind. Because it's rooted in fantasy and mystery. And it speaks of other things. It speaks about duplicity. You can go as deep as you want with sort of Jungian archetypes, the shadow, the masks or the persona, as he called them, right? That we always wear these masks. And then sometimes we just become so unaware that it's a mask, we forget it's a mask. And then that mask creates another mask.

Which is what is interesting about the album title, *Stranger in Us All*. Like I say, they make a reference to that and I think that's cool. Who are we? This is not what Ritchie Blackmore is known for. He's generally not particularly probing. But this song really works for me in so many ways. The music is fantastic and it has a lot of little riffs and a lot of chords. But it always keeps swirling and swirling around this A harmonic minor motif. So it does feel like a masquerade, with all these people dancing around in circles. It's beautiful. I love it.

Pontus: I feel like "Black Masquerade" is this record's "Spotlight Kid." For once there's significant use of keyboards. You almost wonder if this is a send-up of himself or of Yngwie. Because it's very Yngwie Malmsteen-like. I like the Spanish guitar in the middle. And Yngwie used to do this stuff, where things go backwards and forwards between solos, which he copied from Ritchie. But it almost feels like Ritchie copied him back here (laughs).

Steven: Yeah, this is a bit more like it. It sounds like a beefed-up carry-over from the Joe Lynn Turner era. And it's presenting keyboards that are prominent and good for the song, but immediately date this album to its period. Nonetheless, it's got that drama and classical edge that makes so much of what Rainbow and Ritchie did so exciting. I do wish the keyboards were more sympathetic, and yet I do believe that an album should sound like it was recorded when it was recorded. We just look at the seventies and go, "That was the classic era, so it should sound classic." Rainbow came from the seventies, so we think the keyboards should sound classic. It's not Paul Morris' fault, because they had to get through an awful lot of people before we went, yeah, that's the sound that we want.

But we've got a classical guitar solo and I guess we've got something that's meant to be harpsichord in there. I like that too, to be fair. It simply adds more to the epic, classical narrative of the song. And I like the overall energy; the song sounds like it's being played live by a band all in a room together. It sounds like a group of talented musicians that have been allowed to express themselves. And it makes the song an awful lot livelier than the ones where everybody seems to be kept in check. Overall the album lacks for that natural breath to it. This breathes in a natural way. It's a real high point.

It's also one of the better lyrics on the album. It's about looking inside, confronting your darker side. And that fits the mood and the tone of the song. And that has an impact over and above the other relationship-focused lyrics on the album. Because when you read the lyrics and actually think about what they're about, I don't necessarily feel that they connect so much with the music. This connects with the music. It does sound like a lyric that was created for this song or vice versa. My guess is that the music was created first. But this is a song where it all comes together for me.

Martin: "Silence" is my least favourite on the album. I never liked these sort of dark blues songs. It's like the few Black Label Society songs I don't like. Plus it's somewhat of a shuffle to boot. Then there are those braying, inappropriate keyboards designed to sound like horn arrangements. You don't get that with Black Label Society.

Tim: Yeah, I don't like this one either, and the main culprit is what you brought up, those dated faux horns keyboards. I can't believe that in '94 or '95, whenever this is being recorded, they didn't go over to the keyboard player and go, "Can you pick a different patch?" Because it sounds so out-of-place. And "That's the silence of love." What does that even mean? To me, the album ends at "Black Masquerade," because the rest of is throwaway. And of the final three, this is the one I could do without the most, even if it's the only fully-fledged original at the end.

Luis: I actually like this one because it's fresh and not what Blackmore was known for. Like you say, it's a form of heavy blues. There are good instrumental parts and the vocal works. I like that circular, heavy, thunderous riff. What is interesting about it is that it's a 4/4 song, for most part, but it has a triplet feel. It gives it bounce. Plus, at the end of that cycle of 4/4, he throws in that bar of 6/4, which gives it a twist. So it's a bit experimental.

The guitar solo is wicked on this song. But I'm disappointed that the organ is really just acting like a pad. I like the lyrics. "You say you want your freedom/It all gets a bit out of hand/Caught in the ocean as I'm watching you breathe/We all believe what we wanted to believe/And that's the silence of love." It's about the spaces between the words, about the things left unsaid that really carry a lot of the weight in the conversation, where there's just that little bit of courage missing, that little bit of doubt. So the fact that it's a thunderous riff, and that it has that recurring 6/4 bar just to propel the rhythm into stranger territory, and that the lyric is talking about negative space and silence, what you end up with is that the music helps illustrate the words. Yeah, I love this song. It's another worthy Rainbow song that most people will never hear.

Pontus: In "Silence" Ritchie reuses the "You Fool No One" riff but turns it into a shuffle, but it has some bite.

Martin: And actually, Pontus, both the vocal melody and the way Doogie sings it, basically like Glenn Hughes, really connects it to "You Fool No One" as well. And then two songs later, we're going to get a rendition of "You Fool No One" sister track "Still I'm Sad."

Steven: Yes, that's funny, and actually, I went straight to "Sunshine of Your Love" by Cream when I heard that vocal melody. And really in quite an obvious way, to be fair. There's no escaping those cheesy keyboard parts, and as a result, there's a bit of an eighties B-movie soundtrack feel to this song. I don't hate it, strangely enough, but there's an awful lot of distractions going on. And same again, more than anything, it's the keyboards that make you think, okay, this was recorded when it was recorded. Or like I say, its already dated by a decade in 1995. I would even say it sounds a little unfinished.

The lyrics are remarkably repetitive. It seems to be about a confrontational breakup. But the song title is repeated over and over and over and by the end of it, it just has no meaning. You've heard the same part way too many times. It's another one of those songs where it seems like maybe they looked at it and went, "Not much happens here. Can we just tack a really great guitar solo at the end?" (laughs). Can Ritchie come in, crank everything up, rip out a solo, and we'll all go, "Oh, maybe there's something to this one after all. I'd just missed the point."

Martin: Ritchie's got a disease that is "difficult to cure," so with "Hall of the Mountain King," we're back at an old classical piece rearranged in a heavy metal way. I like the upgrade of a lyric stuck on it though, written by Candy and of course sung by Doogie.

Tim: Indeed, this is right in his wheelhouse, so I understand why he did it. But I'm not a fan of adding the lyrics. In the past, you might have had somebody who could stand up to Ritchie, like Roger Glover, who might have said, "Nah, I don't know about that. Do we really want to do that?" If you're going to do a classical piece, sure, go do it, but leave it instrumental. Add some drums to it, of course, but don't try and write lyrics to it. To me, that's a bit Spinal Tap.

Luis: I'm not a big fan of this either. I think that we can all agree that the definitive "Hall of the Mountain King" in the hard rock and metal ethos firmly belongs to Savatage, even though they wrote a whole new original and just used the title.

Pontus: This version is based on, rather than fully adopted. Candice writes the words and it incorporates other motifs from *Peer Gynt*. I think there's "Morning" in the sort of solo section. It's a great ending piece, or it could have been, because it goes faster and faster and faster. It would have been a better way to end the album versus "Still I'm Sad."

Steven: Pretty much everybody disagrees with me, but I've often described "Hall of the Mountain King" as the track that saves the album. This plays to Rainbow's strengths. I've given him a hard time, but just how good is Doogie White on this track? There's a depth and a confidence, a complete believability on this one, that he doesn't quite manage to conjure elsewhere. But man, he does here. He's absolutely on it on this song. I'd love to know—and maybe you do—just how this album was recorded and when it was put together. Because it doesn't always feel like the vocals are consistent. Some of the songs sound fantastic and some of the songs sound not so great. I don't know when the sessions were done, but it's just one of those things where you listen to some of those songs and you go, oh, he's struggling, and then you hear things where you think he's brilliant.

It doesn't matter who he sounds like when it's just really, really good. There's drama aplenty, guitars are often doing very little but to maximum effect. There's little keyboard parts that create the melody. They're just fabulous. There's some really good keyboard work that takes us into Tony Carey territory. I really like it. It's obviously somebody's interpretation of Edvard Grieg's piece of the same name, but they did it so well. Ritchie was such a talented guy at taking these pieces and rearranging them.

As for the lyrics, they are what they are. They create a Dio-era feel because we're backing in that "Man on the Silver Mountain" world. But everything clicks. If you can make it to this point in the album—because we're right at the tail on the album now—you breathe a sigh of relief. Because it started okay and it finished damn fine. In the end you have a solid album. But I'd go so far as to say "Hall of the Mountain King" maybe deserved to be on a better album.

Martin: All right, here we are at the end of the record, and the last Rainbow album ever, as well. There are only ten tracks on *Stranger in Us All*, but the songs average five minutes apiece, in fact without much of a range between shortest and longest. The last one is no exception. It's a tightly-wound version of "Still I'm Sad," thankfully with vocals, but more importantly, festooned with a sharp sense of riff and newly rhythmic arrangement. This is not your father's "Still I'm Sad."

Steven: What is it they say? "Never go back" (laughs). I agree that it's a more than decent version of the Yardbirds classic, but why? Ritchie went and did this yet again with Ronnie Romero. He's covering himself covering himself covering The Yardbirds (laughs). And you're never gonna do it as well the second time around. I just don't understand that as an idea, unless genuinely there was something wrong with what you did before. But to bring in a whole new group of guys when people love what you've done with this music before and expect the results to be anything other than ordinary just doesn't make any sense.

The version on the debut just has so much character. The arrangement is clearer; it's less cluttered. And I just love the manic cowbell action that's on that song. This version has none of that. On its own, there's nothing wrong with this. But the problem is you have something specific to go and compare it to. And I get that with the album as well. You're already thinking about what's come before and it's like we confirm it now. We can all think about what came before because the band is doing it too. That's what's going on here; that's this record's energy.

Just to finish up, there's a slowly building intro from Ritchie on this version, which wasn't on the original version. But again, I don't know anyone that would prefer this over the version that the band had already done before. And I don't need the lyrics. I don't need the vocals on it, to be fair.

Martin: It's strangely poetic that it's the last song on this album, and it's the last song on the only other Ritchie Blackmore's Rainbow album, right? Is he signaling to us that he was well aware that this was the end? There's a profound sense of bookending going on here, or a coming full circle.

Steven: Or you could ask, is there a message in the song title this time around as well? Ritchie doesn't smile in pictures, to be fair, but you turn this CD over, and he couldn't look any less interested. It genuinely looks like he'd been in bed twenty minutes earlier and he showed up and stuck his hat on. It's a good picture, but that big leather coat looks like a dressing gown. The whole presentation just looks to me like he's going, "Do I still have to do this shit?" I mean, we're all standing here, all wearing black, doing not very much. I don't want to be here, thanks. And so why not end the album with, "I've done all this for you guys, and still I'm sad."

Tim: Nice one, Steven (laughs). Yeah, of all the songs they could have redone, they had to redo a song that was a cover to begin with. I would have liked to have heard what this line-up could have done with something like "Sixteenth Century Greensleeves" or "Tarot Woman" or just about anything other than "Still I'm Sad." Not the best use of time, but they saved the worst for the end. The album really runs out of steam for me, but still, it's like three-quarters pretty good. But I will say this, as far as albums that came out in '95, '96, stack this album up against Deep Purple's *Purpendicular* and *Purpendicular* kills it. *Purpendicular* is so much better.

Pontus: For "Still I'm Sad," I'm gratified at least that they wrote a great cadenza for the beginning of it. The original riff is gone, which is sad, because that riff is quite good. They've added a new one, but I'd disagree with you and say that it doesn't add much, or it detracts. It's good to have vocals on this one. Is it fully necessary? I don't think so. But it's a good reading. This version emphasizes the lead vocals as well as choir vocals and stuff like that. But it feels like overkill to cover yourself on your last album. You wonder why he did it.

Martin: It's because it has to be on every single Ritchie Blackmore's Rainbow album!

Pontus: Yes (laughs). It's very weird. And this is actually the longest Rainbow album. It's 51 minutes. They could have taken a song or two off, although in the CD age, it's already alarming to just see ten tracks. But "Still I'm Sad" could have been left off. It could have ended with "Hall of the Mountain King." Or one of those mid-tempo songs could have been axed, making it more concise. But this is 1995 and we're right in the middle of the CD plague where everything was supposed to be long.

Martin: Does anybody want to take a crack at summing up this album, or summarizing it? Like I say, it's the end of the catalogue and it's actually the end of our discussion, the end of this journey.

Tim: Well, okay, I'll add this thought: *Stranger in Us All* sounds exactly like what it is. It sounds like an album that a band that's been dormant for over a decade puts out. It's not an album that sounds like it could have come out in 1985 as the sequel to *Bent Out of Shape*. This sounds like a years-later comeback album, or reconfigured comeback album that's an attempt to say, hey, remember when Rainbow was a thing?

Pontus: Well, here's how I look at it. The title of the album, *Stranger in Us All,* is taken from the "Black Masquerade" song. The album cover is him with his back to the camera with the hat, with the guitar, looking like a scarecrow. And one could imagine that maybe he felt like an old scarecrow. Here he is, leaving Deep Purple again and starting a new band. He is now considered an old statesman of a music form that seems to be on the skids, out of fashion. And then you see that title and you think, maybe he felt that he wanted to be somewhere else.

Of course he wanted to be somewhere else. He formed another band after just one album and one tour. Maybe he felt like a stranger in this loud rock 'n' roll world and that he was telling us he wanted to leave. Let's also not forget he was deeply in love. He was deeply in love with this 23-year-old. Maybe he wants to get rid of the old Blackmore and start again. He's 49 when this album is recorded, and maybe he was in a place where he said, all right, I want to do something different. I'm finished being Ritchie Blackmore.

Steven: I tend to suspect the same thing as Pontus. As is the case with an awful lot of what Ritchie Blackmore's done other than Blackmore's Night in living recent memory, it's as if he doesn't really want to be doing it. It's not a positive album title, I don't think. You've gone from *Long Live Rock 'n' Roll* to *Stranger in Us All.*

Martin: And come to think of it, before that there was *Rising,* and then *Difficult to Cure, Straight Between the Eyes* and *Bent Out of Shape*! It's like, in the beginning, rock 'n' roll is lifting him up, but it eventually becomes a sickness. It then causes him migraines and he ends up bent out of shape. Actually it gets worse. He becomes a perfect stranger, most disconcertingly, to himself.

Steven: Yes, you see, it's all been laid out for us (laughs). And back to the cover again, that's not the album cover of someone that's going, "Put me on the front 'cause I want to be here." We're no longer on the top of the pile or given that glance of what's coming next. We're already off into the distance on that album cover, going, "What's next?" The album feels like it was always going to be a one-off. It was never going to be the main focus. I'm not going to suggest that it was for any specific reasons. I'm sure there were an awful lot people encouraging him to continue with it.

And I personally I saw one of the last Rainbow tours with Ronnie Romero. I walked away with the impression that the enthusiasm from the most important member of the band on stage was so low that the message was, "Well, you asked for it. Now you've got it. You'll never ask about it again, will you?" And I feel that about an awful lot of Ritchie's career after *Bent Out of Shape*. It's the main guy going, "Look, if you're going to make me do it, I'll do it. But you won't want it again, will you?" This album is not as bad as that. I don't dislike the album to that extent. That's really harsh. But I don't feel like everybody's hearts are in this record.

Martin: Luis, how about yourself? Do you see some embedded message in that album title, *Stranger in Us All*? Is Ritchie telling us that we should have expected this to be the end of Rainbow?

Luis: Well, the thing with Ritchie Blackmore is that I've always had the sense that he enjoys taking the piss, right? Out of other people but most often himself. It's that pathological British thing of, well, I can't really take myself too seriously. So I'm going to tell you what I really think, but I'm going to pretend it's a joke.

So maybe that title speaks to this duality that existed within him that is this desire to be a hard rock guitar god but at the same time he's not really. He doesn't think of himself that way. And what's surprising, or possible, is that *Stranger in Us All* got that out of his system. He finally got it out of his system. And then he started doing Blackmore's Night, which he seems happy with it.

So *Stranger in Us All*, isn't that true? We all lie to ourselves, especially about ourselves. It takes a lot of courage and discipline to be truthful about who we are. When we write our story, we tend to make ourselves more heroic than we really are. In some sense, we never really own up to all the questionable things we do. I think it's one of those phrases that's supposed to sound mysterious and I think it achieves that. Because, fundamentally, no matter how well you lie to yourself, you know the truth. So yes, when Ritchie says "stranger in us all," there's an element of self-discovery.

Martin: Interesting; I like that. Well, thanks for this, guys. Yeah, that title, *Stranger in Us All* has always been my favourite part of this album, and my favourite title of all the Rainbow records. I feel much like you guys do, that whether it was intentional or not, or which specific theory you pick from what you guys just said or that I suggested, it tells us something about why Ritchie and Candice have been together since the early nineties and have also been so prolific with Blackmore's Night and even have had two children together.

I guess for those of us who are angry metalheads still, we should be thankful for the fact that if you add Purple to the mix, he's really left us with more than enough electric guitar playing to keep us happy. And I guess in parallel, we should get off his back and let him be the minstrel-type guy he's apparently always wanted to be, right? Okay, enough reflection. Thanks again to all the panellists who spoke to me for this book, and thank you, readers, for joining us on this ride. Now go listen to some Rainbow!

Contributor Biographies

Phil Aston
Phil has had a lifelong passion for music, ignited when he witnessed Deep Purple live in 1974 at the tender age of 14. This transformative experience set him on a path deeply entwined with music, marked by his early days playing in local bands around Birmingham. Phil's career evolved notably as he became the lead guitarist for the NWOBHM band The Handsome Beasts, signed to Heavy Metal Records. His journey continued with stints in Rogue Male alongside Chris Aylmer of Samson and Tantrum, where he contributed music to a film featuring Lindsay Wagner. Phil's songwriting talents were further showcased with London-based Lionheart Music. In 2004, Phil relocated to Cornwall and founded Genius Loci Media, a digital marketing agency tailored to serve the music and creative industries. The agency also ventured into music production, releasing albums for violinist and composer Sue Aston. A pioneer in live streaming, Phil produced a notable performance in the USA featuring members from the bands Survivor and Halford. Currently, Phil runs *Now Spinning Magazine*, which he founded in 2020. The magazine has quickly built a reputation for its honest video reviews, in-depth music features and interviews with many famous artists. Through *Now Spinning Magazine*, Phil continues to share his passion for music, drawing on his extensive experience as a musician and marketer to enrich the music community.

Marco D'Auria
Marco is a passionate filmmaker and music enthusiast. Since 2018, he has been an integral part of the music YouTube channel *The Contrarians*. Additionally, Marco has showcased his directorial and production skills through his award-winning documentary entitled *Standing on the Firing Line: The Story of Mystique*.

Rich Davenport
Rich is a writer, musician and stand-up comedian from Bolton in the North West of England. He's written features and reviews for *Classic Rock*, *Record Collector* and *Rock Candy*, and sleeve notes for classic albums by Rory Gallagher and The Ruts. Rich also hosted a long-running radio show on *Total Rock*. As a musician, he's played with Atomkraft, Radio Stars, Martin Gordon (ex-Sparks), has fronted metal bands See Red and Black Sheets of Rain, and is currently playing with punk band Vicious Bishop and former Radio Stars/John's Children vocalist Andy Ellison. See richdavenport.com for more.

Tate Davis
Tate really got into music after he heard Led Zeppelin's "Heartbreaker" on the radio for the first time at age 13. After he graduated high school, Tate spent time as an on-air personality at 88.3 WMTS in Murfreesboro, TN for two years before becoming a part-time member of *The Contrarians* YouTube channel. His favourite musician of all time is Keith Moon.

Tim Durling
Tim has worked in radio in various capacities, from on-air to commercial writing since 1993. He began his YouTube channel *Tim's Vinyl Confessions* in 2014, as a means of talking about the albums and artists he listens to and collects. He is also a published author, with three books (and more in the works) to his credit, *Unspooled: An Adventure in 8-Tracks*, *Down for the Count: The Y&T Album Review* and *Let It Be Your Guide: The Kansas Album Review*. He lives in the hinterlands of Eastern Canada with his wife Sarah and various pets. Long Live Cats and Dogs!

Nick Ermolovich
Nick is oftentimes a contributor to *The Contrarians* YouTube channel. He's also a part-time musician, a one-time college radio Program Director, a sometimes counsellor to music artists and a long-time fan of rock 'n' roll. A student of bass and piano, Nick played bass in bands throughout high school and college during the 1980s. After a 20-year lay-off, Nick knocked the rust off his fingers to join Jim George in an original rock 'n' blues trio, sharing stages with Gary Hoey, Starz, Humble Pie, Sonny Landreth, Joe Louis Walker and The Holmes Brothers among others. With Jim's passing, Nick looks forward to "one more ride" with a dynamic original artist.

John Gaffney
John is a musician from Tampa, Florida. His past endeavours include the metal bands Sinister Realm and Majesty in Ruin. Currently he records dark electronic music with his project Chamber of Sorrows. John also has a YouTube channel called *Lair of the Alchemist* that discusses all things heavy metal and hard rock. He also commandeers a podcast with the author of this book, called *Kicked in the Teeth: An AC/DC Podcast*.

Peter Jones
Peter has been in love with music his entire life. After starting on piano, Peter began drumming at age nine. Thanks to his two older sisters, he discovered popular music well before his time and spent hours and hours raiding their LP collections. He obtained his BA in music performance while drumming for the world class Millikin University Jazz Band where he toured the Bahamas, Aruba and recorded four albums. Peter has been in rock bands since the mid seventies. He has played in tribute bands to Queen, Cheap Trick, Deep Purple and AC/DC. He also has played with symphony orchestras, dinner theatre shows and local plays and musicals. Peter was also an audio buyer for Laserland back in the late eighties. A lover of all music, Peter's favourite rock bands are Deep Purple, Rush and Kiss.

Peter Kerr
Peter is a lifelong rock/pop music tragic case. Between trawling record stores in Sydney, Australia for that obscure album pressing or propping up the bar at various pubs and clubs in quest of the next killer live act, he runs the *Rock Daydream Nation* YouTube channel.

Jamie Laszlo
Jamie was raised in Pittsburgh, Pennsylvania and listened to the local radio station, WDVE, which helped teach him a lot about popular music. Even though the facts he learned at school faded from memory just days after each exam, the facts he learned about rock music seemed to stay embedded in his head. These days, Jamie is a YouTube music commentator and moderator, regularly contributing to *The Contrarians* and *Sea of Tranquility* music review channels.

Luis Nasser
Luis is a bassist, composer and music lover, founder of Sonus Umbra and an active member of Luz de Riada, Might Could and The Devil's Staircase. He is also a member of *In the Prog Seat*, a show on all manner of progressive rock featured on Peter Pardo's YouTube channel *Sea of Tranquility*. Think of Luis as a mathematical metalhead with a prog-rocker alter-ego. Indeed, Luis is also Professor of Physics at Columbia College Chicago, teaching and doing NSF-funded research on the thermodynamics of musical

harmony. Luis loves touring, writing, recording, collaborating with other musicians and helping incredible yet relatively unknown bands reach a larger audience.

Pontus Norshammar

Pontus is a Swedish journalist based in Stockholm. A music geek and a major record collector since childhood, Norshammar contributes regularly to the YouTube channel *The Contrarians* and has appeared on the British music podcast *The Epileptic Gibbon Music Show*. He is also involved with the Swedish concert scene.

Steven Reid

Steven has been a staff writer with the *Sea of Tranquility* website for over a decade. His impenetrable Scottish twang can now be barely understood as a co-host on the site's *UK Connection* YouTube show and as a regular on *In the Prog Seat* and numerous other music discussion panels. Previously Steven spent over a decade as a writer for the *Fireworks* rock and metal UK print magazine and *Rocktopia* website, with the last four years of that tenure being as Assistant Editor. Steven has also contributed liner notes for albums by Robin George and numerous Eonian Records releases.

Matt Thompson

Matt Thompson is the creator of the zine *Critical Hit Parader: America's Only Rock 'n' Role Playing Magazine* (criticalhitparader.com). The zine provides tabletop roleplaying game (TTRPG) content in the spirit of vintage rock magazines like *Creem, Circus* and *Hit Parader*. His companion newsletter and podcast on the intersection of rock music and TTRPGs is available at criticalhitparader.substack.com. A guitarist and songwriter, some of his music can be found at mtpromise.com.

Special Thanks

A hearty appreciation goes out to Agustin Garcia de Paredes who applied his eagle eye to a copy edit of this book. Agustin is also an admin on the *History in Five Songs with Martin Popoff* podcast Facebook page.

About the Author

At approximately 7900 (with over 7000 appearing in his books), Martin has unofficially written more record reviews than anybody in the history of music writing across all genres. Additionally, Martin has penned approximately 130 books on hard rock, heavy metal, classic rock, prog, punk and record collecting. He was Editor-in-Chief of the now retired *Brave Words & Bloody Knuckles*, Canada's foremost heavy metal publication for 14 years, and has also contributed to *Revolver, Guitar World, Goldmine, Record Collector*, bravewords.com, lollipop.com and hardradio.com, with many record label band bios and liner notes to his credit as well.

Additionally, Martin has been a regular contractor to Banger Films, having worked for two years as researcher on the award-winning documentary *Rush: Beyond the Lighted Stage*, on the writing and research team for the 11-episode *Metal Evolution* and on the ten-episode *Rock Icons*, both for VH1 Classic. Additionally, Martin is the writer of the original metal genre chart used in *Metal: A Headbanger's Journey* and throughout the *Metal Evolution* episodes.

Then there's his audio podcast, *History in Five Songs with Martin Popoff* and the YouTube channel he runs with Marco D'Auria and Grant Arthur, *The Contrarians*. The community of guest analysts seen on *The Contrarians* has provided the pool of speakers used across the pages of this very book. Martin currently resides in Toronto and can be reached through martinp@inforamp.net or martinpopoff.com.

A Complete Martin Popoff Bibliography

2024: Run with the Wolf: Rainbow on Record, Led Zeppelin: A Visual Biography, Queen Live!, Honesty Is No Excuse: Thin Lizzy on Record, Van Halen at 50, Pictures at Eleven: Robert Plant Album by Album, Perfect Water: The Rebel Imaginos

2023: Kiss at 50, The Electric Church: The Biography, Dominance and Submission: The Blue Öyster Cult Canon, The Who and Quadrophenia, Wild Mood Swings: Disintegrating The Cure Album by Album, AC/DC at 50

2022: Pink Floyd and The Dark Side of the Moon: 50 Years, Killing the Dragon: Dio in the '90s and 2000s, Feed My Frankenstein: Alice Cooper, the Solo Years, Easy Action: The Original Alice Cooper Band, Lively Arts: The Damned Deconstructed, Yes: A Visual Biography II: 1982 – 2022, Bowie @ 75, Dream Evil: Dio in the '80s, Judas Priest: A Visual Biography, UFO: A Visual Biography

2021: Hawkwind: A Visual Biography, Loud 'n' Proud: Fifty Years of Nazareth, Yes: A Visual Biography, Uriah Heep: A Visual Biography, Driven: Rush in the '90s and "In the End," Flaming Telepaths: Imaginos Expanded and Specified, Rebel Rouser: A Sweet User Manual

2020: The Fortune: On the Rocks with Angel, Van Halen: A Visual Biography, Limelight: Rush in the '80s, Thin Lizzy: A Visual Biography, Empire of the Clouds: Iron Maiden in the 2000s, Blue Öyster Cult: A Visual Biography, Anthem: Rush in the '70s, Denim and Leather: Saxon's First Ten Years, Black Funeral: Into the Coven with Mercyful Fate

2019: Satisfaction: 10 Albums That Changed My Life, Holy Smoke: Iron Maiden in the '90s, Sensitive to Light: The Rainbow Story, Where Eagles Dare: Iron Maiden in the '80s, Aces High: The Top 250 Heavy Metal Songs of the '80s, Judas Priest: Turbo 'til Now, Born Again! Black Sabbath in the Eighties and Nineties

2018: Riff Raff: The Top 250 Heavy Metal Songs of the '70s, Lettin' Go: UFO in the '80s and '90s, Queen: Album by Album, Unchained: A Van Halen User Manual, Iron Maiden: Album by Album, Sabotage! Black Sabbath in the Seventies, Welcome to My Nightmare: 50 Years of Alice Cooper, Judas Priest: Decade of Domination, Popoff Archive – 6: American Power Metal, Popoff Archive – 5: European Power Metal, The Clash: All the Albums, All the Songs

2017: Led Zeppelin: All the Albums, All the Songs, AC/DC: Album by Album, Lights Out: Surviving the '70s with UFO, Tornado of Souls: Thrash's Titanic Clash, Caught in a Mosh: The Golden Era of Thrash, Rush: Album by Album, Beer Drinkers and Hell Raisers: The Rise of Motörhead, Metal Collector: Gathered Tales from Headbangers, Hit the Lights: The Birth of Thrash, Popoff Archive – 4: Classic Rock, Popoff Archive – 3: Hair Metal

2016: Popoff Archive – 2: Progressive Rock, Popoff Archive – 1: Doom Metal, Rock the Nation: Montrose, Gamma and Ronnie Redefined, Punk Tees: The Punk Revolution in 125 T-Shirts, Metal Heart: Aiming High with Accept, Ramones at 40, Time and a Word: The Yes Story

2015: Kickstart My Heart: A Mötley Crüe Day-by-Day, This Means War: The Sunset Years of the NWOBHM, Wheels of Steel: The Explosive Early Years of the NWOBHM, Swords and Tequila: Riot's Classic First Decade, Who Invented Heavy Metal?, Sail Away: Whitesnake's Fantastic Voyage

2014: Live Magnetic Air: The Unlikely Saga of the Superlative Max Webster, Steal Away the Night: An Ozzy Osbourne Day-by-Day, The Big Book of Hair Metal, Sweating Bullets: The Deth and Rebirth of Megadeth, Smokin' Valves: A Headbanger's Guide to 900 NWOBHM Records

2013: The Art of Metal (co-edit with Malcolm Dome), 2 Minutes to Midnight: An Iron Maiden Day-by-Day, Metallica: The Complete Illustrated History, Rush: The Illustrated History, Ye Olde Metal: 1979, Scorpions: Top of the Bill - updated and reissued as Wind of Change: The Scorpions Story in 2016

2012: Epic Ted Nugent, Fade To Black: Hard Rock Cover Art of the Vinyl Age, It's Getting Dangerous: Thin Lizzy 81-12, We Will Be Strong: Thin Lizzy 76-81, Fighting My Way Back: Thin Lizzy 69-76, The Deep Purple Royal Family: Chain of Events '80 – '11, The Deep Purple Royal Family: Chain of Events Through '79 - reissued as The Deep Purple Family Year by Year books

2011: Black Sabbath FAQ, The Collector's Guide to Heavy Metal: Volume 4: The '00s (co-authored with David Perri)

2010: Goldmine Standard Catalog of American Records 1948 – 1991, 7th Edition

2009: Goldmine Record Album Price Guide, 6th Edition, Goldmine 45 RPM Price Guide, 7th Edition, A Castle Full of Rascals: Deep Purple '83 – '09, Worlds Away: Voivod and the Art of Michel Langevin, Ye Olde Metal: 1978

2008: Gettin' Tighter: Deep Purple '68 – '76, All Access: The Art of the Backstage Pass, Ye Olde Metal: 1977, Ye Olde Metal: 1976

2007: Judas Priest: Heavy Metal Painkillers, Ye Olde Metal: 1973 to 1975, The Collector's Guide to Heavy Metal: Volume 3: The Nineties, Ye Olde Metal: 1968 to 1972

2006: Run for Cover: The Art of Derek Riggs, Black Sabbath: Doom Let Loose, Dio: Light Beyond the Black

2005: The Collector's Guide to Heavy Metal: Volume 2: The Eighties, Rainbow: English Castle Magic, UFO: Shoot Out the Lights, The New Wave of British Heavy Metal Singles

2004: Blue Öyster Cult: Secrets Revealed! (updated and reissued in 2009 with the same title; updated and reissued as Agents of Fortune: The Blue Öyster Cult Story in 2016), Contents Under Pressure: 30 Years of Rush at Home & Away, The Top 500 Heavy Metal Albums of All Time

2003: The Collector's Guide to Heavy Metal: Volume 1: The Seventies, The Top 500 Heavy Metal Songs of All Time

2001: Southern Rock Review

2000: Heavy Metal: 20th Century Rock and Roll, The Goldmine Price Guide to Heavy Metal Records

1997: The Collector's Guide to Heavy Metal

1993: Riff Kills Man! 25 Years of Recorded Hard Rock & Heavy Metal

See martinpopoff.com for complete details and ordering information.